Slow Cooked

Also written or edited by Marion Nestle

Nutrition in Clinical Practice (1985)

The Surgeon General's Report on Nutrition and Health (edited with
J. Michael McGinnis, 1988)

Food Politics: How the Food Industry Influences Nutrition and Health (2002;
revised edition 2007; tenth anniversary edition 2013)

Safe Food: The Politics of Food Safety (2003; revised edition 2013)

Taking Sides: Clashing Views on Controversial Issues in Nutrition and Food
(edited with L. Beth Dixon, 2004)

What to Eat (2006)

Pet Food Politics: The Chihuahua in the Coal Mine (2008)

Feed Your Pet Right (with Malden C. Nesheim, 2010)

Why Calories Count: From Science to Politics (with Malden C. Nesheim,
2012)

Eat, Drink, Vote: An Illustrated Guide to Food Politics (2013)

Soda Politics: Taking on Big Soda (and Winning) (2015)

*Big Food: Critical Perspectives on the Global Growth of the Food and Beverage
Industry* (edited with Simon N. Williams, 2016)

Unsavory Truth: How Food Companies Skew the Science of What We Eat
(2018)

*Let's Ask Marion: What You Need to Know About the Politics of Food,
Nutrition, and Health* (with Kerry Trueman, 2020)

The publisher and the University of California Press Foundation gratefully acknowledge the generous support of the Constance and William Withey Endowment Fund in History and Music.

California Studies in Food and Culture

DARRA GOLDSTEIN, EDITOR

Slow Cooked

AN UNEXPECTED LIFE IN FOOD POLITICS

Marion Nestle

 UNIVERSITY OF CALIFORNIA PRESS

University of California Press
Oakland, California

Library of Congress Cataloging-in-Publication Data

Names: Nestle, Marion, author.
Title: Slow cooked : an unexpected life in food politics / Marion Nestle.
Other titles: California studies in food and culture ; 78.
Description: Oakland, California : University of California Press, [2022] | Series:
    California studies in food and culture ; 78 | Includes bibliographical references
    and index.
Identifiers: LCCN 2022003912 (print) | LCCN 2022003913 (ebook) |
    ISBN 9780520384156 (hardback) | ISBN 9780520384163 (ebook)
Subjects: LCSH: Nestle, Marion. | Women nutritionists—Biography.
Classification: LCC TX350.8.N48 A3 2022 (print) | LCC TX350.8.N48 (ebook) |
    DDC 613.2092 [B]—dc23/eng/20220225
LC record available at https://lccn.loc.gov/2022003912
LC ebook record available at https://lccn.loc.gov/2022003913

Manufactured in the United States of America

31 30 29 28 27 26 25 24 23 22
10 9 8 7 6 5 4 3 2

Contents

Contents

Introduction

For nearly half a century, I have been teaching and writing about the effects of politics on what we eat and, therefore, on our health. I began my career fascinated by nutrients, every one of them, but I ended up viewing foods, diets, and entire systems of food production and consumption as far more significant. Food companies, as I like to explain, are not social service or public health agencies. They are businesses required by stockholders to prioritize profit above all other values—human, social, and environmental.

In saying this, I have always thought I was stating the obvious. Never did it occur to me that I would be considered "one of the country's most hysterical anti-food-industry fanatics . . . the anti-pleasure nutritionist."[1] Not me. I love food, am a foodie through and through, and view the deliciousness of food as one of life's greatest gifts. But I also never could have imagined that anyone could possibly view me as "one of the nation's smartest and most influential authorities on nutrition and food policy," the "leading guide in intelligent, unbiased, independent advice on eating," or "America's foremost public nutrition warrior," let alone "Food Visionary Badass."[2] I also never dreamed that I would hold a professorship named for the glamorous movie star Paulette Goddard.[3]

Since the early 2000s, I have been writing books about food politics. Some have won praise and prizes and are considered highly influential. But as careers go, mine got off to a late start. My first book, *Nutrition in Clinical Practice,* came out in 1985 when I was teaching nutrition—and nutrients—to medical students. It took another seventeen years to produce the one for which I am best known: *Food Politics: How the Food Industry Influences Nutrition and Health.* By then, I was sixty-six years old, a late age to be starting on the most active, productive, and rewarding years of my academic life. The book you are reading is the fifteenth I have written, coauthored, or coedited, and the thirteenth since 2002.

I attribute my late start to having been a Depression-era baby born into a poor family and coming of age in the 1950s, when women, even those from the working or lower middle class, were expected to do nothing more with their lives than marry and have children, and to do so as early as possible. Trying hard to conform to social norms, I did just that. I married at the age of nineteen. Back then, if educated women worked at all, it was as secretaries, teachers, nurses, or, as in my case, laboratory technicians. Any woman who worked was expected to quit as soon as she had children. I did that too. My family, the other adults I knew, and my teachers discouraged ambition, let alone agency, and it took me decades to figure out I had both.

At the dawn of the second wave of the women's movement, which opened up education and job opportunities to women, I went to graduate school in molecular biology. By the time I finished my doctorate in 1968, I had married, dropped out of college, returned to graduate, worked as a lab technician, had two children, been a stay-at-home mom, divorced, and met the man I would marry a few years later. After getting my degree, I held academic jobs, but these were lower-level, untenured positions I could manage along with family responsibilities. Nobody supervising those early positions took my work seriously, and neither did I.

Nevertheless, those jobs gradually allowed me to acquire enough teaching, research, and administrative skills to qualify for a high-

FIGURE 1. On the terrace of the twelfth-floor apartment I have rented from NYU since 1990. This place unites my interests in food, science, and politics. I grow fruits and vegetables in pots. Some of the buildings behind me house NYU science departments; one is the landmarked site of the 1911 Triangle Shirtwaist Factory fire, the greatest tragedy in the history of US labor. Bill Hayes took this photo in 2015 for the Steven Barclay Agency, which represents my public lectures.

level staff position in the federal government, which, in turn, qualified me for a tenured position as chair of the Department of Home Economics and Nutrition at New York University, the life-changing job I started in 1988.

Until NYU hired me, I had never thought about what kind of work I might want to do if I had choices. I did not think I had any. The NYU position came with what I viewed then—and still do—as miraculous benefits: job security as a tenured full professor, a salary adequate to live on with a subsidized rental apartment (figure 1), and a solid platform from which to teach, write, and speak publicly. By then, my children had finished college and were on their own as young adults. I could finally get to work.

The epiphany that launched my career as a critical analyst of the food industry came soon after I arrived at NYU. In 1991 I was invited to speak at a National Cancer Institute meeting about behavioral causes of cancer: cigarette smoking and dietary practices. I was one of two speakers about diet; the other was the *New York Times* science and health columnist Jane Brody, now a longtime friend. The other speakers were physicians and scientists, American and elsewhere, who had worked for years as antismoking advocates. In that pre-PowerPoint era, they showed slide after slide of cigarette advertisements from places around the world, from remote rural villages in the Himalayas to rapidly urbanizing cities in Africa and Asia.

One speaker, John Pierce, a cancer researcher at the University of California, San Diego, particularly got my attention. He showed examples of cigarette advertising like the Joe Camel character that targeted children.[4] I was well aware of those ads, but I had never paid close attention to them. Cigarette advertising was ubiquitous and a normal part of the everyday landscape. This was my "Aha!" moment. I turned to Jane Brody and said, "We ought to be doing this for Coca-Cola."

By *this,* I meant that nutritionists like me ought to be giving just as close scrutiny to the marketing practices of food companies as antismoking advocates were giving to cigarette companies. From then on, I paid attention. I examined and wrote articles about how food companies marketed their products and protected their financial interests. Nearly twenty years later, these articles became the basis for *Food Politics.*

This book is about how I got off to such a late start, finally caught on to what I wanted to do, and did it—and what my personal story might mean for others. I knew early on that I loved food and wanted to study it. I wish I had been able to pursue this goal right from the start. Instead, I did what I could manage at the time. Between raising kids and following my first and then second husband's decisions and moves for work, I tried to make the best of my circumstances, whatever they were.

Why tell this story now? Almost every working day I am asked to respond to questions from students, readers of my work, and media reporters. Usually they ask me about current research studies or business and government decisions about matters related to food, nutrition, and health. But over time the questions became more personal: How did I get interested in food? In nutrition? In food politics? How did I become a source for reporters? How did my NYU department develop programs in food studies? Those are the easy ones.

The more difficult ones dig deeper: What do I eat? What are my earliest food memories? How did I get the courage to take on the food industry? How do I feel about being criticized as a nutrition scold or the voice of the nanny state? Or this particularly tough one: How would I assess my legacy? Students ask me how I prepared for a career in food politics and advocacy and how I got to where I am today. These last questions imply that my career was intentional. It was not, much as I wish it had been. I am far more comfortable speaking and writing about food issues than about my personal history. But these questions persist.

Then came the coronavirus pandemic. Because my age put me at high risk of not surviving this virus, I temporarily abandoned my New York City apartment and moved upstate to Ithaca, New York, to stay with my partner of the past twenty years, Malden Nesheim (we have long had a commuting relationship). Libraries were closed, making it impossible to do my usual kind of research. Sequestered in our house on Cayuga Lake, I had the time and opportunity to ponder these questions and to recall the events that led to the career I've had. Memoirs are about memory and reflection. The pandemic offered what seemed like an endless opportunity to remember and to reflect.

pandemic

FIGURE 2. One of my greatest pleasures is to take my kayak out on Cayuga Lake, the longest of New York State's Finger Lakes. It's where I do my best thinking.

It also gave me the chance to get out in my kayak as often as I could (figure 2).

The story I tell here is unique to me—a statistical N of 1. But as I try to put my professional life into a broader context, I can see several themes that might have wider relevance. The first is the most obvious: the lasting effects of early childhood, which in my case made ambition and agency seem like impossible violations of then-prevailing social norms. A second is the obstacles faced by women in academia, particularly in the sciences.[5] Others are the importance of food in human culture, health, and commerce; the pleasure food brings to daily life; the relentless efforts of food companies to sell products; the ways the food industry uses the political system to protect profits; and the often unrecognized influence of politics on what we eat. Last, I think my career illustrates how following personal values, along with sheer persistence and hard work, pays off in the long run.

A Note on Methods

Memoirs are about what is remembered, but my memory—especially for dates, names, and places—is less than reliable, as I learned when attempting to fact-check this book. I began writing it in June 2020, soon after the COVID-19 pandemic had shut down American society. The pandemic made it impossible to consult books, files, teaching materials, or the papers and photographs held in the NYU library's special collections, which in any case date only from my arrival there in 1988. Before then, I moved a lot, from New York to Los Angeles in 1948, to Berkeley in 1954, to Boston in 1968, to San Francisco in 1976, to Washington, DC, in 1986, and finally back to New York. In each of these major moves and the even more frequent moves within cities, I shed class papers, lecture notes, teaching materials, files, and lab notebooks I assumed I would never use again. I have family photographs, but not many; my family had little money, and film and developing were expensive luxuries. I did save all my publications and interviews about my books in thick binders; these helped.

I don't even have early electronic files. When I first began using a computer in the early 1980s, I used the XyWrite word processing program. When I had to transition to Microsoft Word in the late 1990s, the old XyWrite files were no longer compatible, and I deleted most of them. Luckily I kept and was able to find one folder of XyWrite documents, which can now be opened with Word. In it, I found a log I had kept from 1987 to 1988 when I was in Washington, DC, working for the Department of Health and Human Services.

In 2009, the food writer Judith Weinraub compiled a set of oral histories for NYU's Fales Library, including one with me, which are available online. At the time, I could not understand why so many of her questions focused on my personal rather than professional history; I now appreciate how useful they were.

Beyond those records, I fact-checked what I could, and I have cited sources and references in the notes. The fact-checking led to some unanticipated pleasures. It was a delight to catch up via Zoom and email with the production team for the *Over Easy* television series I did from 1980 to 1982. But some fact-checking led to dead ends. I was never able to find the name of the University of Florida physician-scientist who ran the Howard University workshop on advising minority applicants to medical schools; I owe him a great debt. The notes describe other instances in which facts may have eluded me. But this is, after all, a memoir, as much about what is left out as about what is included. I hope you enjoy reading it.

1   *A Long, Slow Start*

I attribute the late start to my career to the prolonged time it took me to recover and move on from my unhappy family's unique way of being unhappy. I was born during the Depression to impoverished parents, nonobservant Jews who, like those in the 1930 novel *Jews without Money,* were members of the Communist Party.[1] My birth announcement illustrates some of my family's dynamics (figure 3). It was drawn by the New Yorker cartoonist Syd Hoff, whom my parents must have known through Party connections. He wrote the classic children's book *Danny and the Dinosaur,* but also drew political cartoons under the name A. Redfield. The announcement puts my father, Ted Zittel, at the center of attention and misspells my first name. I was supposed to be a boy and to be named Michael; Marion was the compromise. My middle name, Barr, was in memory of my mother's deceased father, despite her despising him for earning so little money that her mother had to sell her knitting to support the family. I dropped it as soon as I could.

To his friends, my father was a larger-than-life figure, big, boisterous, and funny. Yet I hardly remember him, mainly because he was not at home much, but also because he died when I was thirteen, at the low point of my adolescent misery. He started out as a newspaperman but resented authority and never held jobs for long.

FIGURE 3. Even though this birth announcement misspells my name, I like to think it inspired my lifelong appreciation of cartoons.

Throughout my early childhood, he did freelance public relations for folk singers like Richard Dyer-Bennett and Burl Ives until they moved on to bigger-time agents. He also did publicity for labor unions. My sole inheritance from him is a scrapbook of newspaper clippings from 1939 to 1942, the results of his work for a union on strike against Manhattan's Brass Rail restaurant.[2]

Both my parents were first-generation Americans. My father was the oldest of five children, all born in New York. My mother, Tillie, was the middle child of five, but the first to be born in America. Their parents all came to the United States in the early 1900s from Eastern Europe, but the family history was hardly ever mentioned, and I never thought to ask about it.

In the mid-1980s, when I was going through a second divorce, I went to a therapist for the first time. She urged me to interview my mother, then in her late seventies, to get her version of our family history. I spent several well-rehearsed days asking the questions I wished I had known enough to ask earlier. She told me about her dirt-poor upbringing in a two-room apartment over a store in Newark, where she lived with her parents, two sisters, two brothers, and two grandparents. She shared a bed with her sisters. "I never had a bed of my own until I married your father," she said. (They always had twin beds.)

My mother had taken a secretarial job as soon as she graduated from high school because her parents and younger siblings needed support, but she never stopped resenting the unfairness of the family's allowing her older brother to go to college. She married my father in part because he had a steady job that she assumed would free her from ever having to work outside the home. Even though she never did throughout their marriage, my father's intermittent income felt like a betrayal, and she never forgave him.

They fought constantly about money. Once, when I was about eight, my father gave her a watch for her birthday. By then, I knew the rule: no matter what you think of a gift, you must say thanks for it. My mother's response? "How could you spend so much money on something I don't need when we don't have enough for food or rent?" After more such accusations, he walked out. Those interactions were miserable to witness.

Their one area of common ground was politics. They married in 1930 at the beginning of the Great Depression, when the effects of economic and class inequality were especially stark. Many people concerned about those inequalities joined the Communist Party. For my parents, the party was their social life, their community, and their source of meaning. They were rank-and-file members, not leaders, so, unlike many of their friends, they were not harassed by the FBI, fired from their jobs, or imprisoned for their beliefs. Nonetheless, I was to keep their party affiliation a deep secret and never discuss it outside the home.

My parents believed communism would save the world from the harsh inequities of capitalism. Even as a child, I could see the unfairness of the capitalist system. It seemed obvious that people do not choose to be poor, but have poverty thrust upon them; they are born into families with no education or opportunity, paid unfairly for their work, discriminated against, or are just victims of bad luck. Doing everything possible to ensure that everyone—Black and white, rich and poor—has a fair chance at a fulfilling life made sense to me then, as it still does.

But other aspects of my parents' communist beliefs seemed contradictory and did not make sense. If communism was about fairness, equity, decency, and community, why did my parents no longer speak to family members who did not share their political beliefs? How could they condone the Soviet Union's forced removal of peasants from their land, purging of former comrades, or forging a pact with Hitler? I was never convinced by their excuses for these actions, and my skepticism did not make our day-to-day interactions any easier.

With my father away as much as he could be, it was just the two of us—Mom and me—to get along. We did not. I was about eight when her constant sharp comments about how I looked and how I behaved made me think that she neither loved nor liked me. Nothing I did could please her. I viewed this situation as terribly unjust and could never understand it.

One incident particularly sticks. When I was around five, my mother's sister Anna came to stay with us. At lunch one day, I said, "You are older than my mother, aren't you?" Anna, who must have been in her late thirties at the time, burst into tears, left the table, and disappeared behind a closed door. My mother insisted I apologize immediately. But for what? I could not understand how what I had said was so offensive as to bring her to tears.

I tried to behave better, hard as it was to know how, but there was nothing I could do about my looks. My mother, who was considered a beauty, had long, straight hair. Mine is extremely fine and wildly curly, and nobody knew what to do with it. A torment of my early childhood was "What can we do about her hair?" and, later, "Can't you do something about your hair?" My parents took me to men's barber shops to get it cut, and I was often asked whether I was a boy or a girl. In today's terms, I knew I was cis-gender female, but I didn't look it.

One of my rare childhood photographs is shown in figure 4; it's what I looked like at age two and a half. I have never enjoyed getting my hair cut, and for years have cut it myself. Here is one of the great ironies of my life: I am now regularly stopped by strangers on the street who exclaim, "Your hair is so gorgeous!" Go figure.

As a young child, I understood that the adults in my life saw me as difficult, but I thought this too was unfair. My worst problems were with that aunt—I still think of her as the dreaded Aunt Anna—and her husband, Uncle Harry. From the time I was about three, Uncle Harry's pet name for me was "Ugly," as in "Come to the table, Ugly, it's time for dinner." Parents were supposed to love their children. Could

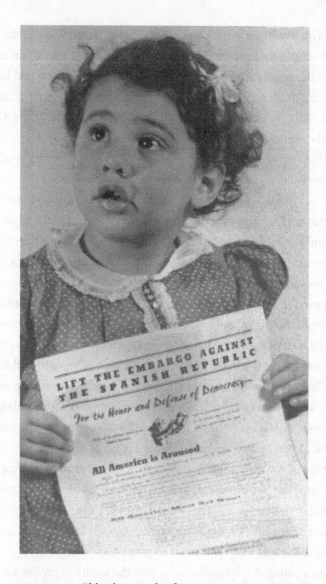

FIGURE 4. This photograph of me at age two and a half appeared in the *Daily Worker* (the Communist Party newspaper) on February 9, 1939, with this caption: "This little girl holds in her tiny hands a poster calling upon democratic America to lift the embargo on the embattled democracy of Spain." It illustrated an article about the Spanish Civil War of 1936–39.

I have been adopted? I could not understand or accept how my mother and her relatives could be so hard on me, and said so. These protests brought on yet another childhood torment—"Why can't you be nicer to your mother?"—from my father as well as my mother's friends and relatives. At no time can I remember an adult friend or relative even once hinting that my mother might be hard to get along with. Only after her death did relatives let me know how difficult they found her. Advice about how to avoid taking her criticisms so personally or how to deflect them would have been enormously helpful, but none was offered. I could not think of any response other than to fight back, which caused even more trouble.

Other aspects of my childhood were also difficult. We moved often, almost always in the middle of school semesters, making it hard for me to adjust and make friends. My parents lived in Brooklyn when I was born but could not afford to stay there, so we moved to Long Island, first to Northport, then to Great Neck. When I was well into the third grade, we moved to Manhattan. My father must have gotten a steady job that paid well enough to move us to a large, three-bedroom apartment on 115th Street, albeit on the cheaper ground floor. I liked living there. Even at age eight, I could walk by myself to school on 109th Street (in what was then a largely Puerto Rican neighborhood), ride my bike in Riverside Park, and take the subway to my unsuccessful piano lessons in Greenwich Village.

The strangest, least expected event in my childhood happened when I was ten. I now had a "sister," Eva, age eighteen. Eva had been living in a Jewish orphanage from which my mother hired babysitters. My mother liked her, invited her to rent our spare bedroom, and became Eva's legal guardian. Eva was pretty and popular, and had a job and a boyfriend. Eight years older than me, she was not someone I was likely to be close to. Thinking of her as a sister made no sense. I knew right away she was joining our family to be my mother's ally, not mine. Sad ...

What was *that* about? In our therapy-induced interview, my mother recalled that she was not getting along with me or my father. She wanted at least one person in the family who loved her, and Eva did. When my father took a job in Los Angeles a couple of years later, Eva moved there with us.

Eva's presence in our household created one more childhood torment: "Why can't you be more like Eva?" As I learned much later, Eva had experienced her own version of this torment, but she interpreted it differently. I heard her version in 1990, when my mother was dying of breast cancer and in hospice care at Eva's home in West Covina. I was deeply grateful to Eva for taking care of my mother during her last months. At that time, I was still new at my NYU job, but I flew out to Los Angeles every third weekend to visit. My mother was on morphine and slept a lot, leaving plenty of time for Eva and me to talk— for the first time, really. Eva had felt my mother's sharp criticisms just as I did. But to my astonishment, she viewed them as expressions of love. Nobody in Eva's life had ever cared enough about her to comment on her looks or behavior until she met my mother. This was love? It never felt like love to me.

But if not love, what was it? When, in our interviews, I asked my mother why she had been so critical of me, her answer surprised me. She recognized how much we were alike. But her life had been deeply unhappy, and she did not want me to have an unhappy life. Her way of expressing love was to try to change me. Sadly, it didn't work for either of us.

I wanted to be pretty, popular, and a joy to be around, but could never figure out how. By the time I was twelve and we moved to California, I saw myself as socially inept, unattractive, and unintentionally but consistently offensive. I had no idea help might be available, let alone how to ask for it. By then, I had concluded that if there were things I wanted in life, I had no chance of getting them. It was best not to want. I was good at only one thing: getting good grades in school. I did not see this as anything special. If I could do well in school, surely anyone could if they put their minds to it. I did not understand, nor did anyone in my life—parents, teachers, friends—ever explain to me, that grades are not ends in themselves: they lead to choices. Only much later did I see that I had choices and could act on them.

Moving to California

My father had two brothers and two sisters, all younger. One brother, my Uncle Bernie, had moved to Los Angeles in 1940. In the summer of 1946, just before Eva entered our family, my father got the job that allowed us to move to Manhattan and also to buy a car, a Hudson. We drove cross-country to visit Uncle Bernie and his family, taking along Sandy Nemiroff, the daughter of friends of my parents, to keep me company on the long trip. We drove through the South, where I got a firsthand view of segregated water fountains and restrooms. Arriving in California, my father was enchanted by the miles of orange groves we passed and the bananas growing in Los Angeles backyards. Two years later, when he was offered a job running the first live theater in Hollywood—for plays, not movies—he moved there to take it. Months later, my mother drove Eva and me across the country to join him.

My father, I must now explain, had a serious weight problem. At five feet ten inches, he weighed more than 350 pounds, highly unusual in that era. Shortly after our first visit to Los Angeles, he had gone on a diet—I wish I knew what kind—and lost more than a hundred pounds. But by the time we joined him in California, he had gained it all back. My mother's unaffectionate first words on seeing him were "You are fat again."

Once again the move occurred in the middle of a semester. I went to the nearby public junior high school in Hollywood, one quite different from my mixed-neighborhood school in New York. Everyone at Bancroft Junior High was white and seemed to have more money than my family did. The kids of movie and early television stars went to that school. David Nelson, the son of Ozzie and Harriet, was in my class. I looked odd (that hair again), spoke with a New York accent, and induced hilarity by my mispronunciation of Yosemite and other California place-names, to my enormous embarrassment. When embarrassed, which was often, I blushed, which only induced further embarrassment. The move was a painful adjustment, soon only to get worse.

In March 1950, a little more than a year after our move to Los Angeles, my overweight, chain-smoking father had a heart attack and died at the age of forty-seven. The theater he managed had not been doing well, and he and my mother were always arguing; these stresses surely added to what we now recognize as multiple risk factors for coronary artery disease. Did his death trigger my later interest in nutrition? If so, I didn't make the connection, although it now seems obvious. I just hadn't been that close to him.

Cold as it may seem, I don't remember feeling much sadness when he died, and I only realized the enormous tragedy of the loss years later. After his heart attack, I was taken to visit him only once during the three weeks he was in the hospital before he died. He had been away from home too much and done too little to help me deal with my mother to be a strong presence in my childhood. What I felt when he died was embarrassment—at both my lack of grief and his abandonment of me. I would now be alone with my mother and Eva. We would have some money from his small life insurance policy, but my mother, who never wanted a job, would now have to get one.

The summer after his death, my mother took me to the East Coast, where I went to camp and she went to Connecticut to live with one of my father's sisters. Eva had a job in California and stayed behind. My mother's plan was to use the summer to refresh her typing and shorthand skills and decide whether to remain in Los Angeles or move back to New York. I wanted to return to New York. We had not been in California long, and I thought I could pick up where I had left off. But my mother decided against that, saying, "The move to California was so traumatic for you, I don't want to put you through that again." I did not believe her, but I had no choice in the matter. Later, during our therapeutic interview, I asked her to explain that decision. She said, "I couldn't afford the rent in Manhattan, and if I had to live in Brooklyn, I might as well live in Los Angeles."

This also made no sense to me—subways joined the two boroughs then as they do now—and I suspected that she might have been involved with one of her party comrades in California, but that was all she told me. She was only forty-three when my father died, and still attractive. She dated a bit, but within a few years announced that she was no longer interested in men, and she lived alone for the next forty years. Now I wonder if she might have preferred women. If so, I doubt she would have been comfortable acting on something so socially unacceptable in that era.

Given our precarious finances, we soon had to move to a smaller, less expensive rental. My mother encouraged Eva to marry her boyfriend, a handsome, decent, and hardworking man to whom she remained married until her death in 2015. (He and I are still in touch.) After I left home to go to college, Eva and I never lived in the same town again, although we continued to see each other occasionally over the years. But from 1951 on, it was just Mom and me. She moved us again, this time to an even cheaper bungalow with one bedroom— the third move in less than three years. I went to high school from that place. I studied and slept in the bedroom, grateful that it had a door I could close. My mother slept on a couch in the living room. Our living situation made it hard to invite friends over and contributed to my overwhelming sense of difference, inadequacy, and lack of options.

The Joy of Food

I have painted a bleak picture of my childhood as unloving, unfair, and limited in choices, which was how I experienced it. But it had moments of pleasure, many of them having to do with food. I have no memory of going hungry, except between meals; nor do I remember much about my mother's cooking except her attempts to disguise canned spinach by mixing it with mashed potatoes. On rare occasions, she produced delicious apple pies.

Before the war, we lived in Northport, then a small Long Island fishing village, and had a victory garden. It produced tiny red tomatoes that I ate like candy. Milk was delivered to our door in glass bottles. In winter, the cream rose to the top, froze, and popped the cap up an inch or two. My parents cut off the frozen cream, thawed it, and used it for cereal and coffee. Every morning, I was forced to drink a tiny glass of fresh-squeezed orange juice (canned juice didn't exist then), to wash down a daily dose of cod-liver oil. It was decades before I willingly drank orange juice. The rare visits to my maternal grandmother were always a treat. On Friday nights, she shaped leftover pieces of challah dough into small birds with raisin eyes—*faygele* in Yiddish—for me and the other grandchildren.

My father's parents were better off. His mother once came to visit us in Northport at the height of the Depression, bringing a gorgeous cake from an expensive Manhattan bakery. But I don't remember enjoying it. My mother was furious: "How could she spend all that money on cake when we need food and rent?"

Once we moved to Manhattan, we were still dealing with food rationing. We saved bacon grease to donate to the war effort. A classmate from a wealthy Chinese family lived up the street from us. My parents must have done them some kind of favor, because they took us to an elegant restaurant in Chinatown where we were the only non-Chinese diners. That was my introduction to real Chinese food, quite different from the chow mein served in local restaurants (although I liked that too). Most schooldays, I came home for lunch, but sometimes I was given a quarter to buy my own lunch, which I happily spent on cream cheese and walnut sandwiches at the Chock Full o' Nuts on 116th Street. I could not imagine anything better to eat.

Back then, I was not particularly adventurous or curious about food; I didn't understand that there was anything to be curious about. Here is an example I still can't get over. The bungalow in Los Angeles where my mother and I lived after Eva got married had a large avocado tree in the back, but we had no idea—and nobody we knew did either—that the rock-hard green things that fell to the ground could be edible, let alone scrumptious. We threw them out.

My One Haven: Higley Hill

I should have been more curious about food, because I knew what real food tasted like. I learned this at the one place I remember being happy—Higley Hill, the summer camp I went to in Vermont. Through Communist Party connections, my parents were friends with George and Bunny Granich, a couple who ran a small camp in upstate New York. But in the summer of 1946 George was dying of cancer, and they moved the camp to a Vermont farm recently purchased by his brother Max (Manny) and his wife, Grace. On the way back from that first cross-country trip to Los Angeles, we stopped at the camp so that my parents could visit George. I liked being there so much that they went on to New York, leaving Sandy and me at the camp for a couple of weeks. The farm occupied more than a hundred acres, with fields, woods, streams, and a pond. There were only a few other campers that first year, and the adults were preoccupied with caring for George. We kids were free to run wild.

I loved Higley Hill, and I loved being away from my parents, but mostly I loved the food. Grace and Manny had lived in China for many years, and Grace knew how to stir-fry ingredients picked fresh from the large kitchen garden. If we campers were good, we got to pick the vegetables for dinner. When it was my turn to pick string beans, I bit into one. It was warm from the July sun, crisp and sweet. Raised on canned vegetables, I had no idea that a string bean could taste anything like that. This was my vegetable epiphany: I've loved fresh vegetables and gardens ever since, and I now cherish the blueberries, raspberries, peaches, figs, tomatoes, and herbs growing in pots on my Manhattan terrace.

Grace would send us kids out early in the morning to pick the raspberries and blackberries that grew wild on the property. These went into pancakes soaked with maple syrup they had tapped months earlier. Higley Hill had its own sugar house. In the spring of 1948, my parents took me there during the sugaring-off season. Manny and some friends collected the sap in buckets, poured it into troughs, and boiled it down into increasingly concentrated and delicious syrup. I got to taste it at every stage of concentration and especially loved the thick, dark syrup poured over fresh snow. My father must have loved it too. He had just taken up painting as a hobby. One of the few pictures he painted before he died showed maple sap collection at Higley Hill (figure 5). I spent another summer at Higley Hill in 1948 and worked there for a few weeks as a junior counselor in the summer of 1950, after my father's death.

Those were the camp's earliest years. During the anticommunist McCarthy era, Higley Hill became a place of refuge for the children of parents who were under investigation by the FBI, jailed, or in hiding because of their communist associations. I was not afraid that my parents would be taken away. My father died before the peak years of anticommunism, and my mother's affiliations seemed more social than political. For me, Higley Hill was the one place where I felt free and could eat glorious food.[3]

FIGURE 5. My father, Ted Zittel, painted this picture of maple sap collection at Higley Hill, the Vermont farm where I went to summer camp, learned to appreciate fresh local food, and had the happiest moments of my childhood.

The Struggle to Escape

Our Los Angeles apartment was on the borderline between two public high-school districts, Hollywood and Fairfax. I went to Fairfax, along with most of my junior high friends. At the time, the Fairfax area was populated with Jewish refugees from World War II, and the school was 90 percent Jewish, 100 percent white, and highly academic: almost everyone went on to college. It included poor kids with single moms like me, but also the offspring of Hollywood producers who got cars or nose jobs for their sixteenth birthdays. The social environment of the school was explicitly hierarchical, and everyone knew the ranks of the many social clubs (essentially sororities and fraternities). The most popular kids, from wealthy, socially prominent families, belonged to the top social clubs, and so on down the line. I was not invited to join any of the clubs until my senior year, when I got a bid from the lowest-ranked club. By then, I was used to being an outsider and too proud to join that club: I declined the invitation.

My friends were also outsiders. All of us intended to go to college, but neither I nor any of the other girls I knew had career aspirations. If we planned to work at all, it would be as secretaries, and we would quit the minute we got married. My three closest friends knew what they wanted from life—to marry a doctor, a professor, and a rabbi, respectively—and they all did just that. I knew only one girl, a year ahead of me, who intended to go to college to prepare for a career: she wanted to be a physicist. But when I ran into her years later, she had instead *married* a physicist. At my twenty-fifth high school reunion, the only one I ever went to, I was the only woman in my graduating class with a doctorate. Hardly any of the women worked, and the few that did were helping their husbands. This, mind you, was an *academic* high school.

I now realize that plenty of women had careers in the early 1950s, but I didn't know any of them. None of my mother's women friends had jobs unless they worked with their husbands. When I turned sixteen my mother insisted I get a work permit—no car or nose job for me. I babysat, wrote letters for a blind woman, and worked as a salesclerk at the May Company department store. The going rate for all that was eighty-five cents an hour. In summers I could earn a couple of hundred dollars as a day-camp junior counselor. Whatever work I did at least got me out of the house and gave me a little money to save for college.

When it came time to apply to college, I knew I could qualify for University of California schools on the basis of my grades, much as I minimized their importance. Most of my classmates opted for UCLA, but I wanted to get as far away from home as I could. I remembered being happier in New York and somehow got the courage to write to Barnard and Radcliffe for applications. I was invited to a Seven Sisters tea held in Los Angeles to meet recruiters for those schools. I did not know anyone else who had been invited, and had no idea what to wear or say. It took every bit of nerve I could summon just to go to it. I felt awkward and out of place.

I never filled out the applications. My mother refused to give me the fifteen-dollar fee for each application—"I don't want you going so far away"—and that seemed like a lot of my hard-earned money to spend on a whim. Even if I did get in, how would I pay for tuition, room, and board? My school counselors were also discouraging: "It's cold in New York and Boston; you won't like it there." Worse, the one recent Fairfax graduate who had gone east to college had committed suicide his first year. Nobody even hinted that I might qualify for a scholarship. Not one person said to me what I routinely tell wavering students: "Apply. You have nothing to lose. If you don't get in, you'll go somewhere else. If you do get admitted, it's your decision." I did not have the confidence—the agency—to figure that out for myself.

I applied to Berkeley and, as my one long shot, Stanford. Berkeley seemed *possible*. In my junior year, I had visited an older high school friend who was a student there. The campus and its view of San Francisco were magnificent. My friend lived in a low-cost student co-op, Sherman Hall. That too seemed possible.

Stanford, a private university, would be prohibitively expensive without a full scholarship. But I took a chance and applied, as did three other students in my class. Perhaps by coincidence, Stanford accepted only the one of us who was not Jewish. Fortunately, my Stanford rejection arrived on the same day as my Berkeley acceptance, which included a scholarship offer. I would be the first in my family to go to college.

UC-Berkeley

Berkeley was nearly four hundred miles from Los Angeles, and I would not be able to get back often. Best of all, Berkeley was affordable. In the 1950s, state legislators still sent their kids to University of California campuses and voted generous funding for the university. (That changed when Ronald Reagan became governor.) My tuition fees amounted to $32 a semester.[4] I had been given a state scholarship worth $300 and had another $300 saved from my high school jobs. My mother agreed to send me $20 a month. That took care of needs. I rarely covet things I can't afford, but even then I regretted not being able to buy the Olivetti typewriter I longed for. It cost a prohibitive $100, and I had to settle for one I could get for $30.

Room and board at the student co-ops cost only $45 a month because residents all had to work five hours a week on whatever was needed to maintain the place. I lived at Sherman Hall and did my hours in the central kitchen, where I peeled huge piles of potatoes under the supervision of Narsai David, the student in charge. He later became a well-known Bay Area restaurateur and is one of my oldest friends.

A Fairfax classmate who was also headed to Berkeley had a car and offered to drive me. Everything we were taking fit easily into his small car, in contrast to what kids bring to college today. With much relief, I said goodbye to my mother, and we drove up the hot Central Valley to the fog-cooled campus. He had arranged to live at a men's co-op, Cloyne Court, and, soon after dropping me off, called to invite me to a party there that night. That was how, on my first night in Berkeley, I met the group of politically active students who would become lifelong friends. Among them was Victor Garlin, whose last name I recognized because our fathers had been friends in New York. Victor introduced me that night to Manny Nestle, who lived at Cloyne Court while attending law school. We soon began dating and married two years later.

This was an exciting time to be in Berkeley, and I felt lucky to have connected immediately with students who actively opposed

1st Husband

McCarthyism, cared about civil rights, and would go on to become leaders of the student movement. My freshman English class encouraged analysis of societal conformity and pushed us to think independently.[5] Social and humanitarian values were honored, not persecuted. Berkeley felt like an adult version of Higley Hill, the home I had never had before.

But I had no idea what to study. One of my mother's friends collected cookbooks, and I enjoyed looking through them, trying out an occasional recipe, and discussing them with her. Knowing that I was interested in food, she suggested I study it. But how? One choice was agriculture. But I was a city girl and knew nothing about farming. The other option was dietetics, a decidedly women's field one step up from home economics. And if I chose dietetics, I would be able to get a job as a dietitian once I graduated.

That choice lasted only one day. My first classes in dietetics were unchallenging, and if classes were easy, I did not value them. The one exception was the five-credit chemistry class required for the dietetics program but also taken by science majors. This class was seriously challenging and therefore worth taking. In my sophomore year I took a class in public health from Henrik Blum, then the health officer of neighboring Contra Costa County. I admired his work and enjoyed the class, but it seemed too easy. It never dawned on me that the reason I found it easy was that I think like a public health person and was a natural fit for this field. Public health is very much about how socioeconomic factors affect disease risk, and if people are hungry or sick, the best preventive strategy is to make sure everyone has access to jobs, good schools, and affordable health care.

My science classes were a struggle, but I thought they were worth it. I was often the only woman in my lab sections but managed to get through them despite the teasing (harassment, in today's terms). I would often open my lab drawer and find a dead rat in it. The guys in my class thought this was funny. I had no idea what I wanted to do and drifted from one major to another. By the end of my sophomore year, I was still undecided, but it no longer mattered. I quit school to get married.

An Army Bride

Everyone I knew was getting married; I went to eight weddings in the summer of 1956. I badly wanted to fit in, and also got married that summer, to Manny Nestle, the man I had met on my first night at Berkeley and the first man I had ever dated seriously. He was eight years older, finishing law school, and about to be drafted into the army. (The Korean War had ended, but young men were still being drafted into military service.) As was almost unquestioned in that era, I took my husband's name. By the time we divorced ten years later, we had two kids, and I kept his name so as to have the same name as my children. I do have regrets about the loss of my Zittel name. I love my Zittell (two-*l*) cousins and do not love the irony of having almost the same name as Nestlé, the multinational food corporation infamous for its history of promoting infant formula in regions where it cannot be used safely (figure 6).[6] My adopted name has no accent on the final *e* and is pronounced like the verb—to nestle—not the company.

Shortly before our marriage, Manny received his draft notice. This was at the peak of the red scare era, when the FBI and Senator Joseph McCarthy's House Committee on Un-American Activities were aggressively identifying and forcing the dismissal of alleged communists or sympathizers from American universities, Hollywood, and government. In 1947, President Harry Truman had signed an executive order establishing a loyalty oath for all federal employees, military as well as civilian. Military draftees were required to swear to support and defend the Constitution and to obey presidential and officers' orders, and universities and schools required teachers to

FIGURE 6. This photograph was taken during a 2012 visit to the Nestlé Alimentarium, the company's food museum in Vevey, Switzerland. Although I have no relationship to the Nestlé family, amused colleagues have suggested that I ought to claim membership as its black sheep.

swear they were not members of organizations considered subversive and would not attempt to overthrow the government. Critics opposed all such oaths on the grounds of civil liberties and the First Amendment, and in the 1960s, the courts eventually agreed and ruled the oaths unconstitutional.[7]

Manny refused to sign the military loyalty oath, and along with others who refused, he was assigned to Fort Ord on the Monterey peninsula. Once he finished basic training, he served his time there as a company clerk. We rented a house nearby in Marina and later lived in Monterey, where I tried and failed to find a secretarial job.

Having nothing better to do, I taught myself to cook from books given to us as wedding presents. I had learned basic cooking techniques in junior high school home-economics classes, including how to make the brown rim cookies and eggs goldenrod so wittily described by Laura Shapiro in *Perfection Salad*. My lab training helped. I quickly discovered that cookbook recipes often do not work even if followed carefully, and I learned to trust my own instincts. As a result of those efforts, I gained fifteen pounds the year after I married.

Manny and I got along well, but we missed our Berkeley friends. The COVID pandemic isolation reminded me of that era. He had his army work, and I had my cooking and reading. I haunted the public library's classics sections and read long Russian novels and Proust. At some point I discovered Monterey Peninsula Community College, which offered courses in marine biology, with field trips. The ocean was right there; it would be fun to explore what was in it. The courses, which required early-morning tidepool explorations, were taught by the smart, engaging, and inspiring Eugene Haderlie, who encouraged me to consider further studies in this field.[8]

Because he had not signed the loyalty oath, Manny was dismissed from the army before he had completed the two-year requirement, and we moved back to Berkeley. He took a research job with a publisher of law books, and I resumed my undergraduate studies. Unfortunately, Berkeley did not offer a major in marine biology. I consulted a faculty adviser to help me find a major that would allow me to graduate in two years. This turned out to be bacteriology, which would qualify me for jobs as a laboratory technician.

Once I completed the requirements for that major, I asked friends majoring in nonscience fields to recommend their favorite courses. I had a wonderful time delving into social movements, political theory, and postrevolutionary French history. I graduated from Berkeley Phi Beta Kappa but took no particular pride in that achievement. I attributed my good grades to hard work and to my ability to almost always be able to predict what instructors would ask on tests. I didn't recognize this ability as proof of discernment or skill. I still thought that if I could get good grades, anyone could.

In the fall after my graduation, I got a job as a technician in the laboratory of Professor Bill Reeves in Berkeley's School of Public Health. His laboratory studied how mosquitoes transmit Western equine encephalitis virus, a rare but dangerous cause of brain inflammation in horses and sometimes in people. I worked there for two years, quitting the day before our first child, Charles, was born in 1961. Our second child, Rebecca, arrived less than two years later. By then, Manny and I had moved to an old farmhouse in Richmond Annex, a few miles north of Berkeley, which we bought for $13,500. I became a suburban stay-at-home mom with two small children. This did not go well. I tried hard to enjoy being a housewife, but the constant demands of child care and household management made me feel trapped. I cried a lot but could not explain my despair. When I read Betty Friedan's book *The Feminine Mystique,* which disclosed the plight of suburban housewives, it hit home, hard. I could see myself in her description of women trapped by societal norms.

Friends urged me to go to graduate school. This seemed like a way out. But once again, what should I study? My favorite undergraduate science professor had been Gunther Stent, whom I admired for his broad interests in literature and culture. He was in the Department of Virology, where faculty studied the structure of viruses and their ability to infect plants, animals, and bacteria as well as humans. I applied and was admitted on the basis of my Phi Beta Kappa grades and previous laboratory experience. I was even given a spot on the department's NIH training grant, which paid a stipend of $200 a month. This would be just enough to cover the cost of five hours a day of in-home child care.

I met with the graduate adviser, Howard Schachman. "By the way," he said, "we gave you the fellowship because no men applied this year. If men apply next year, you may have to give it up." He explained that the department was changing its name to the Department of Molecular Biology to reflect its focus on the newly discovered functions of DNA, RNA, and proteins. This exciting, cutting-edge science was more likely to attract male applicants. From that conversation, I understood that I, as a married woman with two small children, was not going to be taken seriously as a student. I had best not take myself too seriously as a prospective scientist, either.

Men did apply the following year, but I had done well enough in my courses to justify keeping the fellowship and earning Schachman's respect. I never reminded him of that conversation: I was sure he would deny he had ever said anything like that. He was a champion of students, and until his death in 2016, I tried to see him whenever I visited Berkeley. He, in turn, came to my lectures there. He was well into his nineties in 2010 when he attended a talk I gave in the pet food store Holistic Hound about my just-published book, *Feed Your Pet Right*.[9]

But the damage had been done. My sense that I was not going to be taken seriously was reinforced by my difficulty in finding a PhD research supervisor. Several turned me down before I finally ended up with a young assistant professor, Walden Roberts, who was willing to accommodate my 10 a.m. to 3 p.m. schedule, the best I could manage with babysitting arrangements. In my first semester, with a two-year-old toddler and a five-month-old baby, I had to make special arrangements to get to the required 8 a.m. class in physical chemistry. The wife of one of the male students in this class also had just had a baby, and he and I compared notes every morning about how little sleep we had gotten the night before. For me, a good night was six hours in three shifts.

I learned to be efficient and get done what I had to during the five hours available for my graduate studies. I quickly learned that bringing course or lab work home was out of the question—there were too many demands and interruptions. At the lab, I worked. At home, I shopped, cooked, did the laundry, and took care of the kids. That was the way things were in those days. Manny was fine about my going to grad school and probably would have taken more household responsibility if I had asked. But I was doing what women were expected to do. I did not ask.

I managed the graduate courses well enough. I studied hard and did well on tests, but I had a hard time integrating what I was learning into a coherent framework. To do that, I would have had to take responsibility for learning on my own. I did not figure out how to do that until I started teaching, when I had to learn material deeply enough to explain it to students. I failed my qualifying oral examination—a humiliating experience—and had to do remedial classes and tutorials while continuing my doctoral research.

Fortunately, my dissertation project was a straightforward, if uninspiring, project that I could do in limited hours. My task was to purify and characterize an "extracellular" enzyme secreted by bacteria, in this case *Serratia marcescens,* which splits DNA into pieces. I needed to figure out what those pieces were. The answer, it turned out, was single nucleic acids. I liked working with *Serratia.* These are pretty bacteria—bright red in color—stable at room temperature, relatively harmless, and easy to work with.

I was making reasonable progress on my experiments, but Roberts, my dissertation supervisor, was denied tenure and had to leave. He took a job in Colorado while I was still doing my research. We communicated by mail—snail mail in those days—during my last couple of years in graduate school. Despite all that, I finished my degree in five years, faster than the other students in my cohort. I was able to describe everything I'd learned in a dissertation of eighty-three pages, double spaced, which didn't seem like much to show for all that work.[10]

I was a nucleic acid enzymologist before the widespread use of restriction enzymes—those that enable today's sophisticated manipulations of DNA. Anyone now working in the field would view my dissertation research as antediluvian. Even then, I viewed my project as unoriginal. The male graduate students in my cohort reinforced that view by talking about how interesting and scientifically important their projects were compared to mine.

That was how I experienced my years as a graduate student: a glass half empty, just as I had experienced childhood. But twenty-two years later, I went to Denver to give a talk and reconnected with my graduate adviser. He organized a dinner party for me and gave the guests an entirely different interpretation: a glass overflowing. "She had two kids. She only came into the lab a few hours a day. She worked without my supervision for two years. She published three papers from her dissertation, two of them in the top biochemistry journal."[11] If that's what he or anyone else thought at the time, I had completely missed it.

Had I realized how my achievements were viewed, I might have felt better about what I had done—but I have no regrets about having taken my degree in molecular biology. I learned to think critically about science, to recognize good science when I see it, and to distinguish interesting from trivial scientific questions—all immensely useful skills when I switched to nutrition. I am often challenged on my opinions, which is fair, but nobody messes with me about my scientific credentials.

I partly attribute my inability to recognize what I'd accomplished to the other things that were happening in my life at the time. I started graduate school in 1963, at the height of the civil rights movement;

the Berkeley free speech movement erupted the following year.[12] Five students in my graduate program were arrested during the demonstrations, and my husband, Manny, did some of the legal work on their behalf.

Those were heady times. Students were protesting to end the Vietnam War, stop the draft, and open doors for minorities and women. We thought we were changing the world. I felt I was part of this movement despite not being directly involved. I understood why so few women were revolutionaries: they had kids to take care of. I brought my kids to demonstrations, but only to those I thought would be safe. I never dared risk arrest. Who would take care of my kids if I went to jail?

Instead, I engaged in serious, and seriously competitive, home cooking. Our closest friends were foodies, twenty years before the term was coined to describe people like me who are "very very very interested in food."[13] My foodie friends thought nothing of searching out the best places to get fresh-roasted coffee (this was before Peet's, let alone Starbucks), heading over to San Francisco to get the best olive oils, and talking constantly about food as well as cooking and eating it. Once Julia Child's *Mastering the Art of French Cooking* came out, we outdid each other in preparing its recipes—the more complicated, the better.

I enjoyed the food but not the competitiveness or long hours in the kitchen. I learned to throw together meals that could be prepared quickly, tasted good, but looked like they took a lot of time and effort—tetrazzinis, elaborate salads, and soufflés with cheese or Grand Marnier. Once I dropped the competitiveness, what I most enjoyed about cooking was finding whatever happened to be in the refrigerator or pantry and whipping it up into something terrific to eat. That's still the way I most like to cook.

When I finally passed my qualifying exams, I was reasonably sure I could finish my degree, get a postdoctoral position, and eventually find a job that would pay well enough to support my children on my own. By that time, Manny and I were leading separate lives, and our marriage no longer did either of us any good. We separated amicably and divorced. I was already fully in charge of the kids, now ages three and five, and was looking forward to being on my own. I could see how hard the breakup was for my kids, and that hurt. But our shared-custody agreement meant that Manny took the kids on weekends and occasional weeknights. For the first time in five years, I had those times to do whatever I wanted: work in the lab, date other men, read the newspaper, even go to Chicago for my first-ever professional meeting.

Two years later, in the late spring of 1968, I had just finished my last experiments and was about to start writing my dissertation when I went to a party in the hills above Palo Alto and met Zach Hall. He was a postdoctoral fellow at Stanford, a rising scientific star, with a job lined up for the fall in the neurobiology department at Harvard Medical School. He was divorced, with a nine-year-old son who lived with his ex-wife in Washington, DC. We began dating and within weeks rashly decided that I and my kids would move with him to Boston. I had been in Berkeley for sixteen years; I wanted to try something different. Moving to Boston with Zach would be an adventure.

My one regret was that I would have to give up the postdoctoral position I had arranged with Allan Wilson in Berkeley's biochemistry department. Wilson was just beginning to use molecular methods to study evolution, and I was excited by the way his work fused molecular and human biology.[14] For me, that was the road not taken. Instead, I found another postdoctoral position at Brandeis University, starting that fall. By then, I would be thirty-two years old, divorced with two young children for whom I felt overwhelmingly responsible. I had no clear idea of what I wanted to do or even how to set goals and work toward them, but I knew I would be able to use my education to support myself and my kids. Moving to Boston with Zach felt like a real choice but also a great responsibility. I would have to do all I could to make this choice work out well for all of us.

2 *My First Academic Job*

Brandeis 1968-1976

My postdoctoral position was with Larry Grossman in Brandeis University's biochemistry department. My project had to do with how cells repair damage to their DNA, but I wasn't getting anywhere with it. I was much more interested in the work of Maurice Sussman in the biology department. He studied slime molds, soil-dwelling amoebas that reproduce by swarming together to form what look like tiny spore-forming mushrooms. This seemed to be an exciting way to study the chemical signals that cells use to communicate with one another while they are developing into organs. I arranged to transfer to his laboratory the following year, even though everyone warned me that Sussman ran the lab like a boys' junior high school locker room.

They weren't kidding. The lab's windows looked out on steep stairs to an upper level of the campus. Soon after I arrived, Sussman glued a quarter to a step about a third of the way up. Between classes, all the men (boys?) in the lab gathered gleefully at the windows to watch the short-skirted women bend over to try to pick up the coin. Sussman's wife, Raquel, a fine scientist in her own right, ignored such happenings, as did I.

Overall, my eight years at Brandeis were a time of difficult transitions, from divorced to remarried, from postdoc to lecturer to assistant professor, from research to teaching, and from basic science to

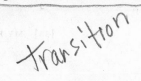

nutrition. All required steep learning curves. On moving to the Boston area, I rented an apartment in Newtonville, but it cost more than I could afford on my Brandeis postdoc salary. Between rent and child care, I was spending more than I earned every month, and I worried about having to dip into what little money I had saved. After the first year, Zach moved in with me, and we shared expenses. But the apartment was crowded with my two children, then aged five and seven, and it was difficult to accommodate the frequent visits from Zach's nine-year-old son. After a year or so, we bought a house in Newton Centre, with rooms for all three kids, and married.

I had to learn how to teach and at the same time to learn the new subject matter my courses required. I had to learn why women—and racial minorities—had (and continue to have) such a hard time in academia, as well as the price of insisting on better treatment. I acquired this knowledge in bursts of revelation—epiphanies, really—beginning with one that explained why my research progress was so slow. In Sussman's lab, I had been attempting to identify the chemical signal that induced slime molds to aggregate. I found it eventually (cyclic AMP, if you care about such things) but wrote only one paper during my three years as a Brandeis postdoctoral fellow, a dismal level of productivity.[1]

The Swimming Pool Epiphany

At this point in my life, I was a postdoc at Brandeis—a temporary position only slightly better than that of a graduate student—whereas my husband, Zach, was a tenure-track assistant professor in a prestigious department at a prestigious medical school. We both viewed his job as more important than mine. The kids were mine from my previous marriage. No matter how much Zach helped with them—and he helped a lot—I felt they were my responsibility. On Saturdays he went to his lab to work; I stayed home with the kids.

In my third year as a postdoc, Brandeis began to offer Saturday morning swimming lessons to children of faculty and staff. These usually lasted less than an hour, and I hung around to chat with the other parents while the kids swam. But on one of those Saturday mornings, the instructor announced a double session. The kids would be in the pool for nearly two hours. This would be time enough for me to pop into the lab and get a little work done while nobody else would be around to distract me.

I was in for a big shock. When I walked into the lab, *everyone* was there: Sussman, his wife, the graduate students, the other postdocs, even the lab technician. Everyone but me, apparently, worked in the lab on Saturday mornings. No wonder nobody took my work seriously. No wonder my progress was so slow. But even if I wanted to be in the lab on Saturday mornings, how could I do it? I doubted I could find, let alone pay, someone to watch my kids. Any thoughts I had entertained of a career as a research scientist ended that morning.

There may have been women scientists who could manage both laboratory work and a family back then, but I was not one of them. I lacked not only the necessary financial resources but also a social or professional support system that might have made it possible. I did not even know such support existed. In January 2020 (just as the coronavirus was making its way out of China) I went to the Congreso Futuro meeting in Santiago, sponsored by the Chilean government. I was one of a small group of visiting speakers who was treated to a side trip to San Pedro Atacama, in the high Andes, to visit the radio telescopes at the Alma Observatory. Among us was a woman who had won a Nobel Prize. We compared notes. Like me, she had married young and had children. But unlike me, she came from a well-off academic family and had traveled extensively, gone to private schools, knew academics, and had any number of scientific mentors. She could afford full-time, live-in child care and was able to go back to her laboratory within days of giving birth. I say this not to minimize

Lab Saturdays

her talent or the problems she faced in her own life, but rather to point out that I had no idea how disadvantaged I had been. At the time, I just thought I wasn't good enough to manage a scientific career.

By the time of the swimming pool epiphany, I was finishing up my postdoc and had started looking for my next position. I had an offer of another postdoctoral fellowship in the lab of an up-and-coming scientist at MIT who later went on to win a Nobel Prize. I turned it down. My kids were eight and ten, testing boundaries, and needed me to be there. When the Brandeis biology department offered me a job as a lecturer—an untenured teaching position—I took it. The job would not be any less work, but it would give me a flexible schedule and allow me to do some of my work from home.

The Teaching Epiphany

As a postdoc, I had agreed to teach a small undergraduate seminar on how to read research papers. It went well, and the department offered me a job running the two-semester laboratory course in animal and plant biology, a required course for biology and premedical majors. I would be teaching students to dissect guinea pigs, mate fruit flies, identify plants and trees on the Brandeis campus, use microscopes to observe corn pollination, and handle radioisotopes. One of my favorite lab sessions involved the dissection of mollusks—small squid that arrived frozen from California. These were edible (at least to students who did not follow kosher dietary laws), and we sautéed and ate what was left over after removing the internal shells.

I had to learn enough basic biology to teach this material. I designed the experiments, wrote the lab manuals, and supervised a couple of longtime staff who set up the labs, as well as half a dozen graduate teaching assistants. In writing lab directions, I learned to be logical and precise. If students didn't understand what they were

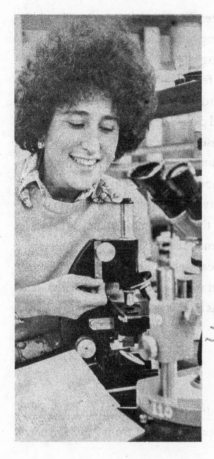

FIGURE 7. This photograph appeared as an illustration in a Brandeis course catalog in 1978, two years after I had left the university. It's the only photo I have of me doing anything scientific, despite working in laboratories for two years as a technician, five as a graduate student, and three as a postdoc, and then teaching laboratory courses for another five.

supposed to do, the experiments wouldn't work. The more attention I paid to what they didn't understand, the better I got at writing step-by-step directions, a skill I consider to be greatly underappreciated. How I wish that people who write manuals for electronic devices would consult me. They seem to have so little idea of—or interest in—what untrained users need to know.

After a year or so, the labs were running well, but some of the faculty complained that I wasn't doing enough and should be teaching more. I could not convince them that I was already plenty busy, and the department assigned me to teach a lecture course on cell and molecular biology on top of running the lab courses. Brandeis classes were small, making it possible to get to know students. I liked preparing labs and lectures but never felt confident that I knew enough to be teaching the material. I absurdly overprepared my lectures.

To do that, I read widely and deeply, tried to anticipate students' questions, and searched the research literature for answers. I was driven by fear, in this case of failing to know something that students would assume any instructor should know. I could see that I was developing another skill: the ability to make sense of vast amounts of research and explain it in a way that is accurate but understandable. Even better, teaching made the material stick. For the first time, I was able to incorporate what I was learning into my own thinking and to draw my own conclusions about what it meant. I still worried that I didn't know enough, but this was mainly because I was always teaching new material.

The Wage-Gap Epiphany

I had been a lecturer in the Brandeis biology department for a year or so when I got an unexpected call one night from Amy Kovner, a friend in Boston.

2nd wave feminism

AMY: Guess what my women's consciousness-raising group discussed tonight?

ME [confused]: Huh?

AMY: We talked about your salary at Brandeis.

ME [stunned]: What? Explain.

What is now known as the second wave of feminism was well under way, and I knew that consciousness-raising groups were places where women shared personal experiences to understand the effects of politics and social forces on their lives.[2] I would have loved to be in one but had not been invited to join any and did not know how to find one that might include me.

So how could it be that Amy's group was discussing my Brandeis salary? Amy laid it out. Myla Zinn was a member of the group. Her boyfriend, Jon Kabat, had just been hired by my department into a lecturer's position just like mine. I knew Myla and Jon as part of the Boston science community, liked them a lot, and was looking forward to having Jon as a colleague. But, as Amy told me, he had negotiated a higher salary than I was getting—$12,000 (mine was $8,000). He had been told he would be getting more than me but to keep this a secret. Myla asked the group's advice. Her friends agreed I needed to be told.

Once I got over the shock, I could see what a gift I had just been handed. The women's movement had reached academia. Colleges were beginning to appoint committees on the status of women; these soon discovered salary discrepancies that became the basis of lawsuits. Women who took their cases to court were winning. I thought I had an airtight case for deserving a higher salary, and I thought I could get it. Zach thought so too and helped work out my strategy.

I met with Jon to confirm the details and make sure he was okay about discussing the issue with the department chair. He was, and I made an appointment with the chair right away. This was not a pleasant conversation. Salaries, the chair let me know, were private personnel matters, and Jon's was none of my business. Besides, Jon needed more money because he and Myla intended to marry and have children.[3] "I already have children," I said. "But you are married," he countered. By his reasoning, Jon would have to provide for Myla, but my husband was already providing for me.

I then invoked the mantra that Zach and I had worked out: "Fix my salary. I do not want to have to go to court over this." I meant it. I wanted the higher salary, but I did not want a legal challenge. I knew

Salary

that if I went to court, I would win the battle but lose the war. I had seen what happened to faculty who fought their departments or universities: they alienated their colleagues and ended up quitting or getting fired. I was fairly certain that Brandeis administrators would recognize the strength of my case and increase my salary. But if they refused, I was fully prepared to take legal action. In the meantime, I could be patient.

Patience was essential. I spent an entire year repeating my mantra to the chair, to a new chair after that one resigned, to one dean after another, and to higher-up administrators. Eventually, somebody figured out that it would be cheaper to pay me more than to go to court over a case the university had a good chance of losing. My salary was raised to $12,500 and my title upgraded to assistant professor—not a tenure-track position, but better than lecturer. Best of all, my colleagues congratulated me on how gracefully I had handled the situation and welcomed me into my new status. I had acquired one more skill: getting things done at universities.

The Minority-Student Epiphany

Because every premedical student had to take the laboratory courses I taught, I got to know many of them. When I was invited to join the premed advisory committee, I said yes right away. At that time, Brandeis students applying to medical schools submitted only one letter of recommendation, written by our committee. We reviewed students' essays, grades, and test scores, interviewed each applicant, and wrote a detailed letter based on the submitted materials and the interview. In effect, we were doing the dirty work—the comparative evaluation— for the medical schools. Our letters could make or break students' chances of getting into any school, let alone their top choices.

At the time I joined the committee, Brandeis had done a good job of expanding the admission of Black students to its undergraduate programs, but none of its Black students had ever been admitted to a medical school. They were not getting the grades they needed in the required premed courses, a situation some of us understood even then as institutional racism. This was shortly after the assassination of Martin Luther King Jr., and what we then called minority groups were demanding greater opportunities in society, including at universities. More than 60 percent of Black medical students were trained at two traditionally Black medical schools, Howard and Meharry, but the Association of American Medical Colleges was now calling on all medical schools to admit students "from geographical areas, economic backgrounds and ethnic groups that are now inadequately represented."[4] The Brandeis premed advisory committee was evidently no help at all to Black students who wanted to study medicine.

My epiphany came when I attended a workshop at Howard University to train advisers to work with minority premedical students. A group at a university in Florida had developed a checklist for evaluating characteristics and experiences of minority applicants that could be used to predict their success in medical school. They gave the workshop attendees sample applications to evaluate. We were to consider grades and test scores but also to look for established predictors of success, such as strong family support, the ability to cope with white institutions, success in overcoming personal and academic hardships, and social connections through membership in clubs, teams, networks, and the like. We soon caught on and were able to identify which applicants had been admitted and which succeeded. The workshop urged appointment of a dedicated minority premedical adviser and suggested specific ways for that person to help applicants succeed in their premed courses. This was worth a try.

I reported back to the Brandeis committee, volunteered as minority adviser, and went to work. I called a meeting of the Black premed students and asked them which classes were giving them trouble and

FIGURE 8. This is a page from the faculty section of the Brandeis University yearbook in 1975. I felt honored to be included in it. The photo appeared under this statement: "Much of my time at Brandeis is occupied with teaching, advising, and just talking to premedical students. I teach a laboratory course that strongly emphasizes analysis of original observations rather than revealed truths. Perhaps because of the experimental and indefinite nature of this experience, I see surprisingly little stereotyped premedical behavior in my classes. I find most students to be genuinely nice people, bright, thoughtful, excited about learning, and necessarily hardworking. Whatever their motivation, students with these qualities are a pleasure for me to teach and get to know."

what kind of help they thought would be useful. I knew all of their premed course instructors and talked to each of them individually. I said—and I swear this is all I said—"I am the faculty adviser for Black premed students, and you have these particular students in your class. Could you please keep an eye on them and let me know right away if they are having any difficulties?" That was the totality of my intervention. I never heard from any of the instructors, but the outcome was extraordinary. All of those students passed all their courses, even organic chemistry, the most challenging. During my remaining time on that committee, every single one of the Black students who applied was admitted to one or more medical schools.

Was this just a coincidence? Were the students better qualified? Did this small intervention encourage the science faculty to adopt more supportive attitudes, consciously or unconsciously? I regret never trying to find out. Without question, the committee wrote much more supportive and detailed letters of recommendation. But I still can't get over how little it took to begin creating a more supportive classroom environment. Working with minority students was one more skill I picked up during my Brandeis years, and such successes gave me more confidence in my ability to teach and support students who needed help.

The Nutrition Epiphany

By 1975, I had been at Brandeis for seven years and teaching for five of them. My academic home, the biology department, had two unusual teaching policies. To make sure we kept up with our fields, instructors could teach the same course for only three semesters in a row and then had to switch to a different course. The lab courses were exceptions, but I changed their content from year to year. Also, we instructors had to teach any course the department needed, whether or not we had a background in the topic. The assumption was that anyone with a doctoral degree ought to be able to absorb new material well enough to teach it to undergraduates. I've never heard of any other university with these kinds of expectations, but they made for great training and, in my case, were life-changing.

I was teaching cell and molecular biology for the third time when biology majors petitioned the department to offer courses in human biology. I was given a choice: teach human physiology or human nutrition. I knew enough physiology to realize that trying to explain the biochemistry of kidney function to undergraduates would not be much fun. And I was already curious about nutrition. Even in the early 1970s, it was in the news. Jane Brody was writing articles about nutrition for the *New York Times.* The Nobel Prize–winning chemist Linus Pauling had written *Vitamin C and the Common Cold* in 1970, and Frances Moore Lappé had published her groundbreaking *Diet for a Small Planet* in 1971. Also in 1971, Michael Jacobson and his colleagues established the Center for Science in the Public Interest (CSPI). In 1975, they published *Food for People, Not for Profit,* an impressively ahead-of-its-time compendium of popular articles on food issues ranging from agriculture to public health.

I thought it would be useful for biology majors to investigate whether science supported the arguments in those articles and books, and I assigned them all in that first class. I could see that nutrition offered a superb way to teach undergraduate biology. Cell and molecular biology are fascinating but highly abstract; it's hard for students to relate matters at the molecular level to their lives. But everyone eats. Everyone has a personal interest in what happens to food in the body. Preparing this class was going to be fun.

But where to start? I needed advice. The only nutrition courses I could find in the Boston area were at Harvard's School of Public Health. These were taught by Jean Mayer, who had been a professor there for decades (but would soon be appointed president of Tufts University). I made an appointment to ask him for suggestions. Not a good idea. Mayer let me know how offended he was by the very idea that someone like me, with no training in nutrition, would be teaching it. He refused to talk to me or offer advice, even about which books I should read. His only suggestion was to go to the bookstore and look at the texts he required for his own courses.

I was taken aback by his reaction. Brandeis encouraged instructors to become biological generalists and to learn what we needed to know to teach whatever we had to. This was my first (but not my last) encounter with academic territoriality. But if Mayer considered me an upstart interloper, there was nothing I could do about it. I went to the bookstore, took notes on what he was assigning to students, and checked out every nutrition textbook I could find from the Brandeis library.

Given my biochemistry training, I thought the best way to begin the course would be to identify each of the nutrients required by the human body and discuss its functions. I opened my half dozen or so books to the pages that listed essential nutrients and spread them out on a table. To my surprise, the lists were different. Some—but not all—included nutrients then known to be required only by animals (boron, for example), needed only when people cannot make enough of their own (carnitine), made by intestinal bacteria (biotin, vitamin K), or not considered essential but known to have health benefits (fiber). Was it possible that nutrition scientists did not agree on which nutrients were required for human health?

I went back to the library and sat down to read the most recent edition of the *Recommended Dietary Allowances* (RDAs), the National Academies' authoritative source of information about the amounts of specific nutrients needed to prevent deficiency symptoms. At the time, the RDA book ran to only 128 pages (it now takes up many thick volumes).[5] Opening it at random, I landed on the section covering the B vitamin thiamine and read the brief descriptions of the studies that formed the basis of its RDA. Again at random, I picked one of the references mentioned in that section and went to find the study in the library stacks.

Symptoms of thiamine deficiency include delirium, confusion, hallucinations, and erratic behavior. To determine what level of deficiency was severe enough to induce such symptoms, the investigators had induced thiamine deficiency by feeding a diet devoid of that vitamin to six women who were patients in a state mental hospital. The investigators then waited to see how long it took for the women to refuse to do chores around the hospital.[6] Really? I could hardly believe what I was reading. These women were already in a mental hospital, presumably because of erratic behavior. Furthermore, they could have been undernourished to begin with. There were only six of them. And not wanting to do chores could have been due to any number of reasons other than vitamin deficiency. This, clearly, was not a well-designed clinical trial.

I tried another one. This time, I landed on a study of vitamin C deficiency done pretty much the same way, except that the study subjects consisted of nine male prisoners in an Iowa penitentiary. During the course of the study, two of the prisoners escaped.[7] This, clearly, was not a well-controlled clinical trial.

This was my first day reading about nutrition, and I was hooked for life. The two examples I had chosen at random raised basic questions of research ethics (the subjects were mentally ill or incarcerated), study design and control, statistical significance (they included very few subjects), and interpretation. Undergraduates in my classes were struggling to read original research in cell and molecular biology. I was sure they would be fascinated by reading studies like these, just as I had been. Nutrition would be a terrific way to teach critical thinking in biology.

Preparing that class was like falling in love, and I've never looked back. I came to it with a passion for food and eating. But I was also engrossed by the challenges and uncertainties of nutrition science—

the difficulty of trying to find out what people eat and how diets differing in foods, tastes, textures, flavors, and cooking methods affect health. To this day, I love the way nutrition research and practice involve not only science but also economics, sociology, anthropology, politics, and psychology. I greatly enjoyed teaching that course. The fifty or so students were mostly premeds, interested in how their own bodies worked, and excited to be taking a course that had never been offered before.

I asked the students to write research term papers that started with some popular question about nutrition and health: Does vitamin C protect against colds? Does dietary fat increase heart disease risk? Does fiber protect against cancer? They were to read the research, come to a conclusion about what the research suggested, and give their personal reaction to those findings. Would they take vitamin C, reduce their fat intake, or increase their fiber intake as a result of what they had discovered?

No matter what topics the students chose, their papers all concluded that the studies they had found were poorly designed and controlled, used too few subjects to draw meaningful conclusions, and did not justify the conclusions drawn from them. Despite all that, students fully intended to change their diets based on what they had read, especially if they were writing about supplements. Just the idea that supplements *might* work, even if the research showed little or no effect, was all it took to persuade students that taking supplements might be beneficial. This taught me that beliefs are stronger influences on human behavior than scientific facts—a good lesson to learn.

Students liked the class so much that they asked for a more advanced version. About twenty of them signed up for a second class the next semester (the department was flexible about last-minute course offerings). I continued to assign original studies but also had students delve more deeply into the sociopolitical issues raised in

Food for People, Not for Profit. I assigned two long essays published in the *New York Review of Books* by the historian Geoffrey Barraclough, then teaching at Brandeis. These dealt with food insecurity in the developing world and its connection to what he called neocapitalism—the subordination of the interests of the poor to those of the rich through the massive transfer of wealth and power on a global scale.[8] To me, it seemed self-evident that food is linked to important social and political issues, but if other people were teaching about such connections, I did not know about them. The students felt they were doing pioneering work, and so did I.

This job was giving me a good sense of what I could do as an academic—teach material I loved, bring social and economic issues into discussions of science, explain how politics promotes inequalities—but I still had a long way to go. I needed to figure out what I wanted to do and to gain the confidence to move in that direction. Those nutrition courses were a good start, but they were the last I taught at Brandeis. My husband had taken a job in San Francisco. Once again, my kids and I would be following him across the country.

3 *Second Job*
A Spousal Hire   — ZachHall- 2nd husband

Zach had come to the end of his faculty appointment at Harvard Medical School and needed to find another job. He had multiple offers, but the one he most wanted was to chair the neurobiology department in the medical school at UCSF, the University of California's health sciences campus in San Francisco. That medical school was in the midst of deliberately transforming itself from an undistinguished clinical training center to a top-tier national research institution. Zach's recruitment was part of that transformation. I loved the idea of returning to the Bay Area but was uneasy about what I would be able to do there. Zach insisted that as a condition of his recruitment, the medical school help me find a job. We flew to San Francisco to interview—Zach as a coveted hire, I as an accompanying spouse.

The medical school dean, Julius Krevans, had already come up with a plan: he offered me a job in his school. And what a job! The offer was for a half-time administrative position as an associate dean, along with a half-time teaching position as a lecturer in the biochemistry department. This meant I would be getting an impressive title, administrative experience, a salary more than twice what Brandeis was paying me, and the opportunity to teach nutrition to medical students.

I was so flattered by the offer that I did not even think to ask about ✗ its potential pitfalls. I was a spousal hire, appointed without a formal search, holding two half-time positions (one of them in a department that would prove unwelcoming), teaching a topic that did not have its own department, and having only loosely defined responsibilities in the dean's office. I did not realize—and nobody told me—that academic institutions do not take spousal hires seriously, or that holding two half-time positions meant I would be reporting to two bosses, neither of whom would feel responsible for my salary increases, let alone career advancement. I would learn these and other hard lessons as I struggled to define my position in the dean's office and to develop a nutrition education curriculum.

Given my experience at Brandeis, I should also have been braced for the implications of being the only woman, untenured, among sixteen other associate deans, all of them male and tenured, and all but me with clearly defined responsibilities (for students, faculty, curriculum, admissions, government relations, teaching hospitals, and the like), and all but one of them white. As we got to know each other, I had a running joke with John Watson, the sole Black associate dean: he never experienced any racism at UCSF, and I never experienced any sexism. To be able to survive and do our jobs at UCSF without being in a constant rage or, in my case, tears, we learned to ignore all but the most egregious daily slights and insults (microaggressions, in today's terms).

Some of these came with the territory. Like my high school, UCSF was decidedly hierarchical. The medical faculty and administrators looked down on the university's pharmacy, dentistry, and nursing schools; they were particularly dismissive of the almost entirely female nursing school. Within the medical school itself, basic biomedical science fields like biochemistry and neurobiology had higher status than anatomy and physiology. At the very bottom were allied health fields like physical therapy. Nutrition? Oh please. It might as well not have existed. Even with my exalted title and my doctorate in molecular biology, I had low status. Having a PhD rather than an MD and not running a research program were particular disadvantages. All of this meant that each of my half-time jobs came with tough obstacles.

The Associate Dean Obstacles

The dean's office paid my salary and gave me an office. If my job title was impressive, my office was even more so. It was the one closest to the dean's and came with a gasp-inducing view overlooking Golden Gate Park clear to the ocean and all the way up the coast to Point Reyes. With an office like that, my job certainly gave the appearance of importance.

But what was it exactly? Officially, I was the associate dean for human biology programs. Bizarre as it now seems, this meant I was responsible for something that did not exist: UCSF's proposed School of Human Biology. The proposed school had been a pet project of Philip Lee, a former US assistant secretary for health, who was then heading up UCSF's health policy institute (which is now named after him).[1] Always ahead of his time, Lee wanted the School of Human Biology to focus on disease prevention, health education, and socioeconomic determinants of disease risk, and to unite UCSF's small but distinguished medical humanities programs in history, sociology, anthropology, psychology, biomedical engineering, and health policy. In theory, the school's aims were a perfect fit with my interests in nutrition.

But in practice, California legislators had never funded the school, and it did not take long for me to realize that they never would. Medical school leaders and the scientific elite viewed the human biology programs as "soft," meaning unscientific, nonrigorous (the most dismissive thing anyone could possibly say about research), and not worth funding. Indeed, they viewed the work of medical humanities faculty as nonresearch. From the perspective of the medical school, which aspired to—and soon attained—high national status, the only research that counted was laboratory-based and worthy of publication in prestigious journals like *Science, Nature, Cell,* and the *New England Journal of Medicine.* Dean Krevans made it clear that my job was to keep the proposed school on a back burner and devote no effort to making it happen. I was too new and uncertain about my position to object or try to do otherwise.

Having no better idea of what I should be doing, I said yes to anything I was asked. Would I take over directing the first-year medical biochemistry course? I would and did. I worked with leading basic science and clinical research faculty to write a grant proposal for a combined MD-PhD program to train physicians to do biomedical research. When the funding came through, I became the program's administrative director. The director of record was a research physician, and the program's advisory committee consisted of the medical school's most prestigious scientists, my husband among them. Although I managed the grants and student admissions, this was staff, not line, responsibility—meaning that I did the work, but the director got the credit. When he left UCSF to become scientific director at one of the early start-up biotechnology companies, he appointed his successor without consulting me. I was erased from the program's history, and I only heard about its fortieth anniversary celebration, in 2017, after the event was over.

I also served on the school's admissions committee and its subcommittee for socioeconomically disadvantaged applicants, created by John Watson in the wake of the Supreme Court's *Bakke* decision. That decision ruled unconstitutional the use of race as a criterion for medical admissions but allowed schools to continue to apply affirmative action, as long as race was not the only criterion for determining socioeconomic disadvantage. Our subcommittee admitted disadvantaged white students as well as those who were Black or Latino. I was surprised to realize that by these criteria, my family's low income, my father's early death, and my being the first in my family to go to college would have qualified me for admission through that subcommittee. Growing up, I never thought of myself as disadvantaged, but most UCSF medical applicants came from wealthier and better-educated families than mine.

In the 1970s, UCSF also began admitting more women medical students, but they were still a minority. The women students had a dreadful time dealing with the overtly sexist environment—instructors who showed slides of naked women to illustrate anatomical points, hit on them, or commented on their appearance or sexuality in front of faculty, peers, or patients. These practices were *normal*. Objections elicited responses that anyone in today's #MeToo era would recognize: "You have no sense of humor," "You are too sensitive," "You better get used to it if you want to survive here."

University administrators appeared untroubled by this kind of faculty behavior and had no incentive to try to stop it. Instead, the student affairs office organized support groups to help women students cope with this kind of environment. The groups were run jointly by a therapist and a faculty member. I volunteered to participate and was assigned to work with Dr. Loma Flowers, a Black psychiatrist. Her first words on meeting me were "I don't understand why I need you to be doing this." I admitted that I knew nothing about therapy, but on the basis of my Brandeis experience—and what now seems like hubris—I assured her that I knew how to get things done at academic institutions. We turned out to be great partners in running that group. She is a breathtakingly insightful clinician, and I did know how to get some problems fixed. We appreciated each other's skills and have been the best of friends ever since. We scheduled our meetings to discuss the group on walks around Stow Lake in Golden Gate Park, a tradition we continue whenever I can get to the Bay Area. I would never have survived UCSF without her friendship and wise counsel.

I needed all the counsel I could get, because I also agreed to chair the newly formed and highly unpopular Chancellor's Advisory Committee on the Status of Women. This gave me license to conduct surveys demonstrating campuswide underrepresentation of women at higher academic and administrative levels (except in the School of Nursing), and to organize a women's faculty association and a task force on child care. The big challenge for these groups was to counter the male faculty members' more blatant displays of sexist behavior.

Here's an example. I was invited to the Department of Medicine's end-of-year dinner to honor students who were finishing their postgraduate residencies. The dinner was held at Trader Vic's, the Polynesian-themed bar and restaurant famous for inventing the mai tai. Although I knew that alcohol was this restaurant's selling point, I was unprepared for how much this party would resemble a fraternity hazing. One man got so drunk that he threw up on our table. The after-dinner speakers roasted individual trainees, not kindly. The chair of the Department of Medicine told an aggressive, raunchy joke in which he used the name of a first-year woman resident. This elicited raucous laughter and hooting at her expense. With as much dignity as she could muster, the targeted resident walked out with her date, to more raucous hooting.

This department chair was the single most powerful clinical faculty member at UCSF. The following Monday, I summoned up all my courage and went to talk to him about the effects of this kind of behavior on women students, residents, and faculty, and why he needed to make it stop. He politely heard me out, but this and other such efforts earned me no applause from the men in power.

Helpful to students, minorities, and women as my work might have been, it did not add up to a job with real authority. That did not concern me nearly as much as it should have, mainly because what I really cared about was getting nutrition into the core curriculum of the medical and other schools at UCSF in any way I could.

The Nutrition Obstacles

The summer before my family moved to San Francisco, UCSF's associate dean for faculty affairs, Bill Reinhardt, whom I had met on the earlier visit, began mailing me journal articles about nutrition in medical education, along with current copies of the student newspaper, *The Synapse*.[2] That's how I discovered why Krevans had created my position. UCSF students had been demanding nutrition content in their courses. The *Synapse* articles described these and additional demands for more diversity in the student body, a greater focus on disease prevention, and more emphasis on socioeconomic causes of poor health. This was reassuring. If UCSF students cared about such matters, I was going to the right place.

I worried that I did not know enough about nutrition to teach it to medical students. That summer I studied every minute I could. Planning a trip to San Francisco to find us a place to live, I asked the dean's office to arrange a meeting with the medical students who were pushing for nutrition instruction. That was when I met second-year medical school classmates Bobby Baron, Jim Cone, and Erica Goode. Bobby had a master's degree in nutrition and would become my closest adviser and collaborator on the nutrition curriculum. Jim and Erica also knew the field. All have been friends ever since.[3]

These students did know more about nutrition—and a lot more about medicine—than I did. When I explained why I wanted to meet them, their response was blunt. "We were hoping for someone trained in nutrition." "I get that," I said, "but I'm a quick study. You tell me what I need to do, and I will get it done." I had one final question for them: "How widespread is student interest in nutrition, preventive medicine, and social justice?" Their answer was, "We are it." That was disappointing, but at least I would have them as allies. I needed allies; I already had enemies.

My appointment as a spousal hire stepped hard on the toes of faculty at both UCSF and Berkeley who had long been lobbying the medical school to let them teach nutrition. I made a special trip to Berkeley to pay my respects to Doris Calloway, a distinguished nutrition researcher and chair of its nutritional sciences department. Her response: "It's obvious that UCSF still has no interest in teaching nutrition to medical students. Don't call on us for help." Ouch. I tried not to take this personally and to look on the bright side; I was now free to do whatever I wanted without seeking her approval.[4] I also introduced myself to Sheldon Margen, a physician who chaired the nutrition program in Berkeley's School of Public Health. He, in contrast, could not have been warmer or more welcoming: "Anything you want, just ask." I did, and often.

As a quasi-half-time biochemistry department faculty member (quasi because I did not have an office in the department and was considered peripheral), I had been allotted a block of five one-hour lectures in which to teach nutrition during the first-year biochemistry course. Bobby Baron told me what needed to be taught, and I followed his advice to the letter. I read everything I could get my hands on. Still worried that students knew more than I did, I overprepared as usual. I tried to relate basic nutrition information to the kinds of health conditions students were most likely to encounter in patient visits—obesity, type 2 diabetes, coronary heart disease, and cancer—and the kinds of questions patients were most likely to ask about personal dietary choices, supplements, and fad diets. From the start, my lectures went well. Preparation helps.

But like most medical school courses, biochemistry was taught by a rotating group of faculty, each covering a specific topic in a few lecture hours. Students hated the course, and I could see why. The lecturers mostly talked about their own research interests, and students were expected to memorize complicated metabolic pathways without explanation of their clinical relevance. I thought I could fix the problems by polling students about what they wanted, recruiting faculty more interested in teaching, and making the curriculum more relevant. Directing the course meant that I could add more hours for nutrition. All those changes made a difference.

I worked closely with student allies, the hospital dietetics staff, and interested faculty to develop the nutrition curriculum. In the late 1970s, when the US Health Resources Administration called for proposals to develop campuswide, interdisciplinary nutrition education programs, we applied for and won one of these grants, which I administered out of the dean's office. We called the program Nutrition-UCSF. We used the grant to fund public lectures (which routinely filled the largest auditorium), develop a four-week clinical elective course, and pay for the teaching participation of faculty in any number of clinical and basic science departments who worked on some aspect of nutrition. I continued to teach nutrition topics in the first-year biochemistry course but also gave lectures in the departments of medicine, pediatrics, and family medicine. I even conducted nutrition ward rounds with interns and residents at San Francisco General Hospital.[5]

The grant made all this possible. As I quickly learned, faculty and staff who were interested in teaching nutrition would be given lecture time in almost any course, as long as NutritionUCSF contributed to their salaries. As little as 5 percent of a faculty or staff salary was enough to legitimize their participation. Although the Reagan administration cut off that grant in 1980, those lectures had become established parts of courses and could continue. Managing this project felt like a real job.

The Public Obstacles

I was teaching just about anything related to diet and health—diets for specific disease conditions, nutrition in the life cycle, nutrition counseling, even the emerging field of parenteral and enteral nutrition (intravenous and tube feeding of hospitalized patients). I gave lectures to the entire faculty of a department or school during "grand rounds." I helped found the Northern California chapter of the American Society for Parenteral and Enteral Nutrition. I read medical and nutrition journals. One lecture at a time, I became a nutrition generalist. If I couldn't answer a question, I researched the topic until I could. But because I was self-taught, I still lacked confidence in what I knew.

In 1979, we still had the federal grant for NutritionUCSF and used it to help organize a conference on nutrition for health professionals, among the first of its kind to be held at a medical school. Interest was tremendous: 1,200 people signed up. I was asked to give the opening talk, an hour-long introduction to basic nutrition principles, with slides. I agreed to do it, but was terrified. I had never given a public lecture, or a slide talk, or faced an audience so large. I spent six weeks working on the slides—this was long before PowerPoint—and rehearsed my talk repeatedly before small groups of friends. I was too nervous to eat and lost weight.

When I gave the talk, the double Nobel Prize winner Linus Pauling was sitting with me on the podium, and Michael Jacobson and Bonnie Liebman from the Center for Science in the Public Interest were in the audience. The talk went fine—my terror does not show, apparently—but questions from the audience felt like attacks, and I handled them defensively. When I went to pick up my slides, the audiovisual technician, a man in his fifties, said "I think you have possibilities as a speaker. Can I give you some feedback?" I was still feeling defensive, but thought I had better hear him out. I'm glad I did. He told me to use pictures rather than words in my slides, use as few words as possible, and set the words in the largest possible font. He also suggested ways to validate and respond to audience questions. His advice was immensely useful, and I have followed it ever since.

If I wanted to continue to reach public audiences, I was going to have to overcome my terror and get better at dealing with questions. I could think of only one way to do that: practice. I accepted every speaking invitation, no matter who the audience, or how small. That was how I agreed to do a series of nutrition segments for *Over Easy*, an award-winning television program aimed at older adults that aired on San Francisco's public station, KQED. One of its producers, Mady Werner (who later changed her name to Iliani Matisse), convinced me to do it even though I had never appeared on television before. I would deliver five- to seven-minute segments—an eternity on TV—before live audiences. Talk about terror. To deal with it, I *really* overprepared: the first segment took more than forty hours of script writing, prop development, and rehearsals. The host was Frank Blair, a former news anchor on NBC's *Today Show*. For my first seven-minute appearance, the script called for him to ask me seven questions about why fresh foods are healthier than highly processed foods. These I was to answer while holding up large models of food packages and nutrition labels, cuing the crew to run video clips, and making sure everything was timed to within ten seconds. After all that rehearsing, I had my part down cold.

But at the actual taping in front of the live audience, Blair got so interested in what I was saying that he threw in an unexpected, unscripted question. I don't remember what it was, but I certainly remember my confusion. This was my first time on TV, and Blair was the experienced host, so I guessed I was supposed to answer his question. I stumbled through it and threw off the entire timing. The crew frantically signaled me to get back on schedule, but the segment was ruined. By the time the ordeal ended, I was in tears. The producers told Blair to stick to the script and had us come back the next day to retape the segment.

This disaster had one good outcome: it ended my stage fright forever—not because nothing worse could ever happen but because of the reaction I got from people who had seen me on TV. One after another, they told me the same things in almost the same order:

"I was just flipping channels."

"I saw you on TV."

"You looked fabulous."

And, after a sheepish pause: "I can't remember what you were talking about."

After hearing these same phrases repeatedly, I got it. I could stop worrying. Nobody would remember what I said anyway. Viewers would only recall that I was on TV and looked as if I was having fun. If any nutrition messages did get across, they would be subliminal.

From 1980 to 1982, I filmed thirteen segments for *Over Easy*. By the time I did my last segments, the host was Mary Martin, the stage star of *South Pacific* and *Peter Pan*, and I loved being on camera with her. She could no longer see the teleprompter or hear very well, and it was up to me to make sure that our conversation went smoothly and stuck to schedule. By then I could do that. Today I don't prepare at all for video interviews, knowing they will almost certainly be edited down to ten seconds anyway. I just try to answer the interviewers' questions as clearly as I can and look like I'm enjoying the experience. It all seems to come out fine.

The *Over Easy* segments I most enjoyed involved the cooking demonstrations. Some of these featured Narsai David, my friend from Berkeley co-op days, who by then was a well-known Bay Area chef. We did one with Craig Claiborne, the food critic for the *New York Times*. Claiborne had health problems and had just cowritten a healthy eating cookbook with Pierre Franey, called *Craig Claiborne's Gourmet Diet*. Their book began with an introduction to nutrition principles by Jane Brody, whose columns for the *New York Times*

FIGURE 9. In a 1981 episode of KQED's television program *Over Easy,* I show the host, Frank Blair (*left*), and the *New York Times* restaurant critic and cookbook author Craig Claiborne (*center*), how much salt is added to processed foods. Claiborne was on a low-salt diet at the time.

lasted until 2022. He gave me a signed copy, which I still have and use. Archived copies of *Over Easy* programs are hard to come by, but I managed to track down the Claiborne episode (figure 9).

Gradually, I became more comfortable speaking to audiences and responding to their questions. I began writing about nutrition by doing short book reviews for the magazine *Medical Self-Care.* Those gave me the courage to review *Jane Brody's Nutrition Book* for the *San Francisco Chronicle.*[6] I started writing articles, book chapters, and letters to editors about nutrition in medical education, diet and chronic disease, dietary guidelines, and hospital nutritional support. At the invitation of the UCSF health policy professor Phil Lee, I coauthored a chapter for a book on nutrition policy—my first entry into this field—with him and Bobby Baron.[7]

Early in 1983, a publisher of medical textbooks, Richard Jones, had heard my talks at conferences and asked me to write a nutrition book for medical students based on my teaching and writing. My husband was taking a sabbatical in Paris, and the dean's office gave me a leave that fall to go with him. There I established the work routine I still use. Mornings, I worked on the book. Afternoons, I did everything else I wanted or needed to do, explored the city's bakeries and bistros, and practiced my American-accented French.

Nutrition in Clinical Practice came out in spring 1985. It summarized everything I thought students and practitioners needed to know about nutrition in fifty-six very brief chapters. This was my first book, and I was proud of it. It got a few good reviews and was adopted as a text for some classes, translated into Greek, and published in an English edition for the Asian market.[8] So far, so good. But within just a few months, Jones must have gone through a midlife crisis. He enrolled in music school and abandoned his publishing business—along with my precious book. I doubt it ever sold more than a couple of thousand copies. But, if you can believe this, a few copies are still floating around, and in March 2021 I saw an unused copy offered on Amazon at the astounding price of $920.99. (The book is badly out of date: if you can't live without one, I'd recommend finding a used copy available for the cost of shipping.)

Despite its sad fate, this book proved its worth. It was my life raft—something positive and constructive I could focus on during a troubled time. My marriage and my UCSF job were coming to a simultaneous end. Working on the book helped me get through this lowest point in my life. It also turned out to be precisely the qualification I most needed for the job I would get after having to leave UCSF and San Francisco.

End marriage & UCSF job. 1985

The Beginnings of the End ✓

spousal appt

over

In 1984, the medical school dean who had hired me, Julius Krevans, moved up to become UCSF's chancellor. I did not understand—and once again nobody told me—that my position as associate dean was essentially a political appointment, meaning that I was expected to offer my resignation the instant a new dean arrived. Untenured, unaware of that inconvenient truth, and not knowing what else to do, I stuck around. In doing that, I got a firsthand education in how the politics of that medical school really worked.

My education began with the search for a new dean. By then, universities were following affirmative action guidelines requiring job searches to be open to all qualified candidates. Krevans appointed a thirty-member search committee—all white men, my husband among them. As chair of the Committee on the Status of Women, I felt that I had to say something. I did, and was appointed to the committee. But then my husband mentioned that he would be attending a meeting I had not heard about. He had been appointed to a small executive committee—all white males, of course—that would be running the show. I complained again and was added to the executive committee.

Nobody I talked to could understand why I was bothering. Apparently, everyone but me knew that you don't ever apply for a dean's job; you have to be nominated. Any candidate who applied for the position clearly did not know how this game was played—an immediate disqualification. In any case, this was a "wired" search. Its outcome had already been decided, and everyone else knew who the next dean would be. My unpopular job on this committee would be to try to make the search process as open as possible.

Bob Fishman, the chair of the neurology department, was heading the nominal search. In the first meeting of the small executive committee, he announced the preselected candidate and apologized for the annoying affirmative action rules that required him to put us through this tedious and unnecessary process. He dutifully recited the names of nominated candidates, among them Virginia Weldon, then vice president of the Washington University Medical Center in St. Louis. "She's out," Fishman said." Her husband is a cardiologist, and UCSF doesn't need any more cardiologists."

> ME [wishing I did not have to do this]: Shouldn't we be considering her candidacy on its own merits?
>
> FISHMAN [with a big sigh]: Oh, all right. She stays in.

Weldon remained in the pool, but when her name came up before the full committee, the same thing happened: "But her husband is a cardiologist." "Oh no," I said, "not this again." Everyone laughed.

At the next meeting of the executive committee, we went through the whole exchange again, but this time Fishman said, exasperated, "Really Marion, you of all people should understand this." As a spousal hire, I ought to know my place. None of the men on the committee, including my husband, said a word. Zach and I brought the tension over that and other such incidents home with us. The strain at work and at home were getting worse, and I was having a hard time dealing with both.

But then Fishman and the search committee were in for a shock. The "wired" candidate turned down the job. By then, all the other candidates had been told they were no longer under consideration. That left the one in-house candidate, Rudy Schmidt, the chair of UCSF's gastroenterology department. As the last man standing, the job was his. In our first meeting, Schmidt said, "I don't understand what you are doing here. If you had an MD degree, you could be teaching nutrition to medical students." I tried to explain that I had been doing just that for the past eight years, but failed to convince him that my work was in any way useful.

His first act was to move me out of the office with the stunning view to one overlooking the hospital driveway, a signal I chose to ignore. He also stopped inviting me to meetings of senior administrators, which meant that I did not know that the state legislature had increased the number of hours of clinical training required for medical students. Because the MD-PhD program required fewer clinical hours, its graduates might not qualify for medical licensure under the new rules. When I finally heard about this and raised an alarm, I expected to be thanked. Instead, I was berated for my incompetence in front of the entire office. Soon after, I was moved out of the dean's suite altogether. David Werdegar, the chair of family medicine, offered me space in his windowless suite in the basement of the parking garage. I gratefully accepted and moved the nutrition education program and everything else I was doing into his department.

At Last, Some Good Advice

I still had the title of associate dean but could no longer ignore the vulnerability of my position. I did not have a mentor. Indeed, I had never even heard the term and had no idea how handicapped I was without one. I sought advice from Phil Lee, who headed the health policy institute. I knew him to be highly experienced in academic and national politics, thoughtful, and generous with his time and attention. During our meeting, I did what women, particularly at medical schools, are never, ever supposed to do: I cried and couldn't stop. Phil heard me out. What he said should not have come as a surprise, but did: "You have to resign. Deans get to choose their own associate deans. Schmidt did not choose you. You need to resign." More tears.

But then he added, "And here's how you do it."

He pointed to my lack of academic credentials in nutrition. I needed to do something about that: "Tell Rudy Schmidt you are sorry things aren't working out. Ask him to help you with the next stage of your career. Ask for two years of salary support while you go to public health school and get a master's degree in public health. Promise him that you will leave UCSF in two years."

I was stunned. Was such a deal even possible? It took me weeks to work up the nerve to act on his advice, mainly because my personal life was falling apart. Couples therapy was not working, my marriage to Zach was ending, and I would soon be moving out of our house. When I finally invoked Phil Lee's script, which I followed to the letter, Schmidt looked surprised, hesitated for a moment, and said he would discuss it with the school's financial officer and let me know. No more than ten minutes later, the time it took to get back to my basement office, I found a message clipped to my office phone: the dean had accepted my proposal and was drafting a confirming letter. For once, being the only woman on the dean's staff worked to my advantage. I would leave quietly, without a fuss, in return for two years of salary support. This would give me time to get my life together, personally as well as professionally.

NB ☆

Letters of Recommendation

While writing this chapter, I happened to run across a tweet from Anne McBride, a graduate of the NYU food studies doctoral program. She was writing a recommendation letter for a student and wanted to make sure she was "not using gendered language that will hinder her chances." She referred to a document put out by the University of Arizona Commission on Women, "Avoiding Gender Bias in Reference Writing."[9] It advised mentioning research and publications, emphasizing accomplishments rather than effort, and keeping comments professional. This took me right back to yet another searing event during my final years at UCSF.

When I moved to family medicine in the late fall of 1984, I asked its chair, Dave Werdegar, for one more favor. I had not had a salary raise in several years (another signal I found easier to ignore). Would he put me up for a merit increase? "No," he said, "I will do better than that. I will put you up for a promotion to adjunct associate professor." At UCSF, that title applied to full-time, nontenured teaching faculty, and included full benefits. This offer was anything but trivial. The promotion would have to go through a formal process requiring extensive documentation; he asked me to give him a list of *thirty* people who might be willing to write supporting letters.

I came up with the names of doctors, scientists, and administrators, mostly men, who had personally observed my teaching, lectures, grant writing, book writing, student advising, management of the MD-PhD program, and work on admissions and other committees. I turned in the list and forgot about it, knowing that the process would take months.

Some weeks later, I happened to be in the dean's office and ran into the administrative assistant for faculty affairs. She, like others there, was sorry about what had happened to me. She pointed to a chair, told me to sit down and not budge, and handed me a folder. "This will make you feel better," she said. The folder was marked "CONFIDENTIAL." It contained my promotion letters.

The letters did *not* make me feel better. Quite the contrary. From having seen tenure committee packets and serving on medical admissions committees, I knew a good letter of recommendation when I saw one. These letters barely mentioned anything I'd done; they mostly said I was nice and worked hard. One, from a faculty member for whom I had given lectures, organized conferences, and written book chapters, mentioned none of those accomplishments; his highest praise was that I met deadlines. Only one letter—from Bobby Baron, by then on the faculty—detailed what I had actually accomplished and assessed its quality. I walked out of the dean's office wondering how I had lasted there as long as I did. Nevertheless, the promotion went through, and my new title turned out to be the determining factor in the success of my negotiations for the job I took at NYU in 1988.

Glimmers of a Future

By the time I moved out of the dean's office, my children were in college and away from home. Work and other issues had strained my marriage to Zach to the breaking point. We separated and soon divorced. Out of a job and a marriage at the same time, I knew I needed to think hard about how I had ended up in this situation and what to do next. I moved into an apartment at the far western edge of San Francisco, overlooking the ocean at Lands End. On rare clear days I could see the distant Farallon Islands, but the coast was mostly fogbound and chilly, and I went to sleep listening to the foghorns and barking sea lions (they moved to Fisherman's Wharf a few years later). Wondering how I had made such a mess of my life and worried about what the future might hold, I wanted to be someplace beautiful and inspiring.

The event that most symbolizes that low point in my life was the struggle to get a credit card. As a wife, I had no independent credit record, and was turned down by every credit card company I applied to, including Bank of America, where I had a checking account. I could not even get a card from Working Assets, which claimed to support social values. I went back to my local Bank of America branch, made my case, and was again refused. At that point I lost it and broke into tears. A clerk came over and asked what was wrong. "Honey," she said, "I've been there. I'll take care of it." I felt embarrassed to have created such a scene, but I left the bank with a credit card in hand and went back the next day with a gift for my new friend.

The rest of that period is a blur, except that I asked Loma Flowers to recommend a therapist. She suggested Nancy Kaltreider, a faculty member in UCSF's psychiatry department, an excellent choice.

Nancy, who later edited *Dilemmas of a Double Life: Women Balancing Careers and Relationships,* had no trouble understanding what I was going through. In our first meeting, she said so, but also said she was puzzled by why I felt trapped. Good point. I still did not feel that I had choices. Recounting my family background and experiences in marriage gave us plenty to talk about.

But then good things started to happen. The UCSF bookstore hosted a book-signing party for the launch of *Nutrition in Clinical Practice.* Bobby Baron invited me to speak at a conference in Nicaragua organized by the Committee for Health Rights in Central America, where I met new people and made new friends. Out of the blue, I got a letter from the John Tung Foundation in Hong Kong offering me funding for a joint program in nutrition education with the American Cancer Society.[10] Money talks: this grant gave me work to do and some credibility at UCSF during those last two years.

While I still had salary support from UCSF, I followed the rest of Phil Lee's advice and went to Berkeley to ask Sheldon Margen about the possibility of entering his master's program in public health nutrition. I had missed the application deadline, but he introduced me to the dean, Joyce Lashof, and I was in. Still, I felt as if I were jumping off a cliff. I was fifty years old, on my own, and needed to find a job. But for the moment, I had something worthwhile to do. I would be going to public health school in the fall to get myself credentialed in nutrition.

4 Back to School

84-2
1986.

Public health school did just what Phil Lee had promised: it opened doors. It also introduced me to terrific classmates. Some of them had worked in public health for a long time but, like me, needed the MPH (master of public health) credential to advance professionally. One was Wendel Brunner, whom I had met a year earlier at the conference in Nicaragua. He was the public health director for Contra Costa County and already had MD and PhD degrees, but he needed, as he put it, the M, the P, and the H. So did the international health consultant Phil Packard. They were my public health school pals, in addition to the five much younger but equally terrific women who were my fellow students in the nutrition specialization program.

I was not entirely convinced that I needed this credential. I already had a doctorate, had just published *Nutrition in Clinical Practice,* and had been teaching nutrition for the past decade. But nutrition is unusual in having different kinds of credentialing. People can call themselves nutritionists with no training at all, or on the basis of online certificate programs based on life experience, whereas others have done years of coursework and research, sometimes with doctoral degrees. Dietitian-nutritionists have to take specific courses, have an undergraduate degree (and, as of 2024, a master's degree), and perform a hospital-based internship. My master's in public health nutrition would qualify me to work in community settings, but did I really need that?

But I quickly understood that this program would be good for me, not least because it was going to be fun. Public health is about how social and political forces determine the health risks of populations. It is about groups more than individuals, prevention of illness rather than treatment, societal rather than personal determinants of health, and using policy to improve health and society. Because it seeks to reduce the socioeconomic inequities that contribute to ill-health, it is also about strengthening democracy. It fit my way of thinking. These were my people.

The public health nutrition program required thirty-six credits, was expected to take two years to complete, and involved the usual lecture courses but also fieldwork consisting of two semesters of part-time work plus a summer working full-time in a public health program or agency. By the time I enrolled in the program, I had only one year of salary left from UCSF. I had promised the UCSF dean I would be gone by October 1986, by which point I would need to find another job. I needed to get this degree done in one year.

Because many of the students in the program were working professionals, the school allowed students to test out of most courses. I took every exemption exam I thought I had a chance of passing, and I did pass some of them. Apparently, I had learned a few useful things about epidemiology and health care administration in my years at UCSF. Having just written a book on the topic, I aced the nutrition exams. Some instructors, like Barbara Abrams, a friend from the time she worked as a nutritionist at UCSF, made generous allowances. Embarrassed as I am to admit it, I still owe her a term paper on maternal and child nutrition.

 I tried to get excused from taking Larry Wallack's course on program planning and evaluation because I already knew how to write grants, but the school insisted I take it. They were right. This was one great course. Wallack taught how to think about public health—to look for the root causes of public health problems, work with communities to overcome them, and develop policies to improve health—skills I've drawn on ever since.

The public health nutrition program simultaneously credentialed students as registered dietitian (RD) and MPH. Back then, qualifying for the RD required most of the same undergraduate courses as it does today, but the nine-hundred-hour internship did not have to be done in a hospital. I had taken most of the required courses, but not the one in food service management. Missing that particular course was the deal breaker. Because I lacked that course, I never did qualify for the RD, despite having met all the internship requirements through public health fieldwork.

The fieldwork was the best part of the program. Its supervisor, Doris Disbrow, suggested I get a head start. The summer before I began taking classes, she arranged for me to visit federal food assistance centers and privately run food banks to find out how they operated, whom they were reaching, and how well they worked. I liked seeing for myself what was happening at such places and comparing what I saw to what I was told. I could observe whether the programs I visited were serving their client populations adequately and how some could do better in kindness and outreach.

For my two-semester fieldwork project, I wanted something more challenging. Homelessness was a new and shocking issue in San Francisco, the result of Reagan-era cuts in welfare benefits and the discharge of people formerly housed in mental institutions. I talked my way into volunteering with San Francisco's Coalition of Homeless Shelter Providers.[1] I spent as much time as I could with this group over the next few months, getting to know the providers and clients, serving meals in soup kitchens, and meeting with leaders of St. Anthony's, the Episcopal Sanctuary, Salvation Army, and representatives of city agencies and other participating groups.

This experience gave me a firsthand understanding of who was living on the streets, why, and what needed to be done to meet their needs for food. Most of the soup-kitchen clients were veterans, former mental hospital patients, people addicted to alcohol or drugs, or people way down on their luck. At the request of one of the coalition members, but against my better judgment, I agreed to give a lecture on healthy eating to a group of homeless men at a shelter. They looked at me as if I were out of my mind. "Ms. Nutrition," one said, "Don't talk to us about what we are supposed to eat. Talk to St. Anthony's. That's who's feeding us." After that, I was "Ms. Nutrition" to the coalition members.

Those men had a good point. The local soup kitchens were sourcing food from wherever they could get it and serving up whatever they got. I often helped prepare and serve meals at the Episcopal Sanctuary and was amazed by what was donated. We were given crates of exotic and expensive red peppers too far gone to sell. We pared away the moldy parts and tossed the rest into the soup. Hunters donated venison; we had to dig out the shot before letting anyone eat it. My favorite donations came from the local X-rated bakery; it contributed enormous leftover cakes baked as chocolate-covered penises and pink-frosted, cherry-tipped breasts, fortunately unrecognizable after slicing. The shelter clients loved them.

The coalition asked me to help design a survey of the health status of mothers who were temporarily housed in a single-room occupancy hotel in the Mission district. I went to the hotel to meet the women, hear their stories, and see what they were up against. I could not imagine how they managed babies and toddlers in such small rooms. The hotel did not allow children to play in the halls. One mother lived with her thirteen-year-old daughter in a room that held two beds, an illegal hot plate, and possessions piled up on the floor. It broke my heart to think that this teenager went to junior high school from that room. Every floor in the hotel had a community room and kitchen, but these were kept locked: nobody was allowed to use them.

It didn't take a genius to imagine what might make life better for those women, starting with community babysitting and meal preparation, but my survey had a different purpose. It was to collect data on food needs, although these too seemed obvious. I worked for weeks with a committee of coalition members to write it. But just when my food part of the much longer survey was ready to administer, I made a bad mistake. One of the coalition members asked what I intended to do with the results. "Publish them," I said. "Nobody knows anything about homeless mothers with children, and this will be valuable information." Wrong answer. The coalition members accused me of exploiting homeless women for my own career gain and stopped the survey cold. It had never occurred to me that what I was doing could be viewed as exploitation: I thought I was helping. This was an important lesson about the complicated role of academics working with communities, and one I've never forgotten.

But now what? Doris Disbrow gave me good advice. She told me to hang in there, continue to go to the meetings, and try to regain the coalition's trust. She suggested I use my term-paper requirement to describe what happened and what I could have done better. I followed her advice. I hung in there, despite feeling awkward about attending the coalition meetings. Weeks later, I got a call from the coalition member who had invited me to speak to the homeless men and who was on the survey committee. He had induced the manager of the hotel to allow nursing students from San Francisco State University to administer the entire survey. I could not imagine how he pulled this off. All he said was that he "had something" on the manager that convinced the man to be more accommodating. "Is your survey ready? The nursing students will give it out for you. Tomorrow. Get it over here."

I never found out what that "something" was or why it was suddenly acceptable to give out the survey, but I ended up with twenty-one filled-out questionnaires. The results were stark. Not a single one of the women who completed the questionnaire was participating in federal food assistance programs, even though they all qualified for food stamps and WIC, the Special Supplemental Program for Women, Infants, and Children. The number of WIC recipients is limited by the size of state grants, but San Francisco's welfare department had set aside two hundred of its allotted slots for women who were homeless. These were going unused.

The results of this survey convinced the city to install a social worker in the hotel to make sure these women got every benefit to which they were entitled. My school project had actually accomplished something! I never published a word about the survey or my observations, but I felt so good about what community public health could accomplish that I wanted to do more of it.

The Job Search

While taking classes, writing term papers, and working with the homeless coalition, I was also job hunting. I was hoping to find a position in an agency or organization engaged in food and nutrition policy advocacy, or a university where I could do policy work. But my skills didn't seem to match what anyone wanted, and I must not have been interviewing well, because I got no offers. I asked everyone I knew for suggestions, including Phil Lee. Although I dreaded the thought of having to leave California, my now-adult children, and my friends of the last thirty years, Phil arranged for me to talk to Mike McGinnis, who ran the Office of Disease Prevention and Health Promotion in Washington, DC, saying, "He's got a big project you'd be perfect for." The project was indeed big: a comprehensive report on everything known about the role of nutrition in health. Since I had just finished writing a book like that, I could indeed be the right person for it. I could see only one possible snag: my meeting with McGinnis was tense, and I suspected I would not have an easy time working for him. But everyone who knew both of us assured me the job would be worth it and I would be able to handle it.

Shelly Margen, my beloved professor at the public health school, suggested I also meet with Marty Forman, the head of nutrition at the Agency for International Development (USAID).[2] But Forman was scornful when I asked about work in international nutrition: "You have no international experience." "Okay," I said, "would there be any possibility of my getting some?" I told him about my summer fieldwork requirement and how, since I still had a salary from UCSF, I would not need to be paid. I could hardly believe it when he offered to send me to Southeast Asia to investigate the extent of malnutrition in rapidly urbanizing cities. USAID would make the arrangements and pay for travel, hotel, and incidental costs. My MPH degree really was opening doors.

When I got back to Berkeley, I told Phil Packard and my other international-consultant classmates about the Southeast Asia plans. They were appalled.

"This is just like USAID, sending someone like you who knows nothing about international work to do something like this."

"Should I not go?"

"Of course you should go; just don't expect to accomplish anything."

With that advice firmly in mind, I got myself vaccinated against all manner of tropical diseases and packed for what turned out to be a full summer of travel and work in Hong Kong, Shanghai, Bangkok, and Jakarta.

Adventures in Southeast Asia

I had never traveled on my own before, or been to Southeast Asia, or worked for an international agency, and I was feeling a lot of appre-

FIGURE 10. My 1986 Southeast Asia travels began with a visit to John Tung, the antismoking philanthropist whose foundation funded my UCSF grant for an education project with the American Cancer Society. This was just after lunch at a lovely restaurant overlooking the Hong Kong harbor. I was glad to have had the chance to meet him; he died later that year.

hension about how this would go. My summer travels began in Hong Kong, where I looked forward to meeting John Tung, whose foundation had given me the nutrition-in-cancer education grant at UCSF (figure 10). He took me to elegant lunches and to dinners where I had my first tastes of shark's fin and bird's nest soups. They were a bit subtle for my taste, but knowing how rare and expensive they were, I hoped I was being sufficiently appreciative. I had an easier time appreciating the sweet bean buns from a stand near the Kowloon ferry. I could see that if Hong Kong was any indication, eating my way through this summer of fieldwork would be exceptionally pleasant.

Neither the Hong Kong visit nor my next stop in Shanghai was sponsored by USAID. Purely by coincidence, I had gotten another, completely unrelated invitation to travel to Southeast Asia, and I could link the two opportunities. Hanmin Liu, the founder of the United States–China Educational Institute in San Francisco, had invited me to Shanghai to teach a workshop for senior Chinese medical scientists headed to the United States to work in research laboratories or hospitals. Because past exchanges had not gone well for either the Chinese scientists or their American hosts, a sociologist had done a survey to find out why. The survey results exposed profound cultural misunderstandings, and Liu had designed the workshop to address them.[3]

Our job would be to teach the Chinese scientists how to cope with aspects of American culture that caused particular cultural misunderstandings. Our first session, for example, was about what to do when they arrived at airports in the United States and nobody was there to meet them. I could see why this would be troubling to Chinese visitors. I had boarded the plane to Shanghai speaking no Chinese and knowing nothing about where I was supposed to go when I got there or even the official name of the program I was joining. It was a relief when I arrived in Shanghai to be greeted by a welcoming committee of at least ten people holding up a banner bearing my name and a welcome in English. Our sessions also dealt with how to respond to questions about what the visitors wanted to accomplish, how to get the resources they needed, and why they needed to say yes right away when invited to dinner (impolite in China, essential in America). The final lesson was about how to eat standing up at a cocktail party.

I was no expert on Chinese culture, but I knew how American universities worked. And I got as much out of the sessions as our students did: this was a cram course on cross-cultural communication. The timing could not have been better. I could finish teaching the workshop before starting my investigative work for USAID.

In 1986 Shanghai, everyone wore blue Mao jackets and rode bicycles. There were few tourists and no signs in English. The Chinese scientists had learned English from nonnative speakers and had as hard a time understanding our accents as we did with theirs. We teachers ate Western-style breakfasts in the hotel, but our lunches and dinners were provided at the school by a young cook who was a chef in training at the Peace Hotel, the only other hotel in Shanghai that took foreign guests. The meals he cooked for us were nothing short of spectacular. He produced incredibly delicious ten-course lunches and fifteen-course dinners every day, with no dish ever repeated unless we begged for it (mostly we begged for fewer courses). Among other marvels, he created savory and sweet pastries in the shape of sea animals. I thought he was a culinary genius, and I never got tired of eating what he cooked for us. I wish I knew what became of him.

Another instructor and I got up early every morning to beat the heat and went for long exploratory walks in the neighborhood around our hotel, the Shanghai Binguan (guesthouse), in the old French Concession. Our walks took us to wet markets where we watched the slaughter of turtles and other exotic animals soon to be eaten. But we could see that China was changing, and fast. Construction cranes were everywhere throughout the city. I did not return to China until 2019, when I went to a UNICEF meeting in Beijing and at last got to see the Great Wall. The difference was stunning. I introduced my UNICEF talks, which were about the food industry's influence on nutrition research and childhood obesity, with photos of my Shanghai visit thirty-three years earlier (figure 11).

After the workshop, it was time to go to work for USAID, where the advice to keep my expectations low proved prescient. I arrived at the Bangkok USAID office only to be told that my official contact had been posted to Cairo the week before. Nobody in the office was expecting me. I had a long list of people I was supposed to interview about the extent of nutritional inadequacies among migrants from rural areas, but the office manager could not help me contact them.

FIGURE 11. I very much enjoyed participating in the Sino-US Workshop on Education and Culture in Shanghai, designed to teach Chinese physicians and scientists how to deal with American culture when they came to work in hospitals and laboratories in the United States.

What to do? Having learned in public health school to just hang in there, that's what I did. I sat at a desk and tried to look busy.

Since I was hard to ignore, the office staff invited me to a farewell party for a staff member. There I met an American consultant whose Thai wife worked for USAID. When I told him my story, he took over. He made the calls, arranged for a car, took me to the places I needed to go, and made sure I met people who could answer my questions. I also got to see some of tourist Bangkok. I visited the floating vegetable and fruit market, of course, but I was also taken on an eye-popping guided tour of the city's sex performance venues by an American—a sex tourist, apparently—whom I had met while waiting for our luggage at the airport. That too was part of my public health education. I could not believe that he and everyone else participating in those performances were not more worried about AIDS, by then well understood to be sexually transmitted.

My next stop was Jakarta, where I was relieved to find my USAID contact in the office, although he was anything but welcoming. "You are one of forty American consultants in Jakarta this week. All of you need cars, drivers, and translators. None of you speaks Bahasa. None of you will learn anything useful." With that, he assigned me a translator and driver, and I was ready to go—except that hardly anyone was willing to meet with me. I was staying at one of the two Jakarta hotels that the agency considered safe for consultants because those places boiled all their water. My hotel had a pool on the roof where I went to decompress after my daily interview attempts, and I soon met a group of Australian bridge-construction consultants with long experience in Indonesia. They assured me they could get me in to see anyone I wanted. But my translator objected that doing so would break protocol and cause trouble—another lesson learned. In the end, I gleaned enough information from the people I did meet and reported what I found out to the USAID officer, who apologized for his early discouragement: "I can't tell in advance who is going to be good, and few are." I considered his comment the highest of praise, proof that I had been able to make a tough situation work.

Back in California, I could not wait to tell Marty Forman about the people I'd met, what I'd learned, and how well I'd done, but he put me off and said we would discuss it when I came to Washington at the end of the summer. Once there, I tried again. He took me sailing on Chesapeake Bay but said he never discussed work while sailing. He never did let me tell him about the trip, and to this day I have no idea why USAID paid for all those weeks of travel, hotels, and meals but nobody wanted to hear about what I had observed. I wondered if I had disappointed Forman in some way. But I could not be more grateful for the experience he gave me and what I learned about working effectively in international situations. My USAID trip was one of the first payoffs from going to public health school. I was glad I had followed Phil Lee's advice. I had learned much more than I expected from the courses I had taken and the community work I was required to do. I felt much better prepared to take on what came next.

And what came next was the job in Washington, DC. Just before I set out for Southeast Asia, Mike McGinnis had offered me the job I had interviewed for earlier. I would move to DC in October. Michael Jacobson, the founding director of the Center for Science in the Public Interest, whom I had met at my first public lecture in San Francisco, told me about apartments available in the building he lived in on Adams Mill Road. In those days, buying an apartment was cheaper than renting, so I bought a small two-bedroom in his building. I liked the feel of the racially mixed Adams-Morgan neighborhood, and I liked knowing someone in the building. I especially liked living right across from a service road into the National Zoo, where I could go for runs every morning to visit the flamingos and pandas.

I was immensely sad to leave friends and family in California but once again felt that I had no choice. The job in Washington was the only one offered to me. Also, if I wanted to get involved in nutrition policy, a nutrition policy job was the right place to start. That alone seemed full of possibilities. But, as I would soon find out, the Washington job was going to be another difficult apprenticeship with another steep learning curve.

NB*

5   *Working for the Feds*

On October 1, 1986, I joined the Office of Disease Prevention and Health Promotion (ODPHP) for a two-year stint as senior nutrition policy adviser to the Department of Health and Human Services (HHS).[1] Here I would have another impressive title, but unlike the one at UCSF, this one came with genuine responsibilities. I would be the project officer in charge of completing the first-ever *Surgeon General's Report on Nutrition and Health*. This project had started a couple of years earlier and was nearly complete, or so I was told. My job would be to write the policy recommendations and oversee the report's release.

ODPHP is a small HHS unit with a big mandate. It is in charge of major public health initiatives, among them Healthy People (the national health objectives issued every ten years); the US Preventive Services Task Force (which grades the effectiveness of medical interventions); and the Dietary Guidelines for Americans (the statement of federal nutrition policy published every five years since 1980). Given my interest in nutrition policy, this was *the* place to be.

ODPHP's longtime director, Dr. J. Michael McGinnis, was a political appointee who—unusually for how things are done in Washington—had kept the job through several changes of administration. He was renowned and highly respected for his skills in negotiating Washington politics, developing immensely important public health projects, and recruiting talented professional staff capable of getting those projects done—no mean feat. He was also infamous for running a tight ship, demanding absolute adherence to government rules about attendance, travel, and conflicts of interest, and micromanaging his staff with heavy criticism and little or no praise. I knew from our interview months earlier that I would not find him easy to work with, but I thought the project—establishing a firm research basis for dietary recommendations—was worth the challenge. I was eager to take it on.

Even so, I greatly underestimated what a hard time I would have in that office. Looking back on that period, I think of it as my two years in federal prison. In our first meeting, McGinnis explained the rules: no matter what the research indicated, the *Surgeon General's Report* would not recommend eating less meat as a way to reduce saturated fat, nor would it recommend eating less of specific foods that were sources of sugar or salt. We were part of the industry-friendly Reagan administration. If the report suggested eating less of any specific food or food group, their producers would complain to the USDA and to their friends in Congress, who would prevent the report from coming out. As I described later in *Food Politics,* this scenario was no paranoid fantasy. Agencies dealing with food issues had learned to avoid congressional interference by resorting to euphemisms, focusing guidelines on nutrients rather than the foods that contain them, and putting a positive spin on advice to eat less of any food category. Whereas "Eat less beef" called the industry to arms, "Eat less saturated fat" did not. Sugar producers could live with "Choose a diet moderate in sugar." Eventually, the *Surgeon General's Report* would recommend the uncontroversial "Choose lean meats" and suggest limiting sugars, but only for people vulnerable to dental cavities (which, if you think about it, means practically everybody).

Given these restrictions on what I could do, you might well ask why I didn't just walk out the door. But I felt I had no other options. I had been turned down for all the other jobs I applied for. I was newly divorced. I had left my children, friends, and home behind in California. Everything I owned was on a truck headed to Washington. While waiting for it to arrive and for my new apartment to become available, I was camped out in a tiny room over the kitchen of the Tabard Inn, a charmingly eccentric hotel (mismatched old furniture, excellent restaurant) near Dupont Circle. The office had promised to pay for my stay in the hotel, but that never happened; some government rule made it impossible.

On the positive side, I could see that my new colleagues, all professionals well versed in getting things done in Washington, were smart and sympathetic, and I would have much to learn from them. I was right about that. I learned things on that job I had no idea I didn't know.

Confronting the DC Culture

The learning curve was indeed steep and fast. In my first week, I was told to go and introduce myself to Suzanne Harris, USDA's deputy assistant secretary for Food and Consumer Services, who oversaw the billions of dollars spent on federal food assistance programs. Her imposing office along the Mall was furnished in overstuffed black leather. Knowing that she was new to Washington and her previous position had been as an assistant professor of nutrition at the University of Alabama, I asked if she was finding the place as strange as I was. "Not at all," she said. "My husband is the head of the Republican National Committee." She showed me her watch with Reagan's picture on it. That was my first lesson in how political appointments work.

In addition to working on the report, I represented ODPHP on several federal nutrition committees. I ghostwrote letters, congressional testimony, speeches, and responses to queries from members of Congress on anything related to nutrition; these went out over

McGinnis's signature. Not knowing how to do such things, I had to ask other staff in the office, particularly my nutrition colleague, Linda Meyers, and McGinnis's special assistant, Peggy Hamburg, who had just finished her medical residency. Cathie Woteki, then at the National Center for Health Statistics, realized right away that I was out of my depth and offered help. All three went on to impressive careers, and working with them was one of this job's most gratifying benefits.[2] Living in the same building as CSPI's director, Michael Jacobson, also helped. We often met for late-night teas, when I could ask his advice about whatever assignment I was struggling with. For the first time, I had a support system to help me get my job done.

I needed it. The culture of McGinnis's office was unlike anything I had known at universities. As an academic, I had almost complete control over when and how to do my work. But in this job, if I came in late or missed work because of a snowstorm, those missed hours were counted against my measly ten days of annual leave. No matter how many hours I worked overtime, they were not permitted to compensate for time missed during the day. I had a particularly hard time with the travel restrictions. To avoid conflicts of interest, the office paid all travel expenses, but that meant having to ask permission to attend conferences or accept speaking invitations. Permission was granted only rarely: "You need to be here in case anything comes up."

Even when I had permission to travel, it could be rescinded at the last minute. At the request of the Indian Health Service (IHS), I was to give a talk to its nutrition staff at a conference in New Mexico. Seeing this invitation as a way to learn about the food issues faced by Native Americans, I prepared extensively for the talk. A few days before I was scheduled to leave, I was told that I was "needed in the office" and someone else would be sent in my place. The IHS nutritionists thought I had blown them off and were deeply offended. I had no way of apologizing convincingly—who outside of government would ever believe I had no choice in the matter?—and the insult was never forgotten. In 2018—thirty years later—when I was in Albuquerque giving the keynote speech at a conference on Native American health, someone there asked me why I had failed to show up for that earlier talk.

Being told what to do, when, and how to do it was also hard to take. I would arrive at the office to find a note on my desk with a list of tasks to be completed that day by COB—close of business, 5 p.m.—and in what order: "Do this one first." I soon learned that it was much better to get the tasks done quickly and in the right order than to worry about doing them well. The punishment for missing COB deadlines—unpleasant conversations, more restrictions on travel, removal from desirable assignments—was far more severe than the response to work poorly done. If what I turned in was acceptable, I never saw it again. If it needed more work, it came back with the comment "This won't do" and additional time to fix it. This system was not fun, but it taught me to write quickly and to turn things in when they were good enough, even if they weren't as good as I wanted them to be.

When I arrived in Washington, I was still writing in longhand, typing what I had written into the computer, printing it out on stacks of perforated paper, editing it, retyping it, and doing that over and over. Two years later, when that job ended, I wrote directly on the computer and could turn out twenty pages of testimony by COB on a topic I had known nothing about that morning. This was fabulous training, for which I remain deeply grateful.

I never could understand why McGinnis and I did not have an easier working relationship. I greatly admired his skills and was totally committed to the report. I wanted it to be authoritative, convincing, and understandable. Surely he wanted that too. I understood the need for getting the report done faster, but its findings were likely to be controversial, and they had to be presented carefully and well. The report had already burned through previous project officers. It was unpopular among Public Health Service agencies: their staff worried that the science was not strong enough to support dietary recommendations and that advice to eat less of anything would cause trouble. Scientists in various federal agencies had agreed to participate, but some of them so reluctantly and with such foot dragging that I suspected them of sabotage.

"Faster" dominated our one-on-one meetings. "Stop trying to do such good work," McGinnis would say. When I objected, he would tell me, "You are not nice. You are hard to work with. You resist supervision. You are bristly." I knew I shouldn't take such comments personally—other staff also got plenty of criticism—but they seemed able to handle it better than I did. They hadn't heard the "not nice" accusation since childhood, as I had. I spent many days in tears. I knew I ought to be seeing a therapist, but nobody I knew, even officials of federal mental health agencies, was willing to recommend anyone. Washington, DC, is not a place where people feel free to say what they really think; the risk of getting into political trouble is too high.

I did not help matters by committing an early act of insubordination. I had been at ODPHP less than six months when Sheldon Margen, the public health nutrition professor in Berkeley, invited me to speak at a small conference on food insecurity. I missed Berkeley and wanted to go, so I offered to make up the time I would miss on weekends. Permission denied. When I showed McGinnis the meeting schedule, he noticed the absence of USDA representatives and insisted I get them invited. I did, and USDA sent two of its staff to the meeting.

The week before that meeting was to take place, my eighty-year-old mother was mugged in a supermarket parking lot and knocked to the ground, causing her to break her hip. For this serious family emergency, I was given permission to use annual leave to visit her in Los Angeles. Since I was paying for the trip, I could book it as I liked. I routed it through San Francisco and went to the Berkeley meeting.

At the last minute, the keynote speaker had not been able to come, and Margen asked if I would stand in and talk about what it was like to be a food policy beginner in Washington. I threw some notes together and talked about how the only thing anyone cared about in DC was whether you were Republican or Democrat, how USDA and HHS were at opposite ends of the political spectrum, how everyone spoke in euphemisms for fear of appearing partisan, and how all written statements had to go through interminable clearance processes. I had fun talking about these things, and my friends at the meeting enjoyed hearing about them.

When I returned to the office, I found a note on my desk to see McGinnis immediately. Busted. John Block, the USDA secretary, had called that morning to complain about what I had said about his agency. McGinnis, understandably, was not pleased. I explained as best I could and left to go to a scheduled meeting at the USDA offices. There I told the two staff people who had ratted on me, "The only reason you were at that meeting was because I got you invited. That's the last time I am doing anything for either of you." By the time I got back to ODPHP, Block had called again to apologize for his "misunderstanding," and all was well. I survived that one, but now understood two things: USDA played hardball, and I was not to do anything like that again.

To minimize conflicts with USDA, one of my tasks was to keep Suzanne Harris in the loop on the report's progress and head off her queries and prodding. During my two years at ODPHP, I probably spent about one-third of my time trying to keep her at bay and another third trying to do the same with McGinnis. That left only a third for getting the report done, which itself was no picnic.

Confronting the Report

The purpose of this first—and, as it turned out, only—*Surgeon General's Report on Nutrition and Health* was to settle the ongoing scientific arguments about the research basis of the Dietary Guidelines for Americans. In 1980 and 1985, the guidelines advised variety, moderation, and avoidance of too much saturated fat, cholesterol, sugar, salt, and alcohol (and, other than dropping the advice to reduce dietary cholesterol, they still do). Nobody objected to recommending dietary variety and moderation, but advice to eat less of any food (rather than of particular nutrients) invariably elicited objections from its producers, as well as from scientists who viewed the evidence as incomplete. The report was intended to consolidate the science and establish a firm basis for public health advice about what to eat. Naive? Perhaps, but the research evidence seemed less complicated in those days.

More than a dozen federal agencies, mostly at NIH, had agreed to take responsibility for preparing one or more chapters. The report would cover the effects of diet on obesity, chronic diseases, childhood development, aging, and behavior; the effects of alcohol and drug use; and dietary fads and frauds. Just before I left California to move to Washington, McGinnis sent me a few draft chapters, which I read on the plane to DC. By the time I arrived, I knew I had work to do. The chapters were incoherent, had no common structure, and had hardly anything to do with public health. The one on dental disease, for example, was entirely devoted to research on the role of vitamin A in the formation of rats' teeth. I assumed that McGinnis knew how inappropriate they were and had hired me to fix them.

I also assumed that our first conversation would be about what kind of leeway I had to revise the chapters, so as not to offend the people who had written the original drafts. Big mistake: "You just got here. How do you know anything is wrong with these chapters? You don't know anything about how Washington works. Unacceptable."

He was right about what I didn't know. Could he also be right about the chapters? I needed to find out. I organized an office read-in. Without telling my colleagues what I thought of the chapters, I asked them to read any chapter that interested them and tell me what they thought of it. No matter which chapter they had chosen, all of my readers began their comments with "I know I must have picked the worst chapter, but . . ."

When I reported all this to McGinnis, he accused me of manipulating the read-in to get what I wanted. It took weeks to convince him to let me edit the chapters. He finally agreed that we would tell the contributors that we were setting a common format and editing their work to fit into it. For revision of the scientific content, I drew heavily on my book *Nutrition in Clinical Practice*. I spent the next year rewriting most of the chapters and writing a few of them from scratch.

I could see why the report had defeated previous project officers. Its preparation involved about fifty individual writers, two hundred peer reviewers, the members of two federal advisory committees, and one editorial advisory committee outside the government. (My partner, Mal Nesheim, was a member of this last one, which is how we first met.) Every review called for extensive revisions. Each chapter and the project as a whole had to be formally approved ("cleared") through our office, as well as through any number of federal offices, committees, and government officials up the chain of command, all the way to the top of the Public Health Service and HHS. I supervised the private consulting firm hired by ODPHP to enter responses to comments, print and distribute chapter drafts, and prepare the final book. By the time the report was done, the piles of drafts filled several warehouse storage rooms from floor to ceiling.

I had to deal with writers who were late turning in chapters or did not follow formatting directions, reviewers' demands for rewrites, draft copies with missing pages, and the endless cycles of comments and responses. The draft chapters often exceeded a hundred pages; they were stuffed with data tables and included dozens of pages of references. A chapter on dietary trends constituted a drama on its own. No fewer than seven doctoral-level nutritionists attempted drafts, one after another. Each was rejected on the grounds of incomplete and inconsistent data; none made it into the final report, not even the version I wrote with Cathie Woteki—but we, at least, got our version published elsewhere.[3]

Forcing the chapters into the newly established format also took work. McGinnis wanted each chapter to begin with a pertinent quotation. In those pre-internet days, finding an appropriate epigraph required hours and sometimes days of library research. So did the sections on historical perspectives. The chapter writers usually handled the scientific background pretty well. But the remaining sections—significance for public health, key scientific issues, and implications for public health policy—were mine to draft, sometimes with help, always with numerous and often contradictory demands from reviewers.

For me the report was my highest priority, but for the other writers and reviewers it was anything but. Progress was slow, and the many other tasks I was assigned slowed progress even more. I pleaded to be allowed to work from home in the mornings, where I would not be interrupted. Eventually I was allowed to. That way, I could block out afternoons for dealing with COB requests and meetings.

I had been working on the report for a year and a half when, in May 1988, McGinnis forced the issue; he imposed a deadline. He set July 27 as a date for a press conference to release the report. Since the only part of the report anyone was likely to read was the executive summary, he informed me that he would write that part himself, and I was not to interfere with or even comment on it. It stung me that after all this time he didn't trust me to write it, but there was no point in arguing.

A Last-Minute Crisis

The report was entirely an ODPHP initiative, but its title implied that it came from the surgeon general's office. This was because

McGinnis wanted nutrition to be taken as seriously as tobacco and for this report to have as much of an impact as that of the 1964 *Surgeon General's Report on Smoking and Health*.[4] In 1988, the surgeon general was Dr. C. Everett Koop, a pediatric surgeon and fundamentalist Christian who had been appointed by President Reagan on the basis of his strong opposition to abortion. But by the time we were drafting the nutrition report, Koop had earned widespread admiration—and my deep respect—for his moral and ethical positions on health issues, particularly AIDS.

Koop had an office in downtown Washington, and McGinnis took me there to meet him in early June. Koop said he was uneasy about pretending to be a nutrition expert and did not want to be involved in the July press conference. I could understand his reluctance. A reporter for *US News & World Report* had just written, "Koop has a diet that would make American Heart Association officials blanch. He eats omelets, steaks, potato chips and honey-roasted cocktail peanuts. He drinks two dry martinis at lunch. He's overweight. He doesn't exercise much." Even worse, the article quoted Koop's response: "If you look and feel as well as I do at 71, call me. . . . There are a lot of people who don't have to worry about getting high fat or cholesterol levels. I eat eggs and red meat. I have good genes."[5] Gulp.

Koop also told us that he had other issues to deal with. Members of Mothers against Drunk Driving (MADD) were camped outside his house to get him to take up their cause.[6] With that and his work on cigarette smoking and AIDS, he did not want to take on yet another controversial issue. McGinnis was able to convince Koop to read a statement at the press conference with the understanding that he could leave immediately afterward. We (meaning me) would prepare the press statement for him, which McGinnis promised to send him within ten days. Good—I would have ten days to write it.

By the end of June, the report was finished and ready to print for its release on July 27. I had ghostwritten Koop's introduction to the report, a foreword from HHS Secretary Otis Bowen, and a preface from Assistant Secretary Robert Windom. I was busy drafting the press conference speeches for Koop and McGinnis when—a crisis. Koop called the whole thing off.

This was the fault of my ignorance. Koop, it seemed, had *two* staff offices: the one in downtown Washington where I had met him, and another in the Parklawn building in Maryland. I had diligently kept his DC staff in the loop at every stage of the report's preparation, but had never heard of his Parklawn office. Its staff had just seen the entire report for the first time. They were dismayed that it did not have a chapter about the nutritional needs of low-income women and children and insisted that it be added. I, of course, would have loved to have socioeconomic issues discussed in the report, but this was way too late in the game. Adding a new chapter at this stage was not possible.

I still do not know how McGinnis did it, but he put his formidable negotiating skills to work and resolved the impasse. I redrafted Koop's introduction to the report to include this statement: "The Report is not intended to address the problems of hunger or undernutrition that may occur in the United States among certain subgroups of the population. All Americans should have access to an appropriate diet, but they do not. . . . [T]he problems of access to food are of considerable concern to me, personally, wherever they may occur."[7]

That was the best I could do to make sure the report acknowledged persistent poverty, inequitable resources, and food insecurity in the United States, problems I had studied in public health school and cared deeply about. But the report's focus was on obesity and chronic disease, then considered to be diseases of affluence. In 1988 the greater prevalence of these conditions among low-income Americans was not widely recognized.

The Response

For me, the July 27 press conference was an out-of-body experience. Dr. Koop read the speech I had written for him with only a couple of wording changes. It felt as though he was channeling me. Speech-writers tell me that they love hearing their words read by famous people, but I did not—I would rather give my own speeches and take credit (or blame) for what I say. If I had known that Koop was going to read my speech essentially word for word, I would have made it much tougher.

But the press conference went well, so well that McGinnis presented me with a now-treasured wooden apple on which he had written, "WHEW!! Very well done!! 7/27/88." "Whew" was exactly how I felt. I was done with the report.

As planned, Koop left right after giving his speech, and McGinnis fielded the questions from reporters. The *New York Times* put its story about the report on the front page, leading off with "The Surgeon General today cited fat as a leading cause of disease that should be reduced in most people's diets and said overconsumption of fats and some other foods was a major national health problem."[8]

Anyone who has followed nutrition in recent years would raise an eyebrow over this statement: we now well understand that overconsumption of calories from carbohydrates, as well as fat, contributes to weight gain and associated health problems. The focus on fat, a nutrient rather than a food, still makes me wince, even though I had been barred from having anything to do with the report's executive summary. Years later, Linda Meyers reminded me that I had objected to the emphasis on fat as reductionist and euphemistic, and likely to induce food companies to manipulate ingredients in food products. Indeed, we soon encountered the "SnackWells phenomenon"—no-fat cookies with almost as many calories as their full-fat counterparts, but from sugars. These flew off the shelves.[9]

FIGURE 12. I'm holding an advance copy of *The Surgeon General's Report on Nutrition and Health* at the press conference announcing its release on July 27, 1988. This was the climax of nearly two years of intensely hard work, emotional as well as professional. The photograph was taken by Michael Jacobson, then director of the Center for Science in the Public Interest.

The report said almost nothing about the role of sugars in weight gain or chronic disease. This was because the FDA had done a comprehensive review of the effects of sugars on health just two years earlier: "Other than the contribution to dental caries, there is no conclusive evidence that demonstrates a hazard to the general public when sugars are consumed at the levels that are now current and in the manner now practiced."[10]

But in 2018, the journalist Gary Taubes, who views sugars as the principal cause of weight gain and poor health, wrote to a reporter who had interviewed me that "the conclusion of my [Taubes's] research in what's now three books (going on a fourth) is that nutritionists of

Marion's generation botched the science of obesity and chronic disease so badly that they couldn't have done more damage had they been paid."[11]

That's not how I see it, of course. The *Surgeon General's Report* reflected the preponderance of research at the time. Earlier in 1988, a report from the World Health Organization's Regional Office in Europe had come to the same conclusion, as did the even longer and more comprehensive *Diet and Health Study* from the National Research Council the following year. Both reports also named fat as the primary culprit in poor diets, making it seem as if the nutrition research community had reached widespread consensus on basic principles of diet and health.[12]

The focus on fat did make some sense. Fat has more calories than protein or carbohydrate (nine calories per gram as compared to four). The assumption was that if people ate less fat, they would automatically eat fewer calories as well as less saturated fat, then and now considered a risk factor for coronary artery disease (although the degree to which saturated fat raises risk is still hotly debated). People do not eat saturated fat on its own; they eat foods containing mixtures of saturated, unsaturated, and polyunsaturated fats. The foods highest in saturated fats are meat and dairy products. In 1988, everyone in government knew it was politically impossible to advise eating less meat or dairy foods. And none of us involved in the eat-less-fat reports could have envisioned how quickly the food industry would reformulate products to replace fat with sugars. Overall, aside from the emphasis on fat, the recommendations of the report for personal dietary choices boil down to Michael Pollan's now-classic advice: "Eat food. Not too much. Mostly plants."[13]

The report elicited widespread criticism on other grounds as well. The *Boston Globe* invoked the specter of the nanny state in the form of "Koop the intruder." A *Washington Post* writer considered the recommendations banal: "Before lecturing citizens on what to eat,

Surgeon General C. Everett Koop ought to avoid choking them. His 712-page report on nutrition and disease is a hard-to-swallow bulk of informational lard, with a shelf date long expired." A *New York Times* editorial complained about the toothless policy recommendations: "Dr. Koop's report calls only for voluntary improvements in food labeling, a meek approach the American Heart Association rightly rejects. Sensible bills now pending in Congress would require food manufacturers to specify fat, cholesterol and fiber content on all package labels. . . . Dr. Koop ought to be in the vanguard of those campaigning to enact them."[14]

Despite insisting that he would not answer reporters' questions, Koop agreed to an interview with the *Washington Post*'s Michael Specter, essentially undermining the entire effort: "'For myself, I'm counting on my genes,' says Koop, acknowledging that he does not normally follow these guidelines. 'If your cholesterol is okay and you think your genes are good, why should you sit on a hill the rest of your life and eat yogurt?'"[15]

I was reminded of all this when in mid-2020, Beacon Press asked me for a back-cover endorsement for Aubrey Gordon's book *What We Don't Talk About When We Talk About Fat*, a searing indictment of the discrimination and hostility faced daily by people who are fat (her term). As is always my practice when asked for blurbs, I read the entire book first. I was glad I did. The book is well worth reading, not only for Gordon's advocacy against stigmatizing obesity but also for her sharply insightful comments on the *Surgeon General's Report*.

The war on obesity, she writes, "seemed to emerge, fully formed" with the report's release. She quotes Koop's press conference speech: 'Of greatest concern . . . is our excessive intake of dietary fat." She notes that "the report called for an increase in food-related public health programs and legislation, but its recommendations largely took the form of individual mandates. . . . Notably, the report stopped short of recommendations that would regulate foods, or the subsidies that provided such cheap and plentiful forms of dietary fat, salt, sugars, and high-fructose corn syrup."[16]

Policy wonk that I am, this sent me right back to the report, which I had not looked at in more than thirty years. I was relieved to see that the chapters held up well, with solid—and critical—reviews of research available at the time. But if I had the chance to redo this report, I would refocus its recommendations on foods rather than nutrients, and on changing the food environment to promote healthier personal choices. But in 1988, such ideas were strictly off limits. Even if I had known enough to write about issues such as farm subsidies (which create incentives for overproducing crops and, therefore, calories), the USDA is the agency responsible for such policies, and HHS had to keep hands off anything within USDA's purview.

Hard as my two years in ODPHP were, I had to acknowledge their invaluable benefits. I now knew how politics worked in practice, how to write things that were "good enough" and let them go, and how to find colleagues who could help me do my work. And, in an entirely unexpected stroke of good fortune, I got credit for what was good in the report and rarely got blamed for its flaws. McGinnis was away from the office for a few months after the report's release, leaving me to accept his speaking invitations. After one such talk, George Blackburn, a medical scientist at Harvard Medical School and a national authority on nutrition and obesity, stood up and told the audience that the only reason the *Surgeon General's Report* ever came out was because of my work. I could never thank him enough for that.[17]

Moving to New York

My ODPHP appointment ran until the end of September 1988. McGinnis occasionally mentioned the possibility of turning my position into something permanent, but whenever he did, I would inadvertently do something to remind him of his difficulties working with me. The turmoil I caused by going to that meeting in Berkeley made me realize I was not cut out for a career in Washington. Everyone I met in DC, no matter their party affiliation, fell into one of two categories: either they preferred Washington to New York, or they preferred New York to Washington. I was clearly in the latter category. My children had settled in San Francisco and Los Angeles, but I doubted I could find a job in California. New York had been my childhood home. If I lived in New York, I would be *normal*.

Late in 1987, I was sitting at the kitchen table in my sunny Adams Mill Road kitchen when I found a small puffy envelope in the mail. Out came the keys to an apartment in New York City. These were from an old friend from my Boston days, Joan Pearlman. She had rented a tiny studio on Charles Street in the West Village but had just moved in with her soon-to-be husband and wasn't using it. I took the train to New York every weekend I could and told everyone I knew I was looking for a job in New York.

I wanted to go back to a university, where I would be free to write and say what I thought. A job chairing a department of nutrition seemed ideal, but to qualify for a position like that I would need to publish more. I was living alone, wasn't dating, and felt so resentful of the office policies and the lack of credit for working overtime that I resolved to do office work only during the hours I was required to be there. Nights and weekends would be mine to work on my own papers. By the time my two years were up, I had managed to produce more than a dozen publications based on the *Surgeon General's Report* and other nutrition policy initiatives.[18]

A couple of months before the report was to be released, I saw postings in nutrition journals for a job as chair of the Department of Home Economics and Nutrition at New York University. Lest I miss it, friends mailed clips of the ad to me: "Marion, here's your job." I soon had a two-inch stack of such notes on my desk. I applied for the job.

I had been interviewing for positions in New York and everywhere else I could, but without success. When I was turned down without a second interview for a job for which I thought I was overqualified, friends urged me to try to find out why. I called the search committee chair, who was kind enough to enlighten me: "You didn't act as if you wanted the job. And when you were asked what management theory you used, you blew it off." The first concern was understandable: even though I thought the job was wrong for me, I should not have let that show. But needing to know about management theory? That was news.

I went straight to a bookstore and browsed books about business management. I found one describing two theories of management styles, called X and Y. Adherents to theory X supposedly motivate employees through tight supervision, rewards, and penalties, whereas Theory Y types see employees as self-motivated and encourage them to take responsibility for their own work.[19] Good thing I checked. I was asked precisely the same question during my first NYU interview. This time I could toss off, "I'm a theory Y type." Everyone laughed, and we moved on. A job offer soon arrived.

But before getting to what happened with NYU, I need to confess to one final act of insubordination at ODPHP. I had seen a notice of a conference at Vassar College organized by the New York–based Health Policy Advisory Center (Health/PAC), which advocated for social justice in health care. I knew hardly anyone in New York and thought this would be an opportunity to meet future friends and colleagues. I asked for one day of annual leave to take a Friday off to go to it. Permission denied. I called my old California therapist, who wisely said: "The Washington job is your past; New York is your future." She suggested, "Call in sick." Really? It was okay to do this? I could not have been more uncomfortable, but I did it and went to the conference. Everyone in the office must have known I was lying, but nobody said a word.

But then, when I had been at NYU for a year or so, I ran across something that forced me to reconsider the entire ODPHP experience. My department had been required to move into a much smaller space, and we had to downsize on short notice and empty a storage room of file cabinets. Hurriedly looking through the file drawers to rescue materials that needed to be saved, I stumbled across the folders dealing with my own recruitment. One held the supposedly confidential letters of recommendation sent to my search committee (at universities, you can never assume confidential letters will stay that way). The one from McGinnis stunned me. He referred to my job as a high-level nutrition policy post in the Public Health Service and described its specific responsibilities, even ones I didn't think he knew about. He said I had performed these "demanding and complex tasks with sound professional judgment, effective leadership, high initiative and integrity, and superb interpersonal skills."

Even if someone else on his staff had written the letter, McGinnis had signed it. Was this what he really thought of me? Now I knew why the other office staff had been able to handle working with him better than I did. They must have understood how deeply he appreciated their work, interpreted his criticisms as tough love (or just theory X management style), and shrugged them off. How I wish I had been able to do that.

6 *Finally, NYU*

In the late spring of 1988, not long after I applied for the NYU job, I got a call from Jim Finkelstein, the assistant dean for planning in NYU's School of Education, Health, Nursing and Arts Professions (SEHNAP, pronounced *see-nap*), saying he was coming to Washington for a conference and wanted to meet me.[1] This was exciting; it sounded like I was being recruited. Finkelstein told me that NYU, a commuter school for the New York region, was working to transform itself into a residential, research-focused university with global aspirations. The Department of Home Economics and Nutrition was financially stable, but its faculty were distinctly old school: they taught well but were not doing research. Chairing this department would be an exciting opportunity to bring it into the twentieth, if not the twenty-first, century. You, he assured me, are the perfect person to do this.

Having been at UCSF during its transformation, I knew how exciting this process could be, and I looked forward to visiting the department and meeting the faculty. Chairing a nutrition department was something I knew I could do. But home economics? I could hardly believe that home economics still existed as an academic discipline, now that women had so many opportunities to enter other fields.

When I arrived for my first visit, I could see right away why transformation was necessary. This was one seriously neglected department. Its offices were shabby. The furniture was worn and mismatched, and rugs were threadbare. The colors clashed: doors were deep purple, couches bright orange. Only one of the four full-time faculty members had a computer; everyone else, including the secretaries, still used typewriters. SEHNAP must have invested nothing in this department for decades. More troubling, the faculty seemed to view the neglect as expected, routine, and acceptable. They seemed frustrated, but I got no sense of outrage.

The department offered degree programs in home economics, nutrition, dietetics, and food service and hotel management, but when I asked to see lists and descriptions of programs, none existed. Eventually, I discovered that these four faculty members ran thirty-seven separate academic programs awarding undergraduate, master's, or doctoral degrees. They also supervised several public education and professional training programs. It was a year before I finally found out what they all were.

I did not understand how this was possible, but I soon learned that unlike any university I had ever had anything to do with, SEHNAP used adjunct faculty to teach most of its courses. At NYU, *adjunct* means professionals well-qualified on the basis of training or experience who teach a course or two on a part-time, temporary basis and are paid a pittance to do so. Despite the advantages of this system in putting students in contact with people who hold important jobs in their fields and are willing to teach for little compensation, I thought, and still do, that this was a terrible way to run an academic department. For one thing, adjuncts get none of the benefits of full-time faculty and have no formal responsibility for advising students. For another, identifying and recruiting adjuncts to teach courses takes up a great deal of faculty time. Also dismaying to learn was that the women who directed the public education programs were not paid at all: they were friends of the faculty, and referred to (behind their backs, of course) as the "rich wives."

I wanted to know what the full-time faculty were researching and asked them to show me their CVs, the standard curriculum vitae summarizing academic training, professional experience, and publications expected of all academics. But these women did not have CVs. Instead, they handed me one-page resumes. Why no CVs? "We aren't looking for jobs."

No computers, no research, no program descriptions, no faculty CVs—and all of this in dilapidated space in a low-status department in a low-status school. My experience at UCSF had shown me how a first-rate university was supposed to operate. Not like this. Here was an academic culture completely outside my experience, yet one with which faculty seemed comfortable. Getting this department in line with departments at "real" universities was going to be like moving the *Titanic*.

Should I even consider taking this job? I called my former therapist in California. She advised, "You've never had job security. Try it. You might like it. If NYU doesn't work out, you can always look for another job."

This sounded like good advice, especially because NYU offered plenty that I wanted. It was in New York City, where I felt at home. I would be a department chair, in charge of my own decisions. I would hold a tenured full professorship with an adequate salary and the possibility of renting a subsidized NYU apartment in Greenwich Village, precisely where I wanted to live. The positives greatly outweighed the negatives, despite the risk of failing to be able to transform the department into something more professionally viable. I decided to take the job.

I returned for a second visit to meet with the associate deans who negotiated the details of new positions. Thinking that this meeting would be perfunctory, I was unprepared for their formal offer: an untenured position at the associate professor level.

Impossible.

Of the four full-time faculty, two were tenured associate professors. A third was Judith Gilbride, an assistant professor who had been serving as acting chair with the assurance that she would be promoted to tenured associate professor for taking on that responsibility. She had also been a candidate for the position of chair. All three would outrank me, and my tenure would depend on their goodwill. But would they have any goodwill? I was being recruited to change practically everything about the way they operated, and I doubted I could count on much support from them. I had to fight back tears—I had no other job prospects—and tell the associate deans I could not accept the position under those conditions.

The search committee was as disappointed by the offer as I was and asked the deans to reconsider. The deans asked me to stay on campus for a few hours while they did some consulting with higher-ups. Ultimately, my UCSF job title of adjunct associate professor saved the day, once I could make the NYU administrators understand that at that particular top-tier university, *adjunct* meant full-time, on full salary, with full benefits. On that basis, the deans upped the offer to a full professorship with tenure, which I accepted with relief.

Months later, when I ran across the file related to my recruitment, I finally understood what had happened. The chair of the department for more than twenty years, Margaret Simko, had retired three years earlier, but previous searches for her replacement had been unsuccessful. A year earlier, the job had been offered and accepted, but the newly recruited chair had withdrawn after receiving a better offer from another university. The search committee must have convinced the associate deans of the desperate need to fill the position.

To me, the NYU offer felt heaven-sent. Two years earlier, I had been pushed out of my position at UCSF. Now I would be a tenured full professor, with lifetime job security. I know plenty of academics who never produced another thing after getting tenure, but for me this was a license to flourish. I could now do exactly what I wanted.

I would have a secure platform from which to teach, research, write, and speak about food and nutrition.

But before I could focus on my own work, I was going to have to get the faculty and the department to become more professional. I knew this would be one tough job from the moment I got there.

"Your Kitchen Is Dirty"

My contract with ODPHP ended on September 30, 1988, but the NYU semester started at the beginning of that month. I wanted to leave ODPHP at the end of August. Permission denied. I would have no time to settle in, but my late start turned out to be a lucky break. Most of my new department's courses were taught by adjuncts, and it was the chair's job to appoint them. Since I did not know anyone in New York, I could not have done this. And just as the semester began, the NYU clerical workers' union went out on strike. I would not have wanted to cross that picket line and felt relieved to be able to avoid taking a controversial political stance at the start of a new job.

By the time I got there, adjuncts had been appointed, the strike had ended, and all four full-time faculty were away at the annual meeting of the American Dietetic Association. I moved into my office, read the welcome notes, and set up get-acquainted appointments.

No matter who was involved, the notes and the meetings followed an identical script. It began with "It's great you took this job; the department really needs you to take charge." Then, apologetically: "I hate to bring this up when you've only just arrived, but . . . "

What could possibly be coming next?

"Your kitchen is dirty."

My kitchen—meaning the department's, of course—was dirty? Were they kidding? I had a doctorate in molecular biology and had just come from a senior policy post in Washington; *this* was what I had to deal with?

When the third person in a row mentioned the dirty kitchen, I knew I had to take a look. The department's teaching kitchen was on the tenth floor of a separate building around the corner from our offices. Getting off the elevator, I was hit by the smell—a distinctly unpleasant but unidentifiable animal-like odor. I walked into a home economics kitchen built in the 1950s. Its walls were the avocado-green color popular in that era, and it had home-style stoves, refrigerators, and cabinets, all so beat up that it was hard to believe they were still in use.

The word *dirty* does not begin to describe what I saw. I ran my finger over a counter; it left a groove in the yellowish greasy coating. This and every other countertop, stove, sink, and worktable was sprinkled with abundant evidence of recent mouse visitation. Surrounding the kitchen were three classrooms and several large storage closets, holding remnants of an abandoned practice apartment for home economics students. One classroom, now in use as a lunchroom, had a clothes washer and dryer, still in use. A storage room, so large it was later used as an office, contained Singer sewing machines piled floor to ceiling. Shelves in the other classroom held dozens of small, open boxes of fabric samples; these too displayed signs of mouse occupation, as did hallway cabinets stuffed with decades-old magazines. I could now identify the smell.

Students were cooking and taking classes in this space? Yes, they were. I could see why friends of the department were so concerned.

I went back to the office and asked, "Who is in charge of the kitchen?"

"Debby."

"Who is Debby?"

"A teaching fellow."

Teaching fellows are graduate students who get stipends for teaching assistance. Debby was a first-year master's student. I asked to see her. Tipped off by the secretaries, she walked into my office and burst into tears. Handing her tissues, I assured her that I did not hold her responsible for the condition of the kitchen, but I did need more information. She told me, among other things, that much of the kitchen equipment was broken. Well, we could start with that: "Find out whether any of it is worth fixing."

A few days later, doing all she could to suppress a grin, Debby reported back: "You aren't going to believe this." She had called a repair service to look at two convection ovens that did not turn on. "The repair guy pulled them away from the wall. The wires were still packed inside. They had never been plugged in."

Unbelievable.

Those ovens had been in that kitchen for at least ten years, and in all that time nobody had noticed or cared enough to try to get them working.

Students were not only learning to cook in this filthy, neglected kitchen; they were running a public lunch program out of it. Once a week, they prepared a lunch served to faculty, staff, administrators, and other guests. I had recently met the chef, cookbook author, and food consultant Rozanne Gold; I asked her to join me for lunch and tell me what she thought. She was rightfully concerned: "You don't have a program here." She told me what I needed to do to improve the program and how to equip the kitchen. I now knew what to ask for.

Cleaning was the biggest task. A one-shot professional steam-cleaning would cost upwards of $2,000, more than the department's entire discretionary budget for the year. SEHNAP was broke; it had run in the red for years and now had to make up for it. Getting the kitchen fixed took months, but the school finally agreed to pay for the cleanup when I threatened to call in New York City's Department of Health. It took the cleaning crew an entire day. When they were done, the result was stunning. The walls were blue, not green—that's how dirty the kitchen had been.

"Your Department Needs Fixing"

Beyond cleaning up the kitchen, I had some ideas about what the department needed to do: encourage faculty to publish (and create CVs), get them computers, write program descriptions, set up a student advising system—the basics of academic life. But all of these actions came up against deeply entrenched neglect. The faculty had grown comfortable with the status quo and were uneasy about doing things differently. They and the whole university needed to modernize: grades on student transcripts, for example, were entered by hand until 1990.

The main barrier to fixing anything was lack of money. NYU is a private university and differed from the state universities I was familiar with in that the department's funding depended almost entirely on the number of credits students took in its particular courses (officially, a "tuition-based resource allocation system"). If a department did not have overhead funding from research grants, which mine did not, its income simply equaled the number of student credits times the price students paid per credit. Against that income, NYU charged the department for space, faculty and staff salaries, and supplies, along with overhead charges to cover shared university expenses, including administration and services such as the library, gym, and student center. Even though the department's enrollments brought in a steady income that well exceeded expenditures, SEHNAP administrators gave us a budget so absurdly low that it hardly paid for copy paper, let alone kitchen expenses.

I was having such a hard time dealing with my new job that I thought I needed therapy. I asked people I knew for suggestions and was referred to Gary Lefer, a Columbia University psychiatrist well versed in academic life. I have no idea what other people talk to shrinks about, but I used him as a management consultant to help me deal more effectively with faculty, staff, and administrators. I admired and appreciated his ability to offer alternative interpretations of office interactions, suggest ways to deal with them, and encourage me to argue more forcefully for what I thought needed to be done.

I needed that kind of help. Even suggestions that I considered trivial elicited active resistance—alphabetizing mailboxes, for example. Nearly fifty people—faculty, adjuncts, staff, doctoral students, and teaching fellows—received mail in the department, but the mail slots were in no order I could discern. If, in those pre-email days, I wanted to leave a message for someone, I had to search through the whole wall of boxes to find the right one. I discussed this with the administrative assistant who had worked for many years with the former chair and acting chair.

ME: I'm having a hard time finding people's mailboxes. How come they aren't in alphabetical order?
RESPONSE: We all know where they are.
ME: But I don't. Could you please put them in alphabetical order?
RESPONSE: How will faculty find their mail?

For her, this request was the final straw. She soon left to work for another department, taking her long and valuable institutional memory with her. Replacing her would not be easy, and the faculty viewed her departure as another strike against me. At the time, I had no idea how I could have done better. Now I wish I had read more of those books about management theory and practice. But by then, my relationship with the faculty was already so strained that they asked if I would be willing to call in a management consultant. I agreed and let them pick the person they wanted—a professor at NYU's business school.

He interviewed me and the faculty and presented his conclusions in the form of a diagram. The faculty and I were at opposite ends of a cultural spectrum. I wanted results. They wanted discussion. They were especially unhappy with the way I ran meetings. As I had been taught at UCSF, I sent out an agenda in advance, expected faculty to come to meetings on time, discuss the agenda items, and come to a decision about them. But they wanted what seemed to me to be interminable discussion. They preferred that I talk to each of them individually and did not want to make collective decisions at meetings. The consultant viewed this as a hopeless conflict in style. He had only one suggestion: "Start your meetings by assuring the faculty that they will not have to make decisions right then." I tried that, and it did seem to help, although not nearly enough.

Still, I pushed for change. Over the next several years, the faculty eventually agreed to close the twenty-five lingering home economics programs (none with more than a handful of students), produce program handouts, reorganize and rationalize curricula, and, yes, write and update their CVs every year. They agreed to change the department's name to nutrition, food, and hotel management to reflect what it was actually teaching.

Some of these changes were forced by events elsewhere on campus. During my first year, the SEHNAP dean was fired. He was replaced by Ann Marcus, a longtime NYU administrator respected for her ability to fix poorly functioning academic units. Her goals were consistent with mine: to make the programs better and more professional as well as fiscally sound. She said what she thought. So did I, and our working relationship was a good one.

Because SEHNAP as a whole, although not our department, had long-standing financial deficits, her first cost-cutting move was to consolidate space. We had to vacate the purple and orange offices and move into new offices built into the classrooms surrounding the kitchen. The stored sewing machines, washing machines, file cabinets, magazines, and unused equipment all had to go. That move triggered my discovery of my recruitment file and the letter from Mike McGinnis.

I thought the space consolidation made administrative as well as fiscal sense. Our offices were now right next to the kitchen, where we could keep an eye on it. But all these changes were painful for the longtime faculty. Over the next few years, three of the four resigned and left. This allowed for new hires, and by the mid-1990s, it was evident to everyone—even me—that the department was running better.

My Food Service Education

Because I had never taken an undergraduate course in food service management, I had not qualified as a registered dietitian. Yet here I was, in charge of a department offering undergraduate, master's, and doctoral degrees in clinical dietetics. I had plenty to learn. Lisa Sasson, a dietitian working with Aramark, the company that ran the cafeterias in NYU's dormitories and student union, thought I needed to understand why it was so hard to get healthy food to students. She invited me to tour the food service operations at eight dormitories. All followed the same menus, and she wanted me to taste the same dish—pasta with broccoli—at each of the eight places. The recipe called for five ingredients: pasta, broccoli, garlic, olive oil, and parmesan cheese. It also called for small-batch cooking to keep the pasta al dente and the broccoli bright green, and for adding the cheese just before serving.

At the first dorm we went to, the dish was delicious, the broccoli crisp and the flavors sharp. I could not understand why Lisa thought we needed to do this. But I soon got her point. In every other dorm, the cooks either left out an ingredient (garlic, cheese, or, in one instance, broccoli), or cooked everything in advance and placed it in a warming tray, leaving the pasta and broccoli gray and soggy. Students always complain about dormitory food. In those dorms, I could see why.

In late spring 1990, I remembered that tour when I was offered a grant by New York City's welfare agency to assess the nutritional adequacy of the meals served in city-run homeless shelters and group houses for children in foster care. I was curious to know what homelessness was like in New York as compared to San Francisco, and to see what New York was doing to help its unhoused population. I also thought it would be good for our department to partner with city agencies. Because I would need help with the nutritional analyses, I asked each of the full-time faculty if they would work with me on this project. All refused: they didn't work summers. I asked Lisa; she said yes immediately.

What a summer we had. It was easy for us to review the menus at the shelters, but we also wanted to know what the sites looked like, how the menu items were prepared and served, how the food looked and tasted, whether anyone actually ate it, and what the people who ate it thought about it. Agency staff agreed to put shelter visits into our contract and took us to places for homeless men, families, women with children, people with AIDS, single-room occupancy hotels, and group foster homes for children and adolescents. These visits were so upsetting that it sometimes took me days to recover from them.

The men's shelters were considered to be dangerous places: guards accompanied us on our visits. At some, food was cooked on site, always in wasteful excess: "We don't want any hungry men around here." At others, meals were supplied by contractors and looked like airline food; these preprepared meals invariably contained less than they were supposed to (fruit cups held just one or two tiny slices of peaches) or were missing entire items. The shelter staff monitored the system as closely as they could, but cheating by contractors was rampant, and by the time the meals were delivered, it was too late to do anything about them. The men who were given meals from contractors complained, understandably, that they did not have enough food.

The foster homes brought me to tears. The children seemed so alone and neglected, and the meal service made me conscious of my white, middle-class values. I thought the staff ought to be sitting at the table with the children, passing the food around family style, and teaching table manners and sharing. I saw none of that. These facilities had cooks, and a few interacted warmly with the kids, but the meals were served cafeteria style, with no adult supervision. In one place, staff brought in fast food for themselves and ate it at a separate table. I thought this a lost opportunity for teaching kids about social interaction at meals and the pleasures food can bring, even under such sad circumstances.

At a foster house in Brooklyn for six teenage girls, the cook put the food out on the corner of a table piled high with laundry and boxes. The girls picked up the food and took it to their separate rooms to eat it. Wouldn't meals offer a good opportunity to teach them how to shop for food and learn to prepare and serve it? Not allowed. That house had a large fig tree out in front, loaded with ripe fruit. I pulled off a fig and bit into it—it was at the perfect stage of ripeness and deliciousness. "Ugh," the girls said. "How can you eat that?" That too, seemed like a missed opportunity.

I filed a lengthy report on our observations and analyses. It included recommendations for changes in the food service operations, better supervision of contractors, training programs for staff, and pilot programs to teach teenagers to cook.[2] But this was just when the new mayor, David Dinkins, reorganized city agencies to cut the budget. Our report disappeared, and we never heard a word about it. Much later, we learned that the city had chosen to go entirely to a contracting system, the opposite of our recommendation. But the project had one positive result: when our department had a faculty position available for someone to run our dietetic internship program, I was able to convince Lisa to leave Aramark and take it, to the department's everlasting benefit.

My Kitchenless Apartment

One great irony of my department's dirty kitchen was that the apartment I rented from NYU had no kitchen at all. My plan in moving to New York was to trade up from my Washington, DC, apartment, but having to stay there until the last minute—I left on a Friday and started at NYU on Monday—gave me no time to look for a place to buy. Instead, I took the NYU rental sight unseen. It was part of the lovely row of old townhouses on the north side of Washington Square, which had been combined on the inside into one apartment building. The elegant facades were straight out of Edith Wharton, but the apartment assigned to me must have been part of the maids' quarters in her day. It was on the top floor facing away from the park, and the rooms were small and dark. A small sink, stove, and wall cabinet lined the entrance hallway. The refrigerator stood in the living room. I complained, but was told nothing could be done. I was in a low-status school and department, and besides, I was told, "the previous tenant had the refrigerator in her bedroom."

I started looking for an apartment to buy right away and visited about forty before giving up. Anything equivalent to where I had lived in Washington would cost three times as much, and I was afraid to take on that kind of financial commitment. My uncle Paul, my father's youngest brother, lived in New York and was helping me with finances. He urged me to ask NYU if I could move to a better apartment.

At NYU, campus housing is negotiated through deans. At the end of my first year, in my earliest meeting with the newly hired dean, Ann Marcus, I pointed out the irony of my living in a kitchenless apartment. She arranged for me to meet with the longtime administrator who ran faculty housing "out of his back pocket," meaning through favors and influence, not policy. We hit it off right away. I told him I missed California and longed for a place with some outside space for a garden. "The Koch apartment has a big terrace," he told me, but "Koch will never move." He was referring to New York's mayor, Ed Koch, who lived in a building now owned by NYU.

The housing guy must not have been reading the *New York Times*, but I was. It reported that Koch, who had just lost his bid for reelection, was giving up the small, rent-controlled Greenwich Village apartment he had held for nearly twenty-five years and moving to a larger apartment at 2 Fifth Avenue. I didn't know Koch, but I had met his sister, Pat, who worked at NYU. Embarrassed as I was to bother her about something so personal, I was sure she would understand. I asked her about the apartment. She said she was helping her brother pack on that Sunday, and I could come look at it.

Once I got past the security guards—"Who are you? What are you doing here?"—all I could see was a chaotic mess. The windows were bulletproof, four inches thick, yellowed, and covered with dark curtains. Stalactites of dark green paint hung from the ceilings. The closets were so stuffed that shoes and clothes fell out when I opened their doors. There was a kitchen, but so tiny that it looked like a closet. The terrace was indeed large, but it was covered with broken tiles, and the railings were rusted and looked dangerously frail. I discussed the situation with my therapist. "You will be living in it for a long time. Put money into fixing it. That's how things work here." I was not enthusiastic about overseeing renovations, but I did want that terrace. I said I would take it.

I had agreed to do a consultation for the World Health Organization in Mauritius over the January break, and I would not be able to move into the apartment until I got back. As soon as I returned, I went to look at it. Nobody told me that the university always renovated apartments between tenants. Workers had cleaned and repainted the apartment, opened up the galley kitchen with a pass-through to the living room, repaired the working fireplace that I hadn't even noticed, retiled the terrace, and replaced the railings.

FIGURES 13 AND 14. Ed Koch, former mayor of New York City, in the apartment he occupied from 1967 until 1990 when I moved into it, and me there in 2013. Following Koch's death on February 1, 2013, the *New York Times* published an article about his living arrangements, illustrated with this photo. Mine was taken for a blog post about our consecutively inhabited apartment.

The biggest surprise was the view, which I had not seen on my earlier visit. The living room had a magnificent, unobstructed view of the Empire State Building and beyond, as far uptown as 53rd Street (today, alas, a new NYU building blocks most of that view). This was going to work out just fine. I have lived in this apartment longer than Koch did. I love it that in addition to its political tenant, the building, built in 1931, has a distinguished food history: James Beard, the patron saint of American cooking, moved into it in 1938.[3]

Talking to the Press

The new apartment, which I moved into in March 1990, made me feel even more certain that New York was the right place for me, even though I was living in the equivalent of a company town: NYU was both my employer and landlord. The university was renting me an affordable place to live in a great location as well as paying me an adequate salary and providing me with a credible platform for speaking and writing about food issues I cared about.

I wanted reporters to ask me about those issues and to frame their stories from my point of view. I like being quoted, and NYU's public relations staff likes it too. In Washington, DC, I had been interviewed on "background" (not for quotation) by Carole Sugarman at the *Washington Post* and Marian Burros at the *New York Times*. Now out of government, I was free to speak to reporters on the record.

In 1991, the USDA was about to release a new guide to healthy diets—a food pyramid—when it abruptly halted publication. The sudden withdrawal and the controversy that followed brought me into contact with reporters all over the country. In the pyramid, food groups were arranged from bottom to top in relation to the quantity of recommended intake: at the bottom were grains and fruits and vegetables, and at the tip, indicating "eat less," were meat and dairy. I have since written detailed histories of the pyramid's withdrawal and revision, and the research basis of its message that some foods really are better for health than others.[4]

My interactions with reporters began with a phone call from Malcolm Gladwell, then at the *Washington Post*. Did I have anything to say about the USDA's hasty withdrawal of its new Eating Right Pyramid? As he had written a couple of weeks earlier, the USDA's stated reason for withdrawing the pyramid was that its design was confusing to children.[5] This was so silly—food guides are for adults—that I immediately suspected meat industry opposition. Gladwell's article, cowritten with Carol Sugarman, quoted me: "The Agriculture Department is in the position of being responsive to the agriculture business. That is their job. Nutrition isn't their job. . . . [T]he food industry has always been involved in dietary guidance."[6]

Late on the night the *Post* article appeared, I got a phone call from one of the USDA nutrition staff members who had ratted on me for attending that meeting in Berkeley a few years earlier. "I saw your quote," she said. "Madigan [Edward Madigan, the just-appointed USDA secretary] is lying about the pyramid. The Cattleman's Association is behind this. I have documents to prove it. We are not allowed to talk to reporters. Could you get what I have to the press?" Feeling like Bob Woodward talking to Deep Throat, I assured her I could.

I soon started receiving documents mailed to me in plain, unmarked envelopes with no return address. These contained illustrations of the withdrawn pyramid along with internal USDA correspondence detailing how it had been researched, developed, approved, cleared by USDA officials, sent to the printer, and then withdrawn. I also got faxes sent anonymously from Washington, DC, hotels. I called Marian Burros at the *New York Times*. Would she like to see what I'd been sent? She would.

Once her first story appeared—headlined "Are Cattlemen Now Guarding the Henhouse?"—other reporters called. I put together a press kit with the relevant documents and sent it to anyone interested. Reporters loved the story, and it remained front-page news for a full year.[7] They could see what it was really about—the USDA's conflicted roles, promoting Big Agriculture while advising the public about diet and health, as well as the undue influence of food lobbyists on federal nutrition policy. By the time Marian Burros forced the issue by publishing what the USDA was considering as alternative food guide designs, I had been quoted in dozens of national and international publications.

A year after the withdrawal, the USDA released a revised version. Retitled the Food Guide Pyramid, it was much the same as the original except for a few details meant to appease critics in the meat industry (such as greater emphasis on eating two to three servings of meat a day). Carol Sugarman quoted me in the *Washington Post:* "It's nice that science finally won out over politics. . . . It's too bad it took

$855,000 additional taxpayer dollars to demonstrate what had already been shown by the first round of research."[8]

As it happened, the pyramid's survival was another result of Mike McGinnis's extraordinary negotiating skills. He brokered the deal, but with typical diplomacy told a reporter that "while there had been 'some disagreement' between HHS and USDA, the Pyramid project involved 'a high degree of collegiality both at the professional staff level and the political level.'"[9]

I had fun talking with reporters about USDA's duplicity. I also enjoyed the cloak-and-dagger aspects of the story. The most fun began with a call from a *Newsweek* reporter asking for a color illustration of the withdrawn pyramid. I had only a black-and-white copy, and blurry at that. The reporter insisted: "I've been told you can get one." Well, I could try. I called someone I barely knew at Porter-Novelli, the public relations agency handling the pyramid's release.

> ME: "Hi. You and I are about to have a weird conversation. I'm
> calling because *Newsweek* wants a color graphic of the pyramid."
> HIM [appalled]: "I can't give that to *Newsweek*."
> ME: "I'm not asking you to give it to *Newsweek*. I'm asking you to
> give it to *me*."
> HIM [after a shocked pause]: "Let me get back to you."

The next day, I had an anonymous message on my office answering machine: "The object you requested will be at the concierge desk of the Four Seasons Hotel in Georgetown at noon, under your name." I called the *Newsweek* reporter, repeated that message, and added that I wanted that object when he was done with it. I still have those color slides of the original pyramid design.

By April 1992, when the pyramid was finally released, I had a good working relationship with a large number of food and business reporters. They kept me informed about current events and current research. When they contacted me, I returned their calls immediately. When they asked questions I couldn't answer, I dropped everything and looked up what I didn't know. I'm still doing that.

By the early 1990s, I was starting to feel better about my life. I liked living in New York, having a challenging but secure job, and seeing a therapist once a week or so to help me through the rough spots. But I was mainly focusing on day-to-day tasks; I still did not have a long-term goal or any clear sense of direction for my own work. That would come soon, as my academic interests expanded beyond nutrition into food.

7 *Joining the Food World*

Along with the freedom to teach and write what I think, and to use my nonteaching time as I wish, an additional privilege of university life has been the opportunity to travel. Invitations to speak at conferences or to give talks are a measure of academic achievement, particularly when they come from other universities in the United States and abroad. I had an early taste of the rewards of academic travel— new places, new people, new information, and all at someone else's expense—when I went to Mauritius for the World Health Organization in 1990, and to Cuba with a scientific and public health group a month after I returned from that trip. With my NYU department running more smoothly, I could accept more speaking and consulting invitations.

Connecting with Oldways

In the spring of 1991, I got a call from Greg Drescher, one of the cofounders of the intriguingly named Oldways Preservation and Exchange Trust, inviting me to speak at a conference he was organizing in New York in collaboration with the James Beard Foundation. I had heard of James Beard (who died in 1985) as the author of popular cookbooks, but not of his foundation. Greg explained that the foundation promoted chefs and restaurants and had just started giving the annual awards that are now considered the Oscars of the food world. I also had never heard of Oldways. This was a newly formed culinary think tank devoted to promoting diets that were not only delicious but also culturally appropriate, healthful, and environmentally sustainable. The prime examples were diets traditionally consumed in regions of the Mediterranean and Asia.[1]

Drescher ran the group's public programs. The other Oldways cofounders were the food writer Nancy Harmon Jenkins and Dun Gifford, a charming, charismatic visionary with links to the Kennedy family, who served as its president.[2] All three had been members of the American Institute of Wine and Food (AIWF). Gifford had chaired the AIWF board but left that group (in deep financial trouble, as was later discovered) to focus more explicitly on the historical and cultural as well as the culinary aspects of food, bringing Nancy and Greg with him.

I accepted the invitation, believing that my NYU department could benefit from connections with Oldways, the Beard Foundation, and the AIWF. If nothing else, their members might provide internships, scholarships, or mentoring for our students. The New York conference was nothing like the science or public health conferences I usually attended. Aimed at food writers, it had an attention-getting title: "Food and Health Writing after the Demise of Oat Bran: Is Anyone Still Listening?" This was at the height of the oat bran craze, when everyone seemed to be pouring it over anything they ate in the hope of reducing blood cholesterol levels (not that easy, alas).[3] Greg invited me to be on a panel to discuss how nutritionists ought to be talking about diets and lifestyles rather than single nutrients or ingredients like oat bran.

Whatever I said on that panel must have fit with the Oldways agenda, because Greg soon invited me to speak at its next conference, this one in Beverly Hills: "From Asia to the Mediterranean: Cultural

Models for Healthy Eating." For the next several years, I was invited to speak at one Oldways conference after another, each more fabulous than the next.[4] These were held in elegant hotels in stunning settings, with talented chefs preparing banquets of foods representative of whatever country we were in. I went to Oldways conferences in Spain, Italy, Greece, Morocco, Tunisia, and Argentina. We were taken on field trips to eat with Bedouins in the high Atlas Mountains; watch camels pulling olive grindstones; see women making couscous; try our hands at making cheese, bread, and orecchiette; and meet farmers as well as historians and scientists. We went to souks, Roman ruins, and no end of food markets. With a small Oldways group, I went to Maui to scope out possible venues for a forthcoming conference. There we ate our way through one gorgeous meal after another in between visits to farms, boat trips, and a breathtaking, if terrifying, helicopter ride into the Haleakalā crater. These trips were so luxurious—and so informative— that I could not believe how lucky I was to be included.

For me, the lasting value of the Oldways conferences was meeting the people who came to them: chefs, restaurant owners, food writers, and academics from all over the world. These were people I would never have otherwise had the chance to meet, united by a common interest in the pleasures and health benefits of diets based on local, seasonal, and sustainable ingredients.

For these conferences, Greg Drescher encouraged me to think and talk about nutrition in a different way from the approach of the *Surgeon General's Report,* and to focus on foods and dietary patterns rather than nutrients. From his perspective and now mine, it made no sense to push manufacturers to reduce the amount of salt, sugar, and fat in what we now call ultraprocessed junk foods. These would just be cosmetic changes. He called such reformulated products "techno-foods, for want of a more pejorative term."

I used this term in the title of the speech I gave at the 1991 Oldways meeting in Beverly Hills: "Cultural Models for Healthy Eating:

Alternatives to Techno-food." In it I talked about how the traditional diets of the Mediterranean, Japan, and Hawai'i were largely plant-based, but now market forces were introducing more profitable, less healthful food products into those areas. I called for education campaigns to encourage traditional diets as well as for policies like price supports, subsidies, school lunch standards, and advertising regulations to make it easier for people to eat more healthfully. I could give that same speech today. I ended it with a comment on changing demographics: "Our society is becoming more ethnically diverse, and ethnic minorities increasingly are becoming ethnic majorities. If these trends continue, the familiar Anglo-German diet, with its focus on meat and dairy foods, might well become just one among a great many traditional dietary models, although as one rather high in fat and low in fiber, to be recommended for consumption only in moderation."[5]

Conflicting Interests? *how Oldways operated*

Much as I appreciated the opportunities Oldways offered and Greg Drescher's influence on my thinking, I had a nagging sense that I ought to be more concerned about how Oldways operated. I was not paying for those glamorous trips, but somebody was. In this case, the somebody was the International Olive Oil Council (IOOC), hardly a disinterested promoter of Mediterranean diets. Thus I must also thank Oldways for introducing me to the conflicts of interest faced by food and nutrition professionals who accept gifts and sponsorship from food companies, a topic to which I later devoted much scrutiny.

Intern'l Olive Oil

The IOOC is a trade association formed under the auspices of the United Nations to promote the quality and integrity of olive oils. Like any trade association, its basic goal is to protect and promote sales.[6] It was no coincidence that Oldways conferences were held in olive-growing countries or in those that might become markets for olive oil. One of the meetings in Hawai'i, for example, was to try to convince Japanese culinary school leaders to substitute olive oil for the fats they traditionally used. It was also no coincidence that most Oldways conferences were about Mediterranean diets, loosely defined as largely (but not exclusively) plant-based, with olive oil as the principal fat. Oldways promoted Mediterranean diets; the IOOC wanted to sell more olive oil. This looked like a win-win, and everyone, including me, conveniently ignored the sales motivation.

In promoting the health benefits of Mediterranean diets, Oldways acted as a public relations arm of the IOOC. In this role, Oldways deserves full credit for introducing the Mediterranean diet—and particularly olive oil—to the American food scene. The free Oldways trips came with a quid pro quo, especially for food writers. They were expected to write articles in the popular press about the benefits of Mediterranean diets and olive oil; if they didn't, they weren't invited back. The bookshelves in Oldways' offices in Cambridge, Massachusetts, sagged under the weight of thick binders of press clippings.

The success of this effort was soon evident. In the early 1990s, it was impossible to find a bottle of good-quality olive oil in New York City outside specialty food shops like Balducci's or Dean & DeLuca. But within just a few years, any local supermarket offered a choice of extra-virgin oils. The 2020 US Dietary Guidelines recommend a "Mediterranean dietary pattern" as a model of healthful eating. This includes fruits, vegetables, grains, nuts, and a full ounce of oil a day— roughly 250 calories' worth. I have no trouble with such recommendations; plenty of research backs up the health benefits of largely plant-based diets and the fats from nuts, seeds, avocados, and, of course, olives. In that sense, Oldways was ahead of its time.

In general, it's the overall diet that counts for health. Oldways called for more research on the benefits of olive oil and other specific foods common to Mediterranean diets. More research is always useful, but asking for research that demonstrates benefits biases the research in that direction. It makes for better science to ask whether an individual dietary component makes any difference to health on its own. I agreed with Oldways' promotion of the Mediterranean diet, but its involvement with the IOOC made me uneasy.

The Mediterranean Diet Conference

Despite my misgivings, I agreed to cochair the first Oldways International Conference on Diets of the Mediterranean, held in Boston in 1993, along with Walter Willett and Dimitrios Trichopoulos, professors of nutritional epidemiology at the Harvard School of Public Health. The speakers were renowned experts, led off by the cardiologist Ancel Keys, then well into his nineties. They included leading international nutritionists—Anna Ferro-Luzzi from Italy, Antonia Trichopoulou from Greece, Elisabet Helsing from Norway—as well as Joan Gussow, chair of nutrition at Columbia University Teachers College, and Sidney Mintz, the distinguished anthropologist from Johns Hopkins and the author of what is now considered the foundational work in food studies, *Sweetness and Power: The Place of Sugar in Modern History.*

I was thrilled by this conference. The speakers were informative and provocative. They raised critical questions about what Mediterranean diets really included, whether anyone actually ate that way, how relevant this diet was for anyone living outside the region, whether olive oil and wine really were all that healthful, and what widespread adherence to a Mediterranean dietary pattern might do to water resources, fish stocks, and the environment. The talks were of such high quality and the questions so insightful that I thought the papers deserved publication. I volunteered to edit them as well as to arrange for their publication as a supplement to the *American Journal of Clinical Nutrition.* As a member of the society that publishes this monthly journal, I knew that it occasionally produced special issues that summarized conference proceedings, paid for by conference sponsors.

Arlene Wanderman, who was the IOOC's public relations representative in the United States, said she would help get the funding. Arlene had graduated from one of my NYU department's home economics programs before I arrived, and I knew her as someone who was smart, straight-talking, and full of integrity. At the Oldways meeting in Hawai'i later that year (the one that established the Chefs Collaborative for healthy and sustainable diets), Arlene and I met with IOOC officials. They agreed to fund the supplement through a $35,000 grant to Oldways. At the time I did not even consider the possibility that IOOC's sponsorship would affect the content of the scientific papers or turn the publication into an advertisement for olive oil. The conference speakers had not taken the benefits of Mediterranean diets at face value: they raised critical questions. And since neither I nor the authors would be paid, I did not think there would be a conflict of interest. Also, the IOOC's sponsorship would be fully disclosed on the title page of the supplement when published in 1995.[7]

In my 2018 book *Unsavory Truth*, I reviewed research on how food-industry funding influences nutrition research and dietary advice, and how poorly that influence is recognized by recipients. Knowing what I know now, I would not have edited that publication. Nor would I have been able to be so deeply involved with Oldways.

I thought publication of the supplement would give Oldways scientific credibility, but this was not Dun Gifford's goal: he had sponsors to please. He wanted Antonia Trichopoulou's name added as coeditor; she had edited or coedited other Mediterranean diet journal supplements sponsored by the IOOC, and he must have thought or known that the IOOC wanted her as coeditor. But I balked: she had contributed a paper to the project but had not worked on any of the others. I thought an academic principle was at stake: authors write, editors edit. Holding to this and one other principle—that debts need to be paid—ended my involvement with Oldways.

The IOOC grant included $20,000 for journal preparation and printing, $1,000 for my NYU office expenses, and $14,000 for undefined purposes (essentially, a gift to Oldways). A year or so after the supplement was published, I ran into the executive director of the American Society for Clinical Nutrition, which published the journal. He had some unwelcome news: "Oldways never paid for the supplement." I could not believe it, but Oldways was stiffing my nutrition society. I was hugely embarrassed and assured the director I would do all I could to get the bill paid. He sent me copies of the correspondence with Gifford's excuses.

With those letters in hand, I talked to Dun Gifford, who told me that Oldways had already spent the money. Worrying that my reputation was at stake, I insisted that the bill be paid. He paid it, but that was the end of our association. By that time, my closest colleagues were gone from Oldways. Arlene Wanderman had died (a great personal loss), Nancy Jenkins was no longer associated with it, and Greg Drescher had moved on to an executive position with the Culinary Institute of America. Not only was I not invited to subsequent Oldways conferences, I was purged. When Oldways held its tenth-anniversary conference on Mediterranean diets in 2003, my cochairing of the first conference was not mentioned in the program materials, nor was the journal supplement on the Mediterranean diets.[8] I never heard from Oldways again until after Dun Gifford's death in 2010, when his partner, Sara Baer-Sinnott, asked me to reflect on Oldways' legacy for the conference's twentieth anniversary in 2013.[9]

From my current perspective, my involvement with Oldways had an overwhelmingly positive influence on my life. Greg Drescher got me thinking about food and nutrition in a much broader context, and his lessons have stuck. Oldways encouraged me to think of diets not

only as nutritious and delicious but also as deeply embedded in social, cultural, agricultural, environmental, and political dimensions,
all at the same time. This way of thinking now has its own name: food
systems. It wasn't just the push to think more systematically that I
found so mind-expanding; it was also learning how hungry (a delib-
erate metaphor) everyone I met through Oldways was to learn more
about food, its role in culture, and its profound effects on health and
the environment. I draw a direct line from what I learned at Oldways
conferences to our establishing food studies as a discipline at NYU.

The most enduring benefits of my involvement with this group
were the people I met through its events, many of whom are now lifelong friends. And while I've never had much interest in celebrities,
there have been a few I've been eager to meet. One was Julia Child.
Oldways made it possible for me to meet her—at her house in Cambridge, no less.

My Dinner with Julia Child

Everyone in the food world has a Julia Child story. Mine began with
meeting Nancy Jenkins at the 1991 Oldways conference in Beverly
Hills. By that time, Julia was so famous for writing *Mastering the Art
of French Cooking* and for her *French Chef* cooking show on television
that she was identifiable by just her first name. She was equally famous for her disdain for nutritionists, who, she frequently stated,
were ruining food for everyone else. The eat-less-fat message of the
Surgeon General's Report had induced complaints about what she
cooked: "Here comes Julia, with all the cream and butter." Nutritionists, she said, were responsible for the death of gastronomy in the
United States. This, she said, was an unnecessary tragedy: "We
should enjoy food and have fun."[10]

I think so too, but am thoroughly convinced that healthy food
can—and should—be delicious, enjoyable, and fun. After hearing me

speak at that meeting, Nancy had an inspired, if overly optimistic, idea: "If Julia met you, she might change her mind about nutritionists." Would I be willing to meet with Julia Child? Would I ever! During my Berkeley years of competitive home cooking, I had used my copy of *Mastering* so much that its pages were stained, spattered, and stuck together, and its binding was falling apart. I loved watching her on TV, and am still in awe of her dribbling hot sugar syrup over a bowl to create a brittle caramel cage—something I would never dare try.[11] Nancy offered to host a dinner party to introduce me to Julia. She set a date in December, months in advance. I felt like I had won the lottery.

Those months went by without a word. A few days before the scheduled date, I called Nancy to make sure we were still on.

"Didn't anyone tell you?" she said. "I broke my foot." Oh no! I managed to stifle my disappointment long enough to commiserate about her injury before blurting out what was really on my mind: "I guess this means the dinner with Julia is off?"

"Didn't anyone tell you? Julia is hosting the dinner at her house."

No, nobody had told me that Julia Child would be cooking dinner for me. I could hardly believe it.

The evening arrived, cold and snowy. Greg Drescher came to collect me from where I was staying in Cambridge and told me who else would be there: Dun Gifford; Barbara Haber, the curator of Radcliffe's Schlesinger Library; Rebecca Alssid, the director of Boston University's master's program in gastronomy (founded at Julia's instigation); and their spouses. Meeting Barbara and Rebecca would be a bonus; I was envious of BU's gastronomy program and the Schlesinger's cookbook collection and wished we had both at NYU. Paul Child would not be there; he was already in a nursing home. Nancy, on crutches and unable to get around in the snow, could not join us.

Greg and I walked in through a side door straight into Julia's kitchen, the very one now on exhibit at the Smithsonian Institution in

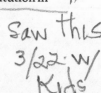

Washington, DC. The other guests around the table stared at us. Greg and I sat down. "And now," Julia said in her warbly inimitable (by me) voice, "Marion will introduce herself." That felt like an opening salvo; it did not feel like a warm welcome. I did my best to say who I was and how much I cared about good food, but could do nothing to reduce the tension. Someone had brought a salad as the first course, and we got through that painlessly, but then Julia served the main course. I am not a vegetarian but prefer largely plant-based diets, so I was unprepared for what came next—the largest slice of beef I'd been given in years, exquisitely cooked, but far more than I wanted. As Julia put it on my plate, she said, "Now, there's nothing like a good piece of meat, is there?" Then came heavily buttered mashed potatoes, also delicious, this time presented with the remark "Butter makes everything better, doesn't it?" Everyone stared at me. What was this nutritionist going to do? Reader, I ate it. Of course I did.

Julia's mean.

I don't remember the evening ever feeling comfortable. I had brought my battered copy of *Mastering* for Julia to sign, thinking that its signs of heavy use would please her. Not a chance. She signed it grudgingly: "Bon Appétit to Marion. Julia Child, Cambridge Mass. Dec. 14, 1991." Still, I consider it a treasure. When I proudly showed it to Marvin Taylor, the curator of the NYU library's food studies collection, he arranged to have the book rebound.

Most people who knew Julia cannot believe this story. She was universally adored for her charm and hospitality. Her behavior to me that night seemed so out of character. Couldn't she tell how much I admired her? Couldn't she see that I appreciated delicious food as much as she did? Years later, when I was in Christchurch, New Zealand, for a conference, I visited Julia's longtime assistant, Stephanie Hersh, who had moved there. At last I could find out what that evening was all about. Stephanie confirmed my impression: Julia had felt trapped into having to meet and prepare dinner for someone she thought of as an enemy of food.

Over the next few years Julia behaved more politely to me but remained suspicious. In 1995, when my department was trying to find a faculty member to head up our new food studies programs, I wrote to ask her for suggestions. Her reply included these comments:

> My great concern with a lot of these academic and administrative positions is that often the people in them have no idea of how really good food is supposed to taste. Three or four years ago, when we had our first AIWF "Taste and Health" meeting here in Boston, some of the nutritionists obviously had no interest in food at all! They did not find it interesting or fun, and felt that food was only to be eaten for survival. They recommended frozen string beans (there is nothing more doleful) because they had the proper vitamins, et cetera, and never considered the flavor or appearance! . . . Meanwhile, good luck with your search.[12]

Once NYU's food studies programs were under way, however, Marian Burros quoted Julia as "delighted" by the creation of these programs.[13] When we invited her to a party to celebrate the construction of our new, state-of-the-art teaching kitchen, I mentioned that her sponsorship of Boston University's gastronomy program had inspired us to create our own programs. In response, she wrote: "I am flattered that you credit the inspiration to me, but think that you should be proud indeed of your accomplishments!"[14]

Later Julia Child wrote an endorsement for my book *Food Politics* when its first edition came out in 2002. Because she rarely endorsed books, I was touched that her publicist, Fern Berman, had been able to convince her to do this one. Her blurb read:

> What a book this is! Of course we have always suspected and known some of the truth, but never in such bold detail! In this fascinating book, we learn how powerful, intrusive, influential, and invasive big

JULIA CHILD PRODUCTIONS, INC.
P.O. Box 5594
Santa Barbara, CA 93150

Dear Marian:

Thanks for your note and birthday greetings. You are kind to remember, and I appreciate your sending a card.

We had a wonderful time in Maine at our annual family gathering, and then went down to Washington, DC to see my Cambridge kitchen installed in the Smithsonian Institution's American History Museum. It was marvelous!

Here's hoping all is well with you. Again, thanks for writing

Julia

FIGURE 15. This postcard from Julia Child, then living in Santa Barbara, came in response to my congratulations on her ninetieth birthday. It is postmarked September 13, 2002. The year before, the Smithsonian Institution installed Julia's kitchen, in which I was once a dinner guest, as part of an exhibition. It is now on permanent display.

industry is and how alert we must constantly be to prevent it from influencing not only our own personal nutritional choices but those of our government agencies. Marion Nestle has presented us with a courageous and masterful exposé.

Julia and I had come a long way since that dinner in 1991. I never had the slightest effect on her low opinion of nutritionists in general, but I was pleased that she considered me an exception. The creation of food studies programs at NYU, which I discuss next, was evidence that I took food seriously, and that's what Julia Child cared about.

8   Inventing Food Studies   1996

It isn't often in academic life that anyone gets to create an entirely new field of study, but that's what we did at NYU in 1996, when my department began offering degree programs in food studies. We were not the first to offer a formal program devoted to the role of food in society—Boston University began offering a master's program in gastronomy in 1991—but we were the first to teach undergraduate, master's, and doctoral students under a more seriously academic rubric. As department chair, I was trying my best to improve the programs I had inherited and to close the ones that no longer attracted students. I was not thinking about adding anything new. But when circumstances forced the situation, the idea of food studies came to me in a flash.[1]

The precipitating circumstance: the department had to give up its food and hotel management courses and degree programs. Hotel management programs? Yes, and these were a big part of the academic mess I had to deal with. The department ran an undergraduate program in food and hotel management along with a master's program in food service management. The latter, however, was run as a hotel management program, with courses taught by adjuncts who worked in the hotel industry. The faculty member in charge of the hotel curriculum had been trained as a dietitian and had a PhD in home economics from NYU but no credentials in hotel management. All of this meant that we were teaching hotel management without a legitimate academic license. This made the hotel programs academically vulnerable. We were not being honest with students. We had no trained hotel academics on our full-time faculty. If anyone who cared about academic integrity knew what we were doing, the programs could be closed or taken away from us.

The previous department chair, Margaret Simko, thought hotel management was the way forward from home economics. She envisioned the programs as evolving into a hotel school like the one at Cornell University, with NYU buying a hotel to be run by our students. I inherited the advisory committee she had established. Its members, mostly from the hotel industry, had been pushing this idea for years and were disappointed—furious, actually—with NYU for not acquiring a hotel for this purpose. I thought the committee was living in a dream world and had no understanding of how universities worked. I doubted that NYU's administration would buy a hotel for a home economics department, staffed by women, none of whom had hotel training. Hotel management was (and, perhaps, still is) a field thoroughly dominated by men, and businessmen at that.

Besides having to get this angry committee to face reality, I also had to deal with Margaret Simko's disapproval. I thought she had badly neglected the department and faculty, but although she had retired, she still occupied her office. During my entire first year her most frequent comment on my actions was "Well, that's not the way I would do it." She held almost daily closed-door meetings with my faculty—two of the four were her former doctoral students, and one other had a doctorate from the department—to give them the same message. A year later, when I needed an office for a visiting faculty member, I was relieved that she gave hers up and left the department.

The hotel management courses made me uneasy for another reason: I had serious doubts about their quality. I was no expert in food service—that was the course I never took when trying to qualify as a dietitian—or hotel management, but I knew enough to worry about the theoretical content of what was taught and whether we were teaching even the applied aspects well. I had reason to worry. One night I ran into one of our graduates at a government-rate (inexpensive, very basic) hotel at a highway crossing outside Washington, DC. I was late getting there and arrived at midnight to be greeted by name by the front-desk clerk, who recognized me from NYU. If our students couldn't get jobs at better hotels than this, I thought, we had no business offering these programs.

But hotel programs attracted tuition-paying students. NYU's School of Continuing Education (SCE) viewed hotel management as a lucrative market and decided to establish the equivalent of a hotel school. As part of this initiative, it wanted to take over our hotel management courses and program titles. Relieved though I was to get rid of them, transferring these programs to SCE would come at a high cost. The undergraduate program alone brought in a million dollars a year in tuition money, and neither my department nor the school could afford to lose that income.

I spent the next couple of years in a futile attempt to work out some sort of cooperative agreement with SCE. Its administrators could not understand why low-status nutrition and home economics faculty were blocking what they wanted to do. Even so, I was not prepared for my conversation with Dean Ann Marcus when she called me in to say that it had become impossible for her to talk to NYU's president about anything else besides moving the hotel program to SCE. She was tired of arguing with him about it. "So," she asked "how would you feel about moving the hotel program to SCE?"

Me, in a flash of inspiration: "It depends on what I get."

"What do you want?"

Another flash: "Food studies."

I knew enough about university politics to realize that I had just been presented with a golden opportunity. The dean's next question: "What's that?" To this, I also had a ready answer: the academic study of food in history, culture, and society. When she asked what I would need to start a program like this, I had an answer for that too. I wanted food studies degree programs at all three levels—undergraduate, master's, and doctoral. We would need a full-time, tenure-track faculty member to develop and run the programs. And we would need the newly cleaned but decades-old home economics kitchen to be replaced by a state-of-the-art professional teaching facility, something in which NYU could take pride. Dean Marcus said she thought she could get us all that. And she did.

While she was doing those high-level negotiations, I was dealing with all the questions that came up when trying to start a new program—how to design a curriculum, recruit students and faculty, and create a supportive academic environment. Fortunately, I had help.

"Food It Up"

While my plan for food studies owed a lot to what I had learned from Oldways, it was not the only source of inspiration. Academic interest in food was in the air, the zeitgeist. The gastronomy program at Boston University was well established, and I had heard of a food anthropology program at the University of Pennsylvania. I also was vaguely aware of the food courses taught at the New School and of talks given at the Oxford Food Symposium, but I thought (not necessarily correctly) that these were more about culinary than academic aspects of food. I knew academics who were teaching courses in food psychology, history, and anthropology, and I had sat in on the "Food as Performance" course my anthropologist colleague Barbara Kirshenblatt-Gimblett taught at NYU soon after I arrived. I knew university instructors who were members of the Association for the Study of Food and Society and of the

Agriculture, Food and Human Values Society, and I had given a talk on the *Surgeon General's Report* at one of their joint annual meetings when I was still in Washington. There were plenty of academics teaching and writing about food, although not in organized programs that could be used as models.

Without models, the practical details of creating the programs required more than inspiration. Here too I had help, particularly from the food consultant Clark Wolf. He had started a specialty food store, the Oakville Grocery, in San Francisco, a place where I and everyone else I knew in that city went as often as we could. Clark was now living in New York and working with hotels to improve their restaurants. He was great friends with Marian Burros, the *New York Times* food writer. In the spring of 1995, she invited both of us to a party celebrating the launch of her most recent book, at the home of the Thai ambassador to the United Nations on the Upper West Side. Clark and I soon discovered that we both lived in Greenwich Village. It was a lovely evening, and after the party we decided to walk the three miles downtown. That gave us ample time to talk.

Clark said he thought the department had exciting possibilities, and he wanted to help with it. But, he said, there was a barrier: he did not want to work with the faculty member responsible for the food service and hotel management programs. Now he had my full attention. Never since my arrival at NYU had anyone even hinted that this faculty member—who raised objections to everything I wanted to do—might be other than an ideal colleague. Clark was the first person (besides my therapist) I could talk to about my difficulties with her and the programs she ran. Unlike the members of the hotel advisory committee, he had a good feel for how universities work. Here at last was someone in the food industry who got it. But how did he think he could help? "Watch me," he said.

He was well connected to New York City's food world and began by putting together a new advisory committee of leading food producers, restaurateurs, chefs, food writers and editors, and culinary professionals. Below I list them and what they were doing in 1995 in appreciation for their contributions to the founding of food studies at NYU.

Clark Wolf, Clark Wolf Company, committee chair
Leonard Barkan, Samuel Rudin University Professor of the
    Humanities, NYU[2]
Raymond Bickson, general manager, the Mark Hotel
Victor Broceaux, vice president, research and development,
    Restaurant Associates
Mitchell Davis, managing editor, James Beard Foundation
    Publications
Cinnamon Dilworth-Broceaux, president, C. A. Dilworth and
    Associates
George Faisan, co-owner, D'Artagnan, Inc.
Betty Fussell, food writer
Dorothy Cann Hamilton, president, French Culinary Institute
Michael Lomonaco, chef, 21 Club
Jeffrey Steingarten, food editor, *Vogue*
Nach Waxman, owner, Kitchen Arts and Letters bookstore

At its first meeting, I showed committee members the curriculum of the food service management master's program. Their analysis: "Your basic program is okay, but you are not teaching enough about food." They wanted their employees and colleagues to know not only what foods are, how they taste, where they come from, and how to prepare them, but also their history and role in culture. This advice was just what I needed.

With a mandate to "food up" the curriculum, a program in food studies made sense. And it would fit with NYU's other academic programs. The university already ran more than a dozen graduate and interdisciplinary programs ending with the word *studies*—Africana, American, cinema, Judaic, and museum studies, for example. During the fall of 1995, we wrote proposals for the revised programs. Perhaps because administrators wanted us to be able to compensate for the lost income from the hotel programs, our proposals sailed through approvals by the school and university in record time, as did the final approval from the State Board of Education early in June 1996.

Clark kept Marian Burros apprised of our progress. She promised to write about the new programs if we gave her an exclusive, to which we readily agreed. Her account, "A New View on Training Food Experts," appeared on the front page of the Living section of the *New York Times* on June 19.[3] It was placed below a large spread on the reopening of the Windows on the World restaurant at the World Trade Center, and next to "Return of the Godmother of Punk," a story about Patti Smith's latest performances. I thought we were in excellent company.

Burros's piece may have been the least prominent story on that page, but it didn't matter. That very afternoon, we had prospective students in our offices holding up clippings of the article and telling us, "I've waited all my life for this program. Sign me up." Two months later, we started teaching our first class of fifteen master's students.

Although the article by Burros had attracted those students, it was anything but the laudatory piece I had expected. It did begin with accolades, noting that our new programs provided "an opportunity for the study of food to achieve the recognition it has always lacked in the academic community." It quoted Julia Child, "who has often referred to dietitians as nutritional terrorists," as "delighted." It also quoted me: "We are designing just exactly the program we all wish we could have taken." (The article identified me, hilariously and never corrected even online, as someone with "a doctorate in molecular biology and a master's in pubic [*sic*] health.")

But then Burros wrote, "Not everyone is as excited about the food-studies program as Dr. Nestle or Mrs. Child." She quoted the celebrated chef of Chez Panisse, Alice Waters: "The program needs real emphasis on the agriculture side. . . . The students should have to go out and grow tomatoes and harvest potatoes." She also quoted the Columbia professor Joan Gussow's misgivings about job opportunities, the Wisconsin biochemistry professor John Suttie's profound doubts ("Interdisciplinary is a big buzzword among administrators, and the people who are trained that way are trained to do nothing"), and the cookbook author Paula Wolfert's dismissal: "I don't think a course at N.Y.U. is going to make any difference." And these comments were from *friends*. Thanks a lot.

Shortly after the programs were under way, Dean Ann Marcus invited me to a dinner party at her home and seated me next to NYU's provost, a theoretical mathematician. His first question was, "Why would anyone want to study food?" Try as hard as I could to explain the basic facts: food is central to human life, has both symbolic and material cultural implications, affects everyone's health, and constitutes an industry worth trillions of dollars, I could not convince him that issues related to something so quotidian were worth investigation. Today, although I still sometimes run into people who are baffled by food studies, such encounters are less frequent.

But the criticisms didn't matter. We had the programs. We had students who were paying tuition to take our courses. We had faculty to teach them. And we had a brand-new, beautifully designed, mouse- and cockroach-free kitchen in which to train students about food.

Recruiting Faculty

When I told Dean Marcus we would need a faculty position for food studies, I knew this was a big ask. We did not yet have students. Even if we did, recruiting faculty at NYU is not easy; candidates have to want to live in New York City, be willing to work for relatively low salaries, and find housing in an overpriced market or rent an apartment from NYU. On top of that, since food studies was not an established academic field, job candidates would have to be drawn from other fields, and the pool would be small. Most academic programs back then reflected our provost's opinion that food was not worth studying, and they discouraged faculty and doctoral students from specializing in food topics.

We advertised in the usual academic channels, but I also requested recommendations from every academic and food professional I knew. I wrote personal letters to every potential candidate I could identify, encouraging each to apply. We ended up with several excellent applicants, but one stood out: Amy Bentley, an American studies historian and an instructor at the University of Colorado who was working on a book about food during the Second World War. She had been teaching for several years, knew how universities worked, and had substantial experience advising and working with students. I was sure she could take over and do the job from the day she arrived. The dean had some doubts: "What will she do if your programs fail to attract students?" I asked Amy to give me a list of courses she felt prepared to teach in the department's existing nutrition and food programs. She divided her list into three sections: courses she could teach immediately, those that would require some preparation, and those she would be willing to spend a lot of time preparing. The dean was convinced. Happily, Amy took the job and did just what I hoped she would.

For the first few years, most of the food studies courses were taught by adjuncts recruited from the local food community. I was constantly on the lookout for qualified people who might be willing to teach for us. I routinely went to the annual Socialist Scholars conferences run by the Democratic Socialists of America, which offered

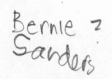
Bernie ?
Sanders

sharp analyses of current domestic and international politics, and I hoped to find people there interested in food issues. There weren't many. But at a conference in the late 1990s, I saw that someone I had never heard of—and from the Culinary Institute of America, of all places—was presenting a paper with *food* in the title. I went to hear it and was impressed by Krishnendu Ray's intellectual power. He was giving a compelling analysis of the importance of food in global society. He had a doctorate in sociology. Why was he at a cooking school when we needed him? He agreed to teach a course on contemporary food issues as an adjunct, and the minute a faculty position became available, we snagged him for it. He went on to win teaching awards and later chaired the department for nearly a decade.

I'm also going to take some credit for recruiting Fabio Parasecoli. When I first met him, he was a journalist who lived in Rome but spent enough time in New York to teach occasional courses for us. He had impressive academic credentials—his doctorate is in agricultural sciences, and he has master's degrees in political science and in languages and literature—and serious interests in food. Once, when I was in Rome for a meeting, I took a train to a studio where he was hosting a television program. After our interview, I put on a helmet, got on the back of his Vespa (how I wish I had a photo), and off we went to dinner at a restaurant he was reviewing for a Rome newspaper. When he applied for and got a job at the New School, I wrote a letter of recommendation for his first appointment, and I continued to write letters for his subsequent promotions. In each of my letters, I said the same thing: "If an appropriate position ever becomes available in our department, we will do everything we can to recruit him away from you." Fair warning. When we were given the funding to hire another faculty member, we begged him to apply, and now the department has another wonderful colleague who can teach anything about food history, culture, and politics, and who produces one valuable book after another.

What I like so much about food studies is its interdisciplinary nature. I hold degrees in molecular biology and public health, whereas the faculty I helped recruit have degrees in history, literature, political science, and sociology, as well as in agricultural science and food studies. I can't take credit for recruiting the economist, Carolyn Dimitri (she came after I stepped down as chair), but she adds enormously to the department's interdisciplinary expertise.

Constructing the Food Laboratory

The decrepit home economics kitchen was a constant worry. If we were going to be training food professionals, we needed a kitchen facility that was up to professional standards. Since we were being forced to give up hotel programs that brought in a million dollars a year in tuition money, it seemed fair that we should at least get a new kitchen in exchange. Dean Marcus persuaded SCE to give us a one-time payment of $350,000. That might be enough to cover the costs of construction and equipment, but the budget would be tight. Fortunately, the kitchen space was near the top of the building, so the outside vents would only need to go up two floors.

I knew nothing about designing kitchens and even less about construction. Again, Clark Wolf to the rescue. He had worked with many kitchen architects and knew what they could do. The two of us, along with the NYU officials in charge of the project, gave prospective architects a tough assignment. We asked for designs flexible enough to serve four purposes: cooking classes for students, cooking demonstrations by faculty and guest speakers, catering for larger events, and an event space. The facility had to be reliably sealed against mice and cockroaches and meet city building codes. And it had to be done on time and on budget. This was essential: construction could not start until classes ended in May, and the new kitchen had to be up to code and ready to use when classes started again in early September.

We interviewed several architectural firms. Most brought in elaborate computerized drawings with terrifyingly expensive plans. Only one, Richard Lewis, whom Clark knew and recommended, actually visited the space and produced quick sketches on the spot. He liked working that way—on his own, informally, doing his own drawings and filing his own permit applications. He understood what we wanted and needed. We thought he would do a great job—and he most definitely did.

All I knew about construction was that it rarely went smoothly and was especially challenging in New York. But, convinced that none of the NYU people on the team would be giving this project the kind of close supervision I was sure it required, I canceled all summer plans and became the de facto construction supervisor. NYU hired the construction crew, who were mostly Polish and spoke little English. We muddled through. All summer I visited the construction zone several times a day. I had no idea what the crew was doing (besides making a mess), but on nearly every visit, the foreman would ask how I wanted him to do this or that. I called someone on the team and got the questions answered right away. I also got the team, including Clark Wolf and Richard Lewis, to meet at least weekly to review progress. We solved lots of problems that way.

I ended up knowing the construction crew really well and learned how important close supervision is, even by someone as ignorant as I was. The one day I had to go to an out-of-town meeting, the crew installed something incorrectly that had to be fixed later on. Otherwise, the project was done perfectly, on time and within budget. The new kitchen was beautiful—industrial gray and stainless steel with movable workstations. We now call it the food laboratory. In constant use for more than a quarter century, it has held up remarkably well, thanks to its flexible design and careful maintenance. And no mouse has ever been seen in it.

FIGURE 16. With Clark Wolf and the *New York Times* food writer Florence Fabricant in my department's new teaching kitchen. It was used that day to prepare nine different turkeys—industrial (three brands), organic, natural, kosher, wild (two), Butterball—for the newspaper's pre-Thanksgiving taste comparison. The organic turkey won. Marian Burros's article about this event, "Tender but Bland Birds Flock to the Feast," appeared in the *Times*'s food section on November 20, 1996.

6.19.96 NYT

Building an Academic Community

Thanks to Marian Burros's article about food studies, we not only had a class of master's students in the fall of 1996 but also two prospective doctoral students: Jennifer Berg, who had been teaching food preparation courses for us as an adjunct since about 1990, and Mitchell Davis, the publications director of the James Beard Foundation, who was on our advisory committee. Jenny was an ally in making the hands-on food courses more professional, and I had relied on her judgment for years. She wanted a doctorate so that she could teach academic courses as well. (This worked; she ended up on our faculty.) Mitchell wanted the credential so that his food interests would be taken more seriously. When the doctoral program opened officially the next year, they were joined by Charles Feldman, who was running the culinary programs at Montclair State College in New Jersey, and Jon Deutsch, who was then just out of college and clearly headed for a stellar academic food career. Faculty and doctoral students at other universities were telling us that their programs did not accommodate their food interests. They wanted contact with people who would take their studies seriously, advise them, and collaborate.

To create a supportive academic environment for faculty and doctoral students who were studying food, we would need additional resources. NYU's Humanities Council offered small grants to faculty engaged in interdisciplinary activities. But I was not eligible: the grants were restricted to faculty in Arts and Sciences. I knew Barbara Kirshenblatt-Gimblett from sitting in on her course and attending a dinner salon she hosted for food academics, but she was in NYU's Tisch School of the Arts and also ineligible. She suggested that we involve Susan Rogers, in anthropology, and we convinced Susan to take the lead on a proposal for a colloquium for food scholars. We got the grant and for the next decade held three or four meetings a semester to which we invited every food scholar we could think of within commuting distance—twenty or thirty at each session. These meetings brought together faculty and doctoral students with shared interests. The colloquium was a haven for all of us.

We tried to be honest with our earliest doctoral students about their limited prospects for getting academic jobs. University departments typically recruit faculty trained in their own fields—history departments hire people with history degrees—but no food studies programs existed anywhere else at the time. Here is one instance in which it was good to be wrong. Food studies programs began opening up at other institutions and were eager to hire our graduates. Nearly all of our doctoral graduates who wanted academic jobs got them. Jenny Berg continues to teach in the department. Jon Deutsch and others went on to distinguished academic careers, and our more recent doctoral graduates have been snapped up for professorial jobs, including positions in traditional humanities and social science departments, even in Ivy League institutions.

We knew we were breaking new ground with food studies, but we had no idea we would be starting a movement. Within the next several years, several universities in the United States, Australia, and Italy started food degree programs of one kind or another. They raised the status and visibility of this new field of study and provided job opportunities for our doctoral students. Departments in more traditional disciplines like anthropology, history, and English literature began to encourage their students to research food-related topics. Publishers issued food encyclopedias. University presses started food-and-culture book series. Libraries competed for food-book collections. The Association for the Study of Food and Society now lists more than fifty national and international food degree programs on its website.[4] Food studies has come a long way, and I am still thrilled every time I see an announcement of a new program.

This is not to say that the early disdain for the academic study of food has entirely disappeared. I still get asked what food studies is. Even within the field, its scope remains a major topic of debate. And I still occasionally come across contemptuous descriptions of food studies like this one: an "academic fetish" having "little to do with legitimate intellectual endeavors like agriculture or nutrition science. Instead, food becomes another lens through which to examine oppression, sustainability, and multiculturalism."[5] Yes, it most certainly does. As I see it, food studies promotes the rigorous examination of major societal problems through the lens of food. In prioritizing healthy and sustainable diets, this field of study is engaged in an overt critique of the industrial food system. Defenders of the status quo cannot be expected to be enthusiastic supporters of food system change. If food studies elicits this kind of criticism, it must be doing something right.

Amassing a Food Library

A new field requires information resources—books, papers, archives—to be accessible to students and scholars. NYU's library did not have much on food, not least because its staff resisted collecting such materials. I knew this because in about 1990, Michael Schrader, a copyeditor and book reviewer for *Nation's Restaurant News,* asked for my help in dealing with this resistance. He had been collecting cookbooks sent to the magazine for review and wanted to donate them to the library in honor of his mother, an NYU graduate. I tried to convince the library to accept his books but got nowhere. ("Cookbooks? Those should go to a public library.") It took until 1994 for the library to agree to take them, and only on the condition that Schrader pay for their cataloging.[6] Also during that time, someone offered to give the library a complete set of bound *Gourmet* magazines. Not a chance: "Not of general interest, not scholarly, no room."

Soon after the start of the food studies programs, I was offered another complete set of bound *Gourmet*s. Unwilling to give up, I gave the library another try. This time, the response was different: "Call Marvin Taylor." He was the new curator of NYU's Fales Library, which housed a prestigious collection of English and American novels dating from the eighteenth century. I had no idea why its curator would have the slightest interest in *Gourmet,* but I called him. His reply: "Of course we want them."

Marvin loved to cook, cared about food, and knew a lot about it. He was already well along in the process of establishing the Downtown Collection, materials related to the 1960s arts scene in Manhattan's SoHo and Lower East Side. Our food studies programs gave him just the excuse he needed to start collecting cookbooks and other print materials about food, especially those related to New York City from the twentieth century on. He knew exactly what food researchers needed, and wanted to acquire all he could. We could not have been more fortunate in our advocate for more and better library resources.

When I heard about a large collection of cookbooks for sale, I immediately let Marvin know about them. A friend in California, Ruth Rosen, a professor of women's history at the University of California, Davis, had forwarded a message sent to historians by Jonathan Ned Katz, a historian of gay sexuality (food is indeed interdisciplinary). He was trying to sell a cookbook collection owned by his aunt, Cecily Brownstone, who had been a food writer for the Associated Press for forty years. Now she was in her nineties and in need of costly full-time care. I knew Jonathan from a feminist seminar we had both attended and got in touch right away. He said she had a lot of cookbooks. Marvin told me to take a look.

Cecily's house was a short walk from NYU. "A lot of cookbooks" was a serious understatement. From the bottom to the top of this five-floor townhouse, cookbooks overflowed from bookcases covering every wall—but they were organized, as if by a trained librarian. Each bookcase was devoted to a specific category: French cooking, of course, but also food from regions of Italy, Asia, and Africa. An entire floor-to-ceiling bookcase held children's cookbooks. Several bookcases were devoted to African American cooking; I had no idea so many existed. There were shelves of books about cheese, wine, and almost any food you might think of, American cooking from every region, and the food of New York City. File cabinets were packed with pamphlets put out by food companies from the 1940s on, along with Cecily's personal correspondence with James Beard, the Rombauers (authors of *The Joy of Cooking)*, and other food professionals who were her close friends. I wanted all of it.

When I reported back to Marvin, he came, met Cecily, and wanted it too. Even though the family was not asking much for what turned out to be about twelve thousand books and six thousand pamphlets and letters, the library did not have the funds. But I did. I had just received the proceeds from a small insurance policy I did not even know I had, and my financial adviser cousin suggested I donate the money to some worthy cause. Here it was. The books Cecily Brownstone had amassed over a career of forty years became the core of a collection that now includes seventy thousand or so books and ten thousand pamphlets, an incredible resource for anyone who studies, as the Fales website puts it, "the evolution of cuisine and food practices in 19th and 20th century America, with a particular focus on the food habits and activity of New York City . . . since expanded to cover international cuisines and other historical periods."[7]

In 2013, to my great embarrassment—shouldn't I be dead before this happens?—all of this was named the Marion Nestle Food Studies Collection. It has taken some time for me to become comfortable with—and proud of—being honored in this way, but I now view this library as part of my legacy to food scholars. My papers are there, too, and I add to them every year. Many other food aficionados have also donated books and papers to the collection. Unlike the rest of the NYU library, special collections like this one are open by appointment to researchers outside the NYU community, and I'm gratified to see how much these materials are used not only by NYU food studies students and faculty but also by scholars from all over the world and from every imaginable discipline.

Planting the Urban Farm Laboratory

I was proud of starting the food studies program in 1996 and rather stung by Alice Waters's implication that we were failing our students by not requiring them to "go out and grow tomatoes and harvest potatoes." When I first saw that comment in Marian Burros's article about our new programs, I thought, "She has to be kidding." NYU doesn't even have a campus or one street free of cars. Did she expect us to plant vegetables in Washington Square Park, right in the middle of the chess players, dog walkers, music makers, and the hordes of people just hanging out? Yes, she did. Alice, as always, was ahead of her time, and it took me years to catch up. Now I firmly agree with her that what we eat cannot be understood without knowing how food is produced.

About ten years after we started food studies, Jennifer Berg, Amy Bentley, and Krishnendu Ray got a grant to develop a curriculum in food systems—the term used to describe the totality of food issues from agricultural production to consumption, along with everything in between. They pushed for a garden to support this new program area, giving it the academically respectable title of Urban Farm Laboratory. In 2008 Jennifer Berg got another small grant to build and plant raised beds in a weedy plot behind one of the NYU's apartment buildings for faculty.

Alice's comment was still nagging at me the next year, when George Reis came to introduce himself as NYU's gardener. I didn't know NYU had a gardener, although I wondered who was growing the kale I'd seen in planters near our office building. George was sneaking vegetables into any place he could, but also had a much grander vision about how to use the small spaces between NYU buildings in more productive ways. Could I help him?

I got everyone I knew at NYU who might be interested in growing vegetables to come to a meeting about how we could convert these small plots into urban gardens. The result was a faculty report calling for gardens to beautify the grounds and improve neighborhood relations. Administrators were unmoved. They raised obstacles: Wouldn't vegetable gardens attract rats, insects, homeless people, and poachers? This seemed absurd. Washington Square Park is overrun by rats as it is, and the homeless question seemed even less relevant, but I did my due diligence. Everyone I consulted said the same thing: rats are manageable (they prefer to nest in ivy and eat meat rather than plants), insects are beneficial, soils can be tested, and unhoused people don't bother gardens. I submitted my reports on pestilence and poaching. They too got nowhere.

When sustainability became a bigger concern, the university began offering "Green Grants." Jennifer Berg and George Reis got me to sign on as the lead faculty member on a plan to survey the extent of open space that might be available for vegetable plantings at NYU, identify faculty who wanted to do research connected with those plantings, and catalog the existing NYU programs and courses that dealt with agriculture and the environment. This and further reports from 2009 to 2011 continued to be ignored.

Still, we persisted. One question was where to put a reasonably sized vegetable garden with adequate sun exposure among NYU's tall buildings. The largest available sunlit patch of land was behind the Silver Towers faculty apartment buildings. These, however, had been designed by I. M. Pei and Landmarked (my capital L indicates the gravity of this designation). Constructing anything around them would not only require permission from reluctant NYU administrators but also sign-offs from neighborhood associations, the Landmarks Preservation Commission, and the I. M. Pei firm, as well as from the Silver Tenants Association and the nursery school housed on the ground floor of one of the Silver buildings.

The next year, students like Daniel Bowman Simon, who had organized a campaign for a White House garden (and later did a doctorate with us), put pressure on administrators to take action on the issue. Eventually, new administrators took over who understood that greening up the campus would be good for the NYU community as well as for community relations. Our faculty broke ground on the land behind Silver Towers in 2013 and officially opened the Urban Farm Laboratory in 2016—seven years after that meeting I ran.

2016
Urb.
Farm Lab

It was worth the wait. We now have 4,500 square feet of raised vegetable beds right alongside Houston Street's six lanes of heavy traffic. The vegetable plantings are so beautiful and unexpected that drivers stop their cars to stare. The Farm Lab is the site of courses in urban agriculture and is used by student, community, and research groups focused on raising mushrooms, sequestering carbon, reducing environmental impact, and other such matters. The department was able to recruit an adjunct faculty member, Melissa Metrick, to supervise the Farm Lab. She oversees the planting, growing, and harvesting of dozens of varieties of summer and winter vegetables, greens, and berries, and teaches how to select, grow, and harvest them, save seeds, and compost waste. My only current involvement, beyond cheering it on, admiring its productivity, and eating an occasional radish, has been to use some of the stipend that comes with my Paulette Goddard professorship to buy a composter and tools for it. I view the Farm Lab as a tribute to Alice Waters's intuitive understanding of the deep connection between food production and consumption—food systems!—for which I now offer belated thanks.

9 *Writing* Food Politics

My landing at NYU in 1988 seemed nothing short of miraculous then and still seems that way. I did not think any other university would have hired me as a tenured full professor. My publication record was weak for faculty at that level of seniority, and the articles I had published were in obscure journals. Also, what I was publishing covered a broad range of topics that did not add up to an easy-to-explain, cohesive research program in an established academic discipline. I knew that "Publish or perish" was no joke. If I was to be taken seriously, set an example for my faculty, and qualify for another academic job, I would have to publish. My department taught nutrition, dietetics, home economics, and food and hotel management. Whatever I wrote would need to fit into those areas.

The *Surgeon General's Report* was about nutrition and food policy. I thought policy could work as an umbrella for my interests. It covered everything I wanted to write about: dietary guidelines, nutrition monitoring, school meals, the pyramid food guide, hunger in America, the role of diet in disease prevention, nutrition advice for minorities and the elderly, and, in a throwback to my molecular biology training, newly emerging concerns about food biotechnology. Whenever I could put *policy* into the titles of my articles, I did.[1]

I wrote reviews, commentaries, editorials, newspaper columns, book chapters, and encyclopedia articles and sent them to any outlet that would take them. My nontraditional writing—plain language, free of academic jargon, interdisciplinary, opinionated, but carefully referenced—was often rejected or treated mercilessly by peer reviewers ("descriptive," "not analytic," "nothing new here"). Pieces like these would have gotten me nowhere at UCSF, where the only work taken seriously was original investigations published in internationally prestigious science journals. But at NYU, many humanities and social science departments produced highly respected research. What I was writing *did* count, which was why NYU was such a good place for me.

I was not even thinking of writing a book. In the basic sciences in which I was trained, books don't count as original research. I wrote as many articles as I could about whatever interested me and encouraged my faculty to do the same.

Food Industry Influence

The epiphany that eventually led to my writing a book came at the 1991 National Cancer Institute meeting I described in the introduction. When I saw how antismoking advocates analyzed the marketing practices of tobacco companies. I realized I should be scrutinizing the practices of food companies in the same way. Wherever I traveled, I took photographs of Coke, Pepsi, and McDonald's advertising on storefronts, café umbrellas, and airport banners. I paid attention to which companies were sponsoring the professional meetings I went to. I looked for evidence of lobbying and campaign contributions and ways in which companies protected their business interests. As far as I could tell, only one other group had been doing this—the Center for Science in the Public Interest (CSPI)—but its newsletter, *Nutrition Action,* had become mostly about how readers could make better food choices.

Personal choices can certainly encourage food-system improvements, but policies make a bigger difference. By the early 1990s, it was apparent that Americans, children as well as adults, were gaining weight. At conferences about obesity, especially childhood obesity, all anyone talked about was the need for education: "How can we teach Americans to make better food choices?" or—and this one really got to me—"How can we educate mothers to feed their children better?" Great. Let's blame childhood obesity on moms. Why weren't nutritionists up in arms about the products being marketed? Why weren't my colleagues outraged by how food companies were enticing kids into pestering their parents for junk food? Why weren't they pushing back against the ways companies sold junk food everywhere, and in increasingly large packages? I wanted nutritionists to stop blaming their clients for making poor dietary choices. I thought we should all be engaging in politics and advocating for policies that would make healthy food choices cheaper and easier for everyone.

This was a niche I thought I could fill. All I needed for researching food industry actions was a computer, a library, and a telephone, and those were all supplied by NYU. I did not need grants. I did not have to be beholden to funding agencies or private donors. I had tenure: I could write what I wanted to. I began to teach, speak, and write about the food industry's influence on dietary choices and on government policy. I searched for examples of ways food companies used the political system to promote and protect sales of their products. I wrote pieces about the meat industry's role in the withdrawal and revision of the USDA's pyramid food guide, the food industry's influence over dietary recommendations, the supplement industry's successful deregulation campaign, the ways in which companies marketed foods to children, and how sellers of junk foods got them into schools.[2]

In 1992 I was appointed as a consumer representative to the FDA's first Food Advisory Committee. This gave me an inside look into how this agency came to approve genetically modified foods (GMOs), and I wrote about that. As members of that committee, we thought we were advising the FDA about how it should handle its thorny food issues. We were mistaken. Officials later told us they used the committee to get reactions to decisions they had already made. But what an education it was to see just how the FDA went about approving GMOs, as well as Procter & Gamble's indigestible and potentially harmful fat substitute, Olestra—another topic I thought well worth writing about.[3]

I wrote some of these articles in collaboration with colleagues at NYU and other universities, such as a long piece about social, behavioral, and political influences on food choice. I wrote an article with CSPI's Michael Jacobson about why dietary advice for obesity prevention focuses on individuals rather than on the food environment created by industry, and why policy approaches—not just nutrition education—are so urgently needed.[4]

The Inside Track

I could write these pieces because I had inside information, not only from my FDA committee work but also because of any number of government insiders I had met during my time in DC. As with the people who sent me documents related to the food pyramid controversy, I had to promise strict confidentiality (and have always kept it). Hardly anyone was willing to talk to me on the record for fear of reprisals. But I could write about whatever documents they sent me. Thanks to my tenure at NYU, my platform for doing this was safe and secure.

Inside information inspired my writing. In the late 1990s, for example, I went to Albany to give a talk to New York State school food directors. Someone in the audience called out: "Why haven't you said anything about pouring rights contracts?" I had never heard of them. Everyone quickly enlightened me: Coca-Cola and PepsiCo were paying schools—even elementary schools—for the exclusive right to sell their products in campus vending machines. Under these contracts, companies selling sugary drinks made lump-sum payments to schools (which the schools typically used to buy scoreboards or sports equipment). Most shocking, they required minimum levels of sales and gave bonuses for additional sales. The more Coke or Pepsi drinks the schools could sell, the more money they got. These contracts gave incentives to schools to push sugary drinks with no thought as to how those drinks might affect kids' health.

My disbelief was so apparent that people started handing me documents and promising more. I ended up with a collection of school flyers advertising soft drinks along with copies of school-district contracts, and even the prototype contract produced by the New York State education department as an incentive to raise money for schools. My article about school pouring-rights contracts was published in *Public Health Reports*.[5] Eventually, opposition to these contracts became so widespread that most primary and middle schools gave them up; few now exist outside high schools and colleges. My own university has a pouring-rights contract with Coca-Cola ("Students want these drinks; we might as well get the money from them"). I regret not fighting harder to get soft drinks off the NYU campus, but without strong and ongoing student support, this was not an argument I could win.

In doing this kind of research, I came across many instances of food companies making donations to professional societies or directly funding the research of nutritionists. Except for Michael Jacobson's early work at CSPI, I had not seen anything written about the evident conflicts of interest caused by researchers' financial ties to food companies. I first wrote about the implications of these ties in 2001 for the British journal *Public Health Nutrition*.[6]

A book!

The Preliminaries

It took years before I realized how these articles might be turned into a book. The existence of the field of food studies made all the difference. It is a humanities and social science discipline, and in such disciplines, as I learned through Amy Bentley, books count. Soon after she joined our faculty, she asked me to tell her on what basis she would be evaluated for promotion and tenure. My department judged nutrition faculty on the basis of articles in professional journals. But how should we evaluate food studies faculty? I contacted the chairs of NYU's humanities and social science departments and asked about their expectations for faculty. They all told me the same thing: for promotion from assistant professor to associate professor with tenure, they expected one published book and another well on the way, along with a couple of articles a year. A book! I could do that. I had a half-year sabbatical coming up. I could take my recent articles and the one about techno-foods from an early Oldways conference and pull them together into a book about food policy and politics.

I didn't give much thought to how I might get this book published. I had written *Nutrition in Clinical Practice* at the invitation of the publisher. Now that I was becoming somewhat known for my work, I assumed I would have no trouble finding a publisher. I did not think to ask other book authors how they got published, whether an academic or trade publisher might be a better option, or whether an agent was needed and, if so, how to find one. I sent off a query to NYU Press, which promptly turned down the idea. Its editor, Niko Pfund, said his press focused on literature and poetry and would not be right for this book. This rejection should have made me take the "how to publish" question more seriously, but it didn't. Pfund's decision had a happy ending. He was president of Oxford University Press when it published my book *Soda Politics* in 2015. I do enjoy teasing him about what he missed when he turned down *Food Politics*.

I was still thinking about *Food Politics* but had done nothing about it in 1998 when my NYU colleague Barbara Kirshenblatt-Gimblett invited me to a party to celebrate the publication of her new book with the University of California Press. She introduced me to her editor, Stan Holwitz, who worked in the Press's Los Angeles office, and told him he should consider the book I was writing. He asked me to send him a proposal. I liked the idea: I was a graduate of UC Berkeley and knew that UC Press published distinguished scholarly works. Not knowing how to write a book proposal, I sent him a version of the same query letter I had sent to NYU Press, but got no response.

Some months later, I was at the reception for the James Beard Foundation's annual award ceremonies and ran into Mitchell Davis, the NYU doctoral student who worked for the foundation. He introduced me to a television agent he knew, Jonathan Russo, who in turn referred me to Lydia Wills, the colleague in his agency who worked with book authors. I went to meet her. She was early in her career as a literary agent but had already represented a number of impressive books. She was bright, lively, and fun to talk to. As the daughter of the historian Garry Wills, she understood academic as well as trade publishing. I told her what I had in mind and confessed my fear that nobody would be interested in a book about the politics of food. "Marion," she said, "my mother will want to read your book." This was love at first sight, and I now had an agent.

And by that afternoon, I had an offer. When I got back to my office, I found a phone message from Stan Holwitz: "We want your book." UC Press had decided to launch a new journal, *Gastronomica*, and to start a book series on food and culture, both under the direction of Darra Goldstein, a food scholar at Williams College. I had been asked to be on *Gastronomica*'s inaugural editorial board. Stan was at an editorial staff meeting in Berkeley, saw my name, and mentioned that he had received my book proposal some months earlier.

The editorial team told him, "Take it." I grew to love Stan—he was involved in three of my subsequent books with UC Press—and was heartbroken when he died in 2018.[7] But we never discussed the content of anything I wrote, and I still joke with UC Press that I don't think he ever read a word of it.

I used my sabbatical, from January to September 1999, to work on this project. I rewrote some of my published articles as book chapters and added new chapters to connect and strengthen my arguments. I was aiming for a book of about 250 pages. For articles in professional journals, a 25-page double-spaced manuscript converts to about 10 pages in print, so I assumed I would need twenty-five such chapters. I was blissfully ignorant of the fact that for books, one manuscript page ends up close to one printed page. Eager to make the issues clear and to summarize the research fairly, I backed up practically every statement I made with a reference. The references alone took up two hundred manuscript pages.

Knowing the book might be controversial, I wanted to avoid errors that would make it vulnerable to attack. I made sure that every chapter was read critically by at least two friends or colleagues, one in the field and one outside it, and more than two for the chapters likely to be most controversial. I was particularly worried about the introduction and asked Mal Nesheim, my friend from the *Surgeon General's Report* advisory committee, to read that one for me. (We became involved a few years later.) At least four intrepid friends read the whole thing; their generosity still astounds me.

In August 2000, after what seemed like endless rewriting, I boxed up what now amounted to about nine hundred pages of text, tables, figures, and references, and mailed it to Stan Holwitz in Los Angeles. His reaction was, "Unpublishable. We can't do it." The references alone would run to one hundred pages of small print. Despite his dismay, he sent the whole thing out to three peer reviewers, as

3 peer reviews

is customary for university presses. I was at an airport hotel in Milan, returning from a trip to Lithuania, when Stan got the reviewers' comments. He sent an email to say that he could not wait to fax them to me; they were the most enthusiastic he had ever seen.

When the pages finally rolled off the hotel fax machine, "enthusiastic" was hardly the word I would use to describe them. Reading them carefully on the plane back to New York, I thought they were devastating. Yes, the reviewers appreciated the content and judged the book worth publishing, but they vehemently objected to its length and recommended it be cut by at least 40 percent. I knew I could consolidate the references by grouping them in the endnotes. But deleting nearly half of what I had written was too painful to consider. I did not think I could do it.

Neither, apparently, did Stan. He recruited a developmental editor, John Bergez, to work with me on the manuscript. I didn't like this idea much—John would be looking for big chunks to cut—but I had no alternative. A few days before Christmas, when NYU's offices were closed, he sent a lengthy fax to a nearby copy shop. Reading it put me in tears. John had created a long table summarizing the number of pages devoted to text and references and offered a few comments on particular chapters. But his most specific advice was to read a book about how to convert a doctoral dissertation into something readable. Was what I had written really that bad?

I contacted my agent, Lydia Wills, who was in Chicago for the holidays. I went back to the copy shop to send her the fax. "Marion," she said, "he's not insulting you. He's telling you that he does not know how to cut your book. You have to call him." How Lydia got that message out of what he had written is still a mystery to me, but his first words when I called were "I don't know how to cut your book." He liked what I had written. "But," he said, "You do not explain enough. If anything, your book needs to be longer."

Longer? This required a conference call with Stan Holwitz. The call had a glorious outcome: UC Press would publish *two* books. I would take out all the chapters dealing with food safety and food biotechnology and save them for the second book. *Yay!*

For the next several months, John taught me how to write for readers. His mantra: Explain. Tell readers why you want them to know what you are talking about and what it means. By the time I did that, the manuscript had increased in length by a third. *Explain...*

The Cover — nxt page

While I was working on the revisions, I heard from UC Press about the cover. The book designer had come up with one that everyone thought perfect (figure 17). "We love this, and know you will too," they said, a statement that always makes me uneasy. What if I don't like it? And in this case I did not. I thought the design was cute, but *Food Politics* was not meant to be cute. It was a serious book, and I wanted it taken seriously. It needed a serious cover. The press agreed to try again.

I was in Woods Hole, Massachusetts, where I had gone to visit friends and finish writing some articles on deadline when, in late August, UC Press sent me two new designs. To my great relief, both were serious, and one was brilliant. Later, a designer friend explained just how brilliant. Visually, it addressed the first question everyone seemed to have: "What does food have to do with politics?" The colors and fonts separated *food* (white on red, lowercase) from *politics* (black on white, all capital letters). The whole thing came together, made sense, and conveyed what the book was about at a glance (see figures 17 and 18). UC Press used the same design, with minor modifications, in the two subsequent editions published in 2007 and 2013.

FIGURES 17 AND 18. *Left:* The University of California Press's first design for the cover of *Food Politics.* I considered it adorable but lacking in academic gravitas. *Right:* The final cover design by Nola Burger.

The 9/11 Index

With the cover settled, all I had left to do was review the index. Usually, authors are responsible for this task, but thanks to Lydia, my contract called for UC Press to pay for a professional indexer. The draft arrived by FedEx on my birthday, September 10, with a two-day deadline for returning corrections. The next morning, a beautiful sunny day, I spread the index pages out on my table, unsure about how to begin to deal with them. But the deafening noise outside made it impossible to concentrate. New York is always noisy, but several helicopters were hovering right over my building and not budging. I gave up and went out on my terrace to see what was going on. The street below was crowded with people looking south, but with my downtown view blocked by tall buildings, all I could see was smoke. When I walked up to the roof of my building, I saw that the smoke was coming from the World Trade Center.

My office building, around the corner, was higher, and I would be able to see better from its roof. I have the photographs I took that day: two smoking towers, one tower, none. An adjunct faculty member and one of our students were at the Windows on the World restaurant that morning and perished. Its chef, Michael Lomonaco, was on our food studies advisory committee. With great trepidation, I called him. I have never been so relieved to hear anyone answer the phone. He had been getting his eyeglasses repaired in a shop on the ground floor and was safe.[8]

Like everyone else in New York City, I was in shock. My apartment was in a lockdown zone. I contacted the press and arranged for an extension on the index. Later that week, my friend Joanne Csete managed to talk her way past the police blockade to help me with it. I needed her help: "Marion, how come your index doesn't have anything in it about nutrition?" Indeed, all nutrition terms had been left out. Reviewing the entries to supply missing terms was a welcome distraction from the cataclysm outside my door. Forcing myself to focus and tune out everything else helped get me through that terrible week.

Waiting for Publication

The publication date for the book was March 2002. I used the intervening five months to begin working with John Bergez on the second book. This would take a year of rewriting and many additions in response to his urgings to *explain*. Late in December 2001, the press sent me my advance copy of *Food Politics*—457 pages long. I thought it was the most beautiful book I had ever seen.

I did not have any idea how the book would be received, but I did have some hopes for what it might do. I wanted nutritionists to stop talking about obesity as if weight gain were strictly a matter of personal choice. I wanted my colleagues to understand how food industry marketing and government policies create a food environment that encourages people to eat more, and I wanted them to take action to counter those policies. I did not ever want to go to another meeting about childhood obesity that failed to recognize how food companies deliberately undermine parental authority by getting kids to demand branded food products. These changes did come soon after the book's release. I would love to think that *Food Politics* had something to do with them.

I also hoped that what I wrote in *Food Politics* would induce the American Dietetic Association (now the Academy of Nutrition and Dietetics) to stop publishing corporate-sponsored fact sheets about nutrition issues. These were brief handouts on controversial topics with advice easily predicted if you knew who had paid for them: chocolate is part of a heart-healthy diet (Mars); the link between salt and high blood pressure is unclear (Campbell Soup); genetically modified foods are safe for the environment (Monsanto). The academy finally discontinued the sponsored fact sheets, but not until 2009.

I had one personal ambition related to the book: I wanted better speaking invitations. For this, I needed my work to get more attention. It was already getting some. I was becoming the subject as well as the source of press articles. The first was for an interview with the *Walking Magazine* (new to me), which described me as "one of the nation's most esteemed and outspoken nutritionists." That interview involved a photo shoot, also my first, in Washington Square Park (figure 19). This was followed the next year by an article by Peter Jaret, a reporter I had met through Oldways, who included me among several other women he deemed responsible for changing the way America eats. He said I was "spreading the good-nutrition gospel."[9]

FIGURE 19. My first professional photo shoot, for *Walking Magazine,* took place in Washington Square Park during the Cow Parade public art project in 2000, in which local artists decorated fiberglass cows placed all over the city. This particular example displayed subway logos. The editors used a photo of me posed in front of a flowering hydrangea to illustrate my interview, but I like this one better, as it reflects the fun of living in New York.

As for speaking invitations, I was getting ten or fifteen a year, but mostly for small, local audiences. I wanted to reach larger, more diverse, and more influential groups, and in more interesting places. You've heard the adage "Be careful what you wish for"? I would soon learn its truth.

10 *The Fun Begins*

The publication of *Food Politics* marked a turning point in my life, if rather a late one; I was sixty-six years old when it came out. Before then, getting attention for my work had been a struggle. I could not get an article published without enduring multiple rejections from editors and peer reviewers. But once the book came out, invitations to write articles poured in. Other rewards also arrived, each more surprising than the last, especially because the earliest reactions to the book were sarcastic and dismissive.

The Early Reviews

On February 22, two weeks before *Food Politics* would be officially published and available in bookstores, Stan Holwitz, my editor at UC Press, called with upsetting news: three terrible reviews of the book had been posted on Amazon.com. He suggested I round up friends and get them to post something better. Maybe other authors do this, but not me. I could not possibly ask people I knew to write favorable reviews of a book they had not yet read.

But I could see why Stan was worried. The reviews were awful. All were posted by "A Customer," and all gave the book only one out of five possible stars. Reading them now, I can see how staged they were, but at the time they stung. The first: "Nestle forgot a not-so-little thing called WILL POWER! Marion Nestle, one of the foremost food nannies in this country, has produced a book that heaps the blame for obesity, diabetes, and heart disease on food producers, marketing executives, and even school principals. Everyone, it seems, is responsible for those love handles except for the very people who are carrying them around."

The second began: "Individuals incapable of thinking for themselves will truly appreciate Marion Nestle's book. . . . [It] only creates the kind of hysteria caused by our litigious society. The Surgeon's General's recent remarks declaring that obesity is a major health problem has greedy trial lawyers considering filing lawsuits against food and beverage companies. This whiny book only helps them 'fuel the fire' and reaches their goals."

And the third: "Marion Nestle's book 'Food Politics' makes clear that the political system she favors is dictatorship—with her in command. Marion is just so much smarter than us all, and so much more virtuous, and so much more in self-control, that she can be the meal planner for the world. If you disagree with anything she says, you're overweight, undereducated and stupid. The author's motto could be 'if it tastes good don't eat it.'"

I was surprised to be considered important enough to warrant the label "foremost food nanny." But was I really the kind of person who can be described as "whiny," "more virtuous," condescending, and not liking food that tastes good? That is not how I think of myself or how I want to be perceived.

While I was fretting over what, if anything, to do about these opinions, a fourth review suddenly appeared on the Amazon site, this one with five stars. It was signed by Sheldon Rampton, whose name I recognized from his tell-all book about the public relations industry, *Toxic Sludge Is Good for You.*[1]

The PR campaign against this book has already begun. For what it's worth, potential readers of Nestle's book should note that the first three "reader reviews" of this book are pretty obviously cranked out by some food industry PR campaign. . . . [T]hey all hit on the same food industry "message points." . . . February 22 is also the date that noted industry flack Steven Milloy of the "Junk Science Home Page" wrote a review trashing Nestle's book. Milloy is a former tobacco lobbyist and front man for a group created by Philip Morris, which has been diversifying its tobacco holdings in recent years by buying up companies that make many of the fatty, sugar-laden foods that Nestle is warning about.

That was great, but the way he ended it was even better: "I haven't even had a chance yet to read Nestle's book myself, but it irritates me to see the food industry's PR machine spew out the usual (. . .) every time someone writes something they don't like. If they hate her this much, it's probably a pretty good book."

After reading this, I went right to Steven Milloy's piece on the Fox News website. His point: *Food Politics* is junk science. "Nestle, who portrays herself as an above-the-fray professor of nutrition at New York University, spends more than 400 pages accusing the food industry of 'influencing' the government, 'co-opting' nutrition professionals, 'exploiting' children, and 'corrupting' schools all in the name of profit."[2] Guilty as charged.

Rampton's review made me feel much better. Those nasty reviews were not attacks on my intellect or scholarship: they were attacks on my political views. Putting "politics" in the title of a book was a red flag. I should have expected pushback like this from people with opposing points of view.

The lesson not to take comments like these personally came just in time, because other attacks soon followed. One came in the form of a threatened lawsuit from the Sugar Association. The letter charged that during a radio interview, I had made "numerous false, misleading, disparaging, and defamatory statements about sugar." Sugar is defamable? Who knew? Apparently, I had made "the false and inaccurate statement that soft drinks contain sugar" and, as I should have known, soft drinks "have contained virtually no sugar (sucrose) in more than 20 years." Furthermore, if I did not "cease making misleading or false statements regarding sugar or the sugar industry . . . the only recourse available to us will be to legally defend our industry and its members against any and all fallacious and harmful allegations."

At this, I could not stop laughing. The lawyer was quibbling over a matter of semantics, and biochemical semantics at that. He was using *sugar* to refer only to sucrose (table sugar). Most soft drinks produced in the United States are sweetened with high-fructose corn syrup (HFCS), not sucrose. But both sucrose and HFCS are made up of the same two sugars, glucose and fructose. In sucrose, glucose and fructose are bonded together, but digestion quickly separates them. In HFCS, the sugars are already separated. The difference is a matter of politics more than biochemistry. The Sugar Association represents the producers of sugar beets and sugarcane (which yield sucrose); the Corn Refiners Association represents the producers of corn and HFCS.

Still laughing, I forwarded the letter to Michael Jacobson at CSPI. He was not amused. He viewed the letter as an opening salvo in a defamation lawsuit like the one the beef industry had brought against Oprah Winfrey in the late 1990s. Winfrey won the suit, but at the cost of $1 million in legal fees. He insisted I consult a lawyer. I didn't have one, but I mentioned the letter to a friend who worked for a high-end Wall Street law firm. She was not amused either and arranged an informal consultation with a libel expert. I followed the expert's suggestions and wrote a point-by-point rebuttal.[3]

A few months later I ran into the head of the Sugar Association at a meeting in Washington, DC, and told him how much fun I was having with his lawyer's letter. I had been showing slides of it in talks and got laughs every time I did. He responded tersely, "We are glad that you are speaking more precisely now." By this, he meant that I was using *sugars*, plural, when talking about the sweeteners in soft drinks.

Also attesting to my sudden rise to prominence was my designation as a "Crankster" in an online list maintained by the industry-funded American Council on Science and Health, and as a "key player" by the industry-funded Center for Consumer Freedom, which still describes me as "one of the country's most hysterical anti-food-industry fanatics" and "the anti-pleasure nutritionist." *Restaurant Business* put me on its "dishonor roll" of new enemies, along with Eric Schlosser, whose book *Fast Food Nation,* an exposé of the meat industry, had come out the previous year, and Osama bin Laden, whose attack on the World Trade Center apparently had not been good for the hospitality industry.[4]

I also got hate mail: "Only a communist would suggest that our food supply be regulated by the government. . . . You and your ilk scare the hell out of me as you shape the minds of our youth." I can't remember whether I replied to that one, but if I did I would surely have pointed out that our food supply is already regulated by the government through many agencies and in countless ways, and that I wrote *Food Politics* in the hope of refocusing those regulations to promote public health and environmental sustainability rather than corporate profits. And yes, I am doing all I can to encourage young people to advocate for that refocusing.

Then Came the Rewards

The first sign that *Food Politics* might get some appreciation and do some good came when I got a call from Derek Yach at the World Health Organization. I knew of his work as an international antismoking advocate and wondered why he was calling me. "I've given copies of your book to my staff. I'm meeting with food industry executives in a couple of weeks. What will it take to get you to come to this meeting?" Wow. I booked a flight to Geneva right away.

I felt like a visiting dignitary. Yach introduced me to WHO officials, from his staff all the way up to its director, Gro Harlem Brundtland. What, exactly, would he like me to do at the food industry meeting? "Nothing. Just sit there. With you in the room, they will know I mean business." At that meeting, and at another a month later at the Benetton headquarters in Italy, Yach pressed food companies to stop marketing junk foods to children. The WHO was taking on the food industry and making *Food Politics* part of that effort.[5] I could not have asked for better recognition.

The Book Tour

Because my first book, *Nutrition in Clinical Practice,* had been printed by a medical publisher who went out of business, I was unfamiliar with publicity expectations. UC Press set up a formal book tour, including visits to Washington, DC, Chicago, and West Coast cities for bookstore talks and media interviews. As an unknown author, I had more than my share of disheartening experiences. Bookstore readings were sparsely attended; on a really good day, I might sign ten books. University events went a bit better. Television bookings were rare. I made a special trip to Chicago for a television interview that got canceled at the last minute.

But there were lots of radio interviews—more than a hundred by the time I was done. UC Press had recruited a publicist to work with me, and her philosophy seemed to be the more the merrier, no matter who they were with. The first interviews were challenging, especially the talk shows with hosts whose listeners called in from cars and complained about the nanny state. I had done twenty or so such interviews and still was feeling uneasy about them when I landed in a studio in Washington, DC, for an interview with a woman who was a well-known (but not to me) right-wing commentator. A few minutes into a tense discussion of what food could possibly have to do with politics, she asked: "And what's your position on abortion?"

Unprepared for that question and having no idea how to respond, I blurted out, "I'm prochoice."

"See," she said. "So what's the point of your book?"

I left the studio furious with the PR person who had put me in that position and called to tell her that I did not see the purpose of being booked to appear on shows whose listeners would never buy, let alone read, my book. But as soon as I had finished venting, I knew exactly how I should have responded.

I soon got my chance to test this flash of inspiration. In my next interview with a hostile host, I said, in the sweetest tone of voice I could possibly muster, "I can tell by your question that you must not have had a chance to read my book." Bingo! He spat out: "Read your book? It was just handed to me fifteen minutes ago." Again in the sweetest possible tone, "Then let me tell you a little about it." I never had that much trouble with an interview again.

Media Attention

Food Politics got lots of press attention and reviews. The first article to appear was a full-page discussion in *Fortune*, which involved a photo shoot on Bleecker Street.[6] When I saw the photo (figure 20), I thought I'd made a terrible error. Wearing an inexpensive pantsuit and no makeup, I thought I did not look nearly elegant enough to appear in a magazine read by wealthy executives. I have never used makeup (I never thought it helped much), but I immediately went out, bought some, and got the store clerk to teach me how to use it. I also spent more than I had ever spent previously on clothes to buy

FIGURE 20. The first article about *Food Politics* appeared two weeks before its publication date in *Fortune,* on February 18, 2002. Seeing this photo made me think I needed makeup and more professional clothes for public appearances like this one.

three business suits. I wore them like uniforms to all subsequent talks and interviews. I still have and use two of them; the other was threadbare by the time I gave up on it.

Like the *Fortune* interview, some of the press attention seemed so far out of my league that I could hardly believe it was happening. I was invited by the ABC News anchor Peter Jennings to interview for a special he was doing on obesity. When I went to the studios for the taping, Jennings told me he had read *Food Politics* and it had given him the idea for the program. I was so stunned that I can't remember another thing about that interview.[7]

The following year, I heard that *Time* and ABC News were jointly hosting a summit on obesity. Jennings's staff called to say that he wanted to know what I would be speaking about at this event, but I had not been invited. They soon called back to tell me that Jennings had said, "If she's not going, I'm not going." The meeting invitation arrived soon after.[8] I didn't speak at it, but enjoyed being in the audience, particularly because Richard Carmona, the US surgeon general, gave me a shout-out: "She taught me nutrition in medical school!" He had taken the month-long clinical elective in nutrition that I ran with Bobby Baron at UCSF in the early 1980s. When Peter Jennings died in 2005, I felt as if I'd lost a friend.

Lecture Invitations

Here's where "Be careful what you wish for" comes in. I was deluged with speaking invitations from universities, foundations, food and nutrition societies, and business groups. I had more than fifty speaking engagements in 2002 and was traveling constantly while trying to keep up with my administrative duties, teaching, and writing. I had met Eric Schlosser when we both spoke on a panel at a Socialist Scholars Conference, and I asked him how he handled his speaking invitations. He advised me: "You have a platform. This is your chance to get your ideas known. Go for it." In 2003, I gave almost a hundred lectures. The publication of *Safe Food* in March of that year only added to the requests.

I had a hard time refusing invitations, especially those to glamorous events that also seemed out of my league, like *Fortune* conferences in Aspen and Laguna Beach and the World Economic Forum (WEF) in Davos, where I spoke on a panel with Francis Collins, then

(SWITZ.)

head of the US National Institutes of Health. The WEF panels, as explained to me, were intended to keep the accompanying spouses and staff amused while the real movers and shakers had private meetings. Even so, I felt privileged to be in the room when a CNN executive suggested that journalists covering the Iraq war had been targeted by US troops (he was forced to resign as a result), and when the actress Angelina Jolie stood up in the middle of a public session on poverty in Africa, announced a large donation, called for more, and quickly raised a million dollars, to the quite evident embarrassment of the African leaders on stage. I had the same privileged-outsider's reaction when I attended the WEF again in 2017 and heard Xi Jinping announce China's intention to be a major force in globalization.[9]

Awards and Recognition

Positive attention for *Food Politics* came from unexpected places. I was at a meeting in San Francisco when people started asking me if I had seen the new issue of *Vanity Fair,* not a magazine I usually read. There I was in its "Food Snob's Dictionary," the only living person besides Alice Waters listed in a separate entry. Mine, listed alphabetically between "Mouthfeel" and "Niman Ranch," read: "Leading American food scholar, renowned for her unintimidated takedown of evil Big Food, *Food Politics: How the Food Industry Influences Nutrition and Health,* and her stewardship of New York University's Department of Nutrition, Food Studies, and Public Health. Snobs pride themselves on knowing the correct pronunciation of her last name (*nessle,* not *nest-lee*)."[10]

I thought of *Food Politics* as a niche book, and I had not been told that UC Press had submitted it for awards. In 2003 the book won awards from the Association of American Publishers, World Hunger Year (the Harry Chapin Media Award), and the James Beard Foundation (in the literary category). The Beard Foundation also included me in its *Who's Who in Food and Beverage in America*. Then the book was translated into Chinese and Japanese.[11] While never a *New York Times* best seller, *Food Politics* did well by the standards of academic presses. I produced a revised edition for UC Press in 2007, with a new foreword and afterword, and a tenth-anniversary edition, which came out in 2013. For that edition I was thrilled when Michael Pollan wrote its foreword.

I also received other awards, some of which were tremendous fun. In 2005, for example, I received a Health Quality Award from the National Committee for Quality Assurance (NCQA), a group that works to improve standards for health care. The awards dinner took place in Amtrak's magnificent Union Station, in Washington, DC. The other recipients were Dr. Brent James, representing Intermountain Health Care in Salt Lake City; Mary Tyler Moore, for her work with the Juvenile Diabetes Research Foundation; Hillary Clinton, for attempting to create a national health care system; and—I still can't get my head around this—Newt Gingrich.[12] At the time, Gingrich was a strong proponent of a national health care plan; only later did he ferociously oppose the Affordable Care Act and do all he could to foster political divisiveness and partisanship.[13]

 Also unexpected was an article in *Ms.* magazine titled "The Feminist Food Revolution." Jennifer Cognard-Black, a professor at St. Mary's College of Maryland, wrote it to highlight gender issues in the food movement. She began by observing, "From farms to community gardens to restaurants, women are taking food back into their own hands. So why do men keep getting all the credit?"[14] Her piece focused on the difference in press accounts of the promotion of healthy, sustainable food by the British chef Jamie Oliver (laudatory) and First Lady Michelle Obama (dismissive), as well as the attention given to the "small group of white men who have turned a national interest in sustainable food into cults of foodie personality." She was referring to Eric Schlosser, Michael Pollan, and Morgan Spurlock (the director of the film *Super Size Me*, in which I briefly appear). She urged readers "to not forget to also read Marion Nestle's watershed book *Food Politics*."

It had never occurred to me to think about the food movement in terms of gender politics. I should have. But my only concern about "foodie personalities" had been whether they helped to advance the food movement, as these men most definitely did. I felt honored to be included among them. But I learned my lesson, and I am now paying closer attention to gender issues in food politics.

I also got a kick out of some of the publicity that came with my speaking invitations. I was a minor panelist at the conference organized by Slow Food in San Francisco in 2008. This was a glorious event at which Alice Waters took over the plaza in front of City Hall, planted a vegetable garden, and organized a banquet served at block-long tables facing that garden. I kept running into people who said I needed to look at a local magazine, *San Francisco 7 × 7*. I could not find a copy anywhere, but my daughter Rebecca, who lives in San Francisco, knew the editor and arranged for us to pick one up at the magazine's downtown offices. No wonder people thought I should see it. There I was among the pantheon of the Roman "Gods of Food" (figure 21).[15] My daughter managed to get me a copy signed by the designer, Marty Blake. I had it framed right away.

One award touched me so deeply that I still can't get over it: Bard College's John Dewey Award for Distinguished Public Service. It was presented to me at the Woodbourne Correctional Facility in the Catskills, at a celebration for graduates of Bard College's Prison Initiative (BPI). I was their chosen graduation speaker. Max Kenner, who runs this program, told me that some of the students had read *Food Politics* in their classes and were inspired to ask for and be allowed to plant an organic garden in the prison courtyard. They asked that I be invited to speak at their commencement. I cannot conceive of a greater honor.

Gods of
Food –

FIGURE 21. Marty Blake's illustration from an article in the August 2008 edition of *San Francisco* 7 × 7 publicizing the Slow Food conference. *Top row:* Food writer Michael Pollan; Carlo Petrini, the Italian founder of Slow Food; Eric Schlosser, the author of *Fast Food Nation*. *Bottom row:* Alice Waters, the owner of the restaurant Chez Panisse; Gavin Newsom, San Francisco's mayor (later governor of California); and me hugging the supersized tomato.

Bard Prison Initiative

BPI offers courses leading to associate of arts and bachelor's degrees. The Woodbourne graduates were mostly Black or Latino. All of us were in full academic dress for the ceremony, in which Bard's President, Leon Botstein, awarded the degrees and my medal. I had never been in a prison before. I brought my Berkeley doctoral robe, but I had to leave everything else—purse, pens, cell phone—at the entrance, which meant I could not take photographs. To this day I am in awe of what these men had achieved. The speeches given by the graduates, many of whom had been incarcerated for decades, were far more scholarly and moving than mine. In accepting my award, I pointed out that John Dewey firmly believed that education has a social as well as individual purpose: to encourage students to become effective members of a democratic society. "In growing a garden and producing food for yourselves and for others under these particular and peculiar circumstances, you are carrying out John Dewey's ideals better than he ever could have imagined."[16] notes p. 258

Meanwhile, Back at NYU

While dealing with the press interviews and travel invitations elicited by *Food Politics,* I was still teaching and chairing my NYU department. I gave copies of the book to my faculty, and one day a couple of them invited me to lunch at Capsouto Frères, a restaurant in Tribeca (sadly now closed) for what turned out to be a surprise celebration. My colleagues were all wearing tee shirts displaying the *Food Politics* cover. I don't know whether any of them ever wore their shirts in public, but I still treasure mine.

Looking back on it, I don't know how I managed to keep up with my teaching, administrative duties, lectures, travel, and the preparation of *Safe Food.* But in a complicated although painful way, I got lucky. In 2003, my chairing of the department came to an end, and I was left free to concentrate on my own work.

My school at NYU, then called the School of Education, had de-cided to close a department that served very few students and asked whether mine would take on its only viable program, a master's in public health education. By then, my department had established a master's degree program in public health nutrition, so it seemed to make administrative sense to put the two MPH programs in the same unit.

I had no strong feelings one way or the other, but I could see a downside to taking on faculty with no interest in food or nutrition. I called a department faculty meeting to consider the request. To my astonishment, the faculty, one after another, said they thought it was a good idea, as it would strengthen our offerings in public health. Af-ter the meeting, Jennifer Berg commented that I must be proud of how the faculty had been able to come so quickly to a decision like that, which I was. I informed the dean that this was a go, and we took on the program. At subsequent meetings, we changed the name of the department to nutrition, food studies, and public health. I liked this change, as the new title reflected the scope of my academic interests.

Some months later, I learned how badly I had misread what hap-pened at that meeting. I had never fussed much about my own NYU salary, which I considered adequate, and I had instead done every-thing possible to get my faculty better compensated. The gap be-tween their salaries and mine had greatly narrowed. I had not had a raise in several years and thought it was time to ask for one. This made Dean Ann Marcus realize that I had chaired the department for fifteen years without ever having undergone a performance evalua-tion. She sent her associate dean to meet with my faculty to find out how they thought I was doing. The associate dean reported back to me that the faculty had stored up plenty to complain about. They viewed me as dictatorial, citing the transfer of the public health education program as the prime example. They had not wanted the program moved into the department but felt that I had not consulted them or given them any choice in the matter.

I felt blindsided. I thought I *had* consulted them. How could I have misread their views so badly? I called my old therapist and asked for a consult. His first question: "How much longer do you intend to keep doing this?" That was all it took. I had been chairing the department for fifteen years, much longer than the typical term. It was way past time for me to resign. As it happened, I was meeting Dean Marcus for dinner that week. NYU had a new president coming in, and she too was resigning. "Don't worry," she said. "I will take care of you."

I called an emergency meeting of the faculty, announced my resignation, and said that by not telling me what they really thought, they had put me in the impossible position of misrepresenting their views to the dean. I could no longer continue as chair. A few of the faculty were dismayed, but most seemed relieved. These were people I had hired and for whom I had lobbied for higher salaries, promotions, and larger apartments. When I asked why they hadn't said what they really thought, one after another said, "You are bossy." "You never asked me." I felt unappreciated and betrayed, yet it was obvious that my departure was long overdue. I also realized that I had just been handed a priceless gift: time to focus on my own work.

Ann Marcus had promised to take care of me, and did she ever. I would take a sabbatical from June 2003 to September 2004. When I returned, I would have to teach only one course a semester and serve on only one committee, an exceptionally light faculty load. I lightened it even more by telling Judith Gilbride, who had chaired the department when I was first hired and would now be replacing me as chair, that it was best if I stayed out of her way and did not go to faculty meetings. I moved into an office so remote that nobody could find it, where I could work without interruption. I loved that top-floor office. It had two large windows with views all the way to Brooklyn,

high ceilings, and only one drawback: when it rained, the roof leaked.
Buckets were essential, and sometimes umbrellas.

But I now had the perfect job. I could do anything and everything
I liked, with no administrative headaches and no time-consuming
committee responsibilities. And once *Food Politics* came out, I was
never again asked to serve on another federal committee. The agencies rejected my nominations on the grounds of partisanship, or so I
was told.

All of this meant that I could stay home mornings and write. I
could travel when I wanted to. And I began dating the recently wid-
owed Mal Nesheim. We had met when he was an adviser for the *Surgeon General's Report*. Back then, in the late 1980s, he had just become Cornell's vice president for planning and budgeting, after
having long chaired the university's Division of Nutritional Sciences,
and he would soon become Cornell's provost, its chief academic officer. I thought he was especially wise about interpreting nutrition research and the politics of nutrition in academia. I enjoyed talking to
him about such things and valued his advice and friendship. Over the
years, we stayed in touch and met for dinner whenever he happened
to be in New York City. When his wife of many years, Diva Sanjur,
died late in 2002, I sent a condolence note, and we continued to
speak occasionally during the months that followed. At some point
things got more serious, and we have been partners ever since—one
of the best results of my long-overdue resignation as department
chair.

11   *How I Do It*

Lucky me. The things I most like doing—researching, teaching, and my version of public service—are exactly what university professors are supposed to do. Promotions and salary increases depend on accomplishments in all three areas, but published research counts most. Academics joke about the aphorism "Publish or perish," but the system really does work that way. For me, research means studying how science, economics, and politics interact to affect food choices and public health, as exemplified by the influence of the food industry. I write articles and books about these topics (research), talk about them with students (teaching), and discuss them on my blog, in public lectures, and in interviews with reporters (public service). I get asked questions about my work all the time: How do I keep up with what's happening in food and nutrition? How do I organize my teaching? How do I manage dealing with the public? How do I do everything I do? What I read underlies all of that.

Keeping Up

To teach myself what I needed to know about nutrition, I started with basic textbooks. But, as I learned during my graduate work in molecular biology, real understanding of a subject requires reading the original research behind the textbook summaries. This means looking up the references cited in research articles and consecutively checking the citations until nothing new comes up. Applied to nutrition research, this technique served me especially well when I was teaching medical students at UCSF.

As a graduate student, and as a postdoc and faculty member at Brandeis, I routinely read scientific journals at the library. I made copies of articles I thought I might refer to later and started a system for filing them. At UCSF, when I was preparing lectures on heart disease, cancer, diabetes, osteoporosis, or other health conditions, I read everything I could about them. In those preelectronic days, filing all the articles on those topics required a more elaborate system.

At UCSF, all the other associate deans subscribed to the *New England Journal of Medicine* and talked about what was in each issue the day it arrived. If I wanted to be in on those conversations, I had to subscribe too. As I expanded the scope of my teaching, I subscribed to other journals in science, medicine, nutrition, public health, and, eventually, food studies.

Keeping up with those journals was a chore, and the unread ones piled up quickly. I would take big stacks of journal issues on plane trips, tear out the articles I wanted, and leave everything else behind. Filing got done in binges. My folders and subfolders eventually filled more than thirty file drawers at my NYU office. This was a cumbersome system, but one that paid off. I didn't have to read the articles before I filed them; I just needed to put them someplace where I could find them right away. When reporters called with nutrition questions, I could pull the relevant files and have the research right at hand. I also created files for everything I was writing about. Each new topic and every new book required another file drawer. Once the NYU library started collecting my papers, I could pass along boxes of file folders on topics I did not think I would be writing about again. I did this for years, until everything went digital.

Now, because journals send the table of contents for each issue by email, I can quickly look them over, download the articles I want, and file them in my equally elaborate online filing system. I now subscribe to journals only in digital format, but I also subscribe to many online news feeds. It takes a couple of hours a day to go through all of them, but keeping up with publications has been a career-long habit *NB* and not one I am ready to give up. I use this material right away for the blog I've run since 2007, to support my teaching, and to inform whatever I happen to be writing about at the moment.

Teaching

Some people can tell you their philosophy of teaching. I never had a formal one. For me, teaching has always been about trying to explain nutrition concepts clearly, in a way everyone can understand. Doing this requires a lot of reading and thinking, which I enjoy, particularly because it makes the material stick. I have always taught new material, developed new courses, and almost entirely revised my existing courses from year to year.

Early on at NYU, I taught whatever nutrition courses were needed for undergraduates or graduate students. These covered many facets of nutrition: basic, community, international, geriatric, contemporary issues, fieldwork, research, writing. I also ran and particularly enjoyed the department's doctoral seminar, in which students reported on their research progress and helped each other get past the hurdles they encountered. When we started the public health nutrition program, I taught the history of public health, program planning, and social and behavioral determinants of health. For food studies students, I taught courses in nutrition, food ethics, and food writing.

Once *Food Politics* came out, I began to teach much more about food systems policy, politics, and advocacy.

Sometimes I have taught in collaboration with colleagues. In 2001, for example, I taught a course at NYU on the health and nutritional effects of industrial agriculture with Corinna Hawkes, who now heads the food policy center at City University in London. She was living in the US at the time and asked the students to pick a food product and trace every step of its path from production to consumption. This was my introduction to food supply chains, and the students' term papers were object lessons in how hard it is to get accurate information about how food comes to us.

Through Oldways, I met the anthropologist Sidney Mintz. I adored him, and we had an ongoing flirtation that his wife, Jackie, didn't seem to mind. He kept saying that he'd like to teach with me. Sid was in his eighties and long retired from Johns Hopkins when, in 2004, we had the inspired idea of teaching a three-week course for graduate students during the January intersession—in Puerto Rico. That's where Sid had done his original ethnographic field research with sugarcane workers. We called the course "The Bitter and the Sweet: Puerto Rico, Sugar, and History."

Our deal was that he would give lectures if I took care of all the administrative and logistical aspects. The logistics turned out to be horrendous: we were there during Puerto Rico's January holidays, and everyone was on vacation. Mal Nesheim and I had just started seeing each other, and he joined me after the first week of the class. That helped because he speaks workable Spanish, had been to Puerto Rico many times, and knew several Puerto Rican university professors who had done their doctoral work at Cornell. They could help teach the course, meet with students, and answer questions about what was really going on in Puerto Rico.

I have no idea whether the students realized how fortunate they were to have this opportunity, but I viewed teaching with Sidney

P. 253 note

Mintz as the most extraordinary privilege. He was a hero in Puerto Rico for the research he had done there and was honored by the university while our course was in progress. I've had a deep interest in Puerto Rico ever since.[1]

In 2006, the chair of NYU's sociology department, Dalton Conley, invited me to join his department. I hadn't realized it, but in writing *Food Politics,* I was practicing sociology—but without a license. Okay. If I was now a sociologist, I had best learn something about sociology. I could not think of a better way to do that than to teach a graduate course in food sociology. I followed my usual practice; I took some introductory sociology books out of the library, and started reading them. As a senior at Berkeley, I had taken William Kornhauser's course on social movements, and I thought I could do something like that for food. This was hubris. Modern sociology involves theory and methods I would not be able to master without lots of work. At the precise moment I realized I was in way over my head, Troy Duster came to my rescue. He is a highly distinguished sociologist who taught at Berkeley but was spending half his time at NYU. A friend of Alice Waters, he thought this would be a good opportunity to learn more about food and offered to coteach the course with me. I was saved.

We structured the class around the question of whether food advocacy constitutes a social movement. Although enormous numbers of groups work on food issues, their goals are more diverse than those of the civil rights, women's rights, or environmental protection movements. Food advocacy groups focus on such matters as eliminating food insecurity, improving school food, discouraging consumption of sugar-sweetened beverages, reducing the use of antibiotics and pesticides, protecting farm workers, and promoting regenerative agriculture. The students' term papers were thoughtful, critical, and enlightening. I understood more about food movement sociology and would have liked to teach the course again. I was bereft when Troy went back to Berkeley full-time.[2]

☺ The lesson about academic hubris is one I never seem to learn. I'm curious about new topics and want to know about them. When the political maneuvering for the congressional Farm Bill of 2012 got under way, I was having a hard time understanding what the fights were about. Once again, I could not think of a better way to learn about the Farm Bill than to teach a course on it. In fall 2011, I took that on. The Farm Bill gets reworked every five years or so. It covers hundreds of programs, from agricultural subsidies to food stamps—each with its own constituencies, lobbyists, and arcane rules—and takes up hundreds of pages of exceedingly small print. The students and I muddled through together, although they soon tired of hearing me say that the bill was too big and complex for any one person to understand. I wrote an article about this experience for *Dissent* and later updated it for *Politico*, which gave it just the right title: "The Farm Bill Drove Me Insane."[3] Lesson learned, maybe. Since then, I have stuck to teaching food systems policy, politics, and advocacy. Teaching is still the best way I know to keep up with current events in food politics.

Among the privileges of academia is getting to teach in other places. In 2006, 2007, and 2015, I taught at UC Berkeley, first in the public policy and public health schools and later in Michael Pollan's science journalism program. In 2016, I had a fellowship at the University of Sydney, where I gave lectures and began the research for the book that became *Unsavory Truth*. I wrote early chapters of that book as a Fulbright Specialist Scholar at the Institute for Public Health in Cuernavaca in 2017, where I also gave lectures. I officially retired from NYU in September 2017 but have continued to teach an occasional short course on food systems.

For lecture classes, I use PowerPoint slides, just as I do for public talks. As I was instructed to do in my very first talk, I set them up with images rather than words. I decide what I want to say, in what order, and then search for an image to illustrate each point. The slides cue what I want to say so I do not have to read from notes. I plan on less than one minute per slide, so the images move quickly. By now, I have thousands of slides filed by topic. Even when teaching a course I've taught before, I introduce new slides covering more recent events. I want everyone who listens to my lectures to be able to analyze current events just as they are happening and to come to their own opinions about them.

When the COVID-19 pandemic hit, I immediately started teaching "Food Systems in the Coronavirus Era." I used this opportunity to talk about how the pandemic had exposed the power of food corporations to protect profits at the expense of the health of low-wage workers in the meat industry, grocery stores, and restaurants. For the pandemic courses, I had to learn new teaching skills. I taught an asynchronous undergraduate class online, for which students viewed prerecorded lectures at their own convenience. NYU sent professional recording equipment—camera, remotes, microphones, lights, diffusers, tripods—and I prepared a series of thirty-nine short videos, with built-in test questions. My students took the class from places like Dubai, Abu Dhabi, Croatia, Turkey, Mexico, Singapore, and three cities in China. Given how much work these videos were to prepare, I was relieved when students said they liked watching them. But the class was not much fun for me. What I most love about teaching is getting to know students, and the back-and-forth exchanges. This is not easy when students appear as two-dimensional pictures on a computer screen. I am trying my best to teach in this new online world.

Public Engagement

For academic purposes, the work I do outside the university falls into the category of public service. This includes service to the profession, such as membership on committees and on journal editorial boards and peer reviews of manuscripts submitted to professional journals.

FIGURE 22. At the invitation of students in my NYU food ethics class, I spoke at an Occupy Big Food demonstration in New York City's Zuccotti Park on October 19, 2011. This was part of the much larger Occupy Wall Street demonstrations. No microphones were allowed. I had to shout out one sentence at a time. The crowd shouted a repeat of what I had said so others farther away could hear.

I am still doing my share of all that. But my public service activities also include my daily blog, articles I write for the media, lectures to nonprofessional audiences, answering questions from reporters, and joining an occasional public demonstration (figure 22).

I must confess to a few failures in public engagement, starting with my appearances on the Food Network in its very first week. Late in 1993, I was contacted by Sue Huffman, whom I knew through our shared interest in healthy diets. She was consulting with Reese Schonfeld, the founder of CNN, who was just starting this new television channel focused on food. They took me to lunch and asked if I would be interested in doing an ongoing show. That sounded like *Over Easy,* and I said yes right away. But it turned out that what they had in mind for me did not have much to do with educating the public about nutrition. I would be paired with Tony Hendra, a British humorist best known (to me, at least) for having performed the role of Ian, the band's manager, in the mock documentary *This Is Spinal Tap.* We were to do five-minute "he said, she said" segments on nutrition issues. This was hardly my style. I gamely filmed five episodes with him one afternoon; these aired during the network's chaotic first week. During that week, I was called back at one hour's notice to do more filming. This was not going to work for my tightly scheduled academic life, and I was not invited back, although I later made one-time appearances on Food Network shows hosted by David Rosengarten and Donna Hanover.[4]

Another failure began in 1996 when the cookbook editor Maria Guarnaschelli asked me to ghostwrite the introduction to the forthcoming revision of *The Joy of Cooking* and to help ensure the accuracy of the book's information about nutrition and food safety. For this she would pay me the highest fee I had ever been offered: $15,000. I knew the book well, having long cooked from a well-worn 1960s edition written by Irma Rombauer and her daughter, Marion Rombauer Becker. I got right to work.

Maria's development of the 1997 edition was renowned for its Shakespearean level of drama, the hirings and firings of dozens of writers and recipe developers, and vast outlays of cash (said to have come to $5 million).[5] In my case, the drama merely involved frequent late-night phone calls and one emergency meeting called on New Year's Eve, of all times, to settle an urgent question: What would the book say about the safety of raw-milk cheeses? I suggested a cautious statement: raw-milk cheeses ought to be safe if aged and dried appropriately, but the soft, wet ones are riskier. Never mind. As published, the book includes this cheerfully optimistic comment on page 1070: "It *is* worth seeking out raw-milk cheese; any potentially harmful bacteria die during ripening." Fingers crossed.

But I have no complaints about how I was treated. I was, after all, paid to be a ghostwriter. Just before publication, I read the entire book to vet the nutrition information, and Maria incorporated most of the changes I asked for. I get credit in the book for my work on the introduction, its title changed from "About Food" to "Diet, Lifestyle and Health." But almost nothing I wrote made it into the book, and the parts that did were edited beyond recognition. My original draft, in which I tried to channel the Rombauers' format and voice, ran to nearly eight thousand words. I wrote "About" sections on diets, foods, calories, nutrients, alcohol, food safety, and sustainable food. I think only one of my sentences, about our industrialized food system, survived intact: "But there are hidden costs: the impact of the overuse of fertilizers and pesticides on the quality of our land, water, and air; the despoiling of tropical forests and jungles to produce our meat and winter vegetables; and the damage done to the birds, frogs, and pollinating insects with whom we share our ecosystem."

Weirdly, whoever ended up rewriting that chapter quoted me by name. After mentioning the expansion of organic farming, farmers' markets, and public interest in food issues, the text reads: "But to ensure that these trends continue, as Marion Nestle, professor and chair of Nutrition and Food Studies at New York University, reminds us, every one of us ought to take an active interest in the way our food is produced and processed."

I ended my original draft with recommendations about where to get further information ("Keeping Alert"). I still think what I wrote would have worked better than what finally appeared, but Guarnaschelli was determined to drop any hint of Rombauer's voice. Ultimately, the *New York Times* called the book's new editorial tone "corporate," and this 1,136-page doorstop edition was replaced by newer and slimmer versions in 2006 and 2019.[6]

Social Media

I've run an almost daily blog—now at FoodPolitics.com—since 2007. This is another habit I'm not yet ready to break, ironic given how reluctant I was to start doing it. When Farrar, Straus & Giroux (FSG) was about to issue the paperback of my book *What to Eat*, its marketers wanted to experiment with social media and asked if I would be a guinea pig. I worried that writing a blog would require yet another steep learning curve, take inordinate amounts of time, and be of questionable value. But when FSG offered to pay for constructing the website and asked only that I try it for a few months, I agreed.

This was a good decision despite the time it took me to figure out how and what to post on it. Its domain name seemed awkward: WhatToEatBook.com. I already had another website called FoodPolitics.com, although I relied on a student to run it for me, and I was starting work on what ended up as two books about pet food. Eventually, I thought it made more sense to consolidate the two sites under a domain name that reflected all my work, could be used as a source of information about my books, articles, media interviews, and public lectures, and set up so I could run it myself. I tracked down the WhatToEatBook.com designers, Rachel Cunliffe and Stephen

Merriman of Cre8d Design in Auckland, New Zealand, and they figured out how to consolidate everything in one site. The new version of FoodPolitics.com launched in January 2009, and I've been posting items to it almost every weekday ever since.[7]

The blog forces me to stay current, and it also works as an electronic filing cabinet. I can post links to original documents and find them easily through WordPress's efficient search tool. It is a source of information for reporters and for students working on food policy research projects. At NYU, blogs count as faculty community service, and while I was teaching full-time, I could pay for it out of my university stipend for academic expenses. Now that I am retired, I pay for it myself.

I post about topics I find intriguing, relevant, outrageous, or funny. I typically write something about the food industry on Mondays ("Sponsored Study of the Week"), current events on Tuesdays and Wednesdays, collections of articles on a specific topic on Thursdays, and a book or report I think worth recommending on Fridays ("Weekend Reading"). I write the posts casually and quickly, rarely spending more than two hours a week on them. I can always find something to write about. As the USA Today reporter Beth Wiese once told me, "Food is a full-employment act."

At first, the site permitted readers to post comments, but I had to stop that when the trolling got too hard to handle. One (or perhaps more) anonymous writers, using false email addresses, started posting disparaging comments about my age, looks, ethnicity, and opinions, and called on NYU to fire me. I wasn't worried about that (a benefit of tenure), but the comments were so unpleasant that readers complained. With much regret, I had to ask my New Zealand site managers to turn off the comment option. Now the only way I know people actually read my posts is through the emails they send whenever I make an error.

The blog has a daily readership of a few thousand (small by social media standards). But links to my posts appear automatically in my

Twitter feed, @marionnestle, which has had about 140,000 followers for years. *Time* named @marionnestle one of the top 10 Twitter accounts in health and sciences in 2011, *Science* ranked it in the top 100 in 2014, and the *Guardian* rated it #2 in health care, science, and policy in 2015.[8] In 2022, at the insistence of a friend who thought I needed to reach younger audiences, I opened an Instagram account at marionnestle.

The San Francisco Chronicle *Columns*

Although almost everything is published online these days, I still think of print as more authoritative, and I write for print publications much more carefully than I do for the blog. Each of the 800–1,200-word columns I wrote for the *San Francisco Chronicle* from 2008 to 2013 took me many hours to prepare. This was another case of being careful what you wish for. I first dreamed of writing a newspaper column that might reach a large audience in the 1980s, when I was working at UCSF. I even enrolled in a night class on feature writing taught by a *Chronicle* reporter. She had us interview restaurant chefs or people with AIDS and write sample pieces. Mine were competent but took hours to write, and I found them a slog to do. Other students seemed to just whip theirs off, and with livelier results. When the instructor recommended me for a gig writing a column in a local fitness magazine, I turned it down. I did not have the confidence to take it on.

I had forgotten that lesson twenty-five years later when Michael Bauer, the executive editor of the *Chronicle*'s prize-winning food and wine section, asked me to write a nutrition column. My editor would be Miriam Morgan, whom I liked and respected. She would make it easy for me; I could do it as a Q&A. I enjoy answering questions; they keep me up on what people want to know. We called the column Food Matters.

But this too was a slog, and it never got easier, mainly because readers hardly ever submitted questions. I had to decide what to write about every month. I kept the column going because I loved being part of the *Chronicle's* food section team, and I visited the offices every time I could get to San Francisco. This was the heyday of the paper's food section. It had its own building, with whole floors of test kitchens, pantries, and wine collections. When the *Chronicle* closed that building and eliminated the separate weekly food and wine section, it was time to stop the column, which I did with mixed relief and regret. By that time, I had written more than fifty columns on such topics as calories, high-fructose corn syrup, fussy eaters, horsemeat, school lunches, and Mexico's soda tax.[9]

Media Interviews

Reporters send me questions nearly every day. I try to respond right away, understanding their deadline pressures. If they are writing about research, they send me the relevant articles. I can read scientific papers quickly, and this is a great way to keep up on current research. Interviews are easy for me, too. In decades of doing them, I have almost never been misquoted, and I rarely say anything I later regret. I don't keep track of the quotes and only see them if someone sends the article to me. In some years, NYU's public relations staff tracks faculty media involvement and gives me a list of the articles that quote me; before the pandemic they ran to about two hundred a year.

Sometimes I'm photographed but not quoted. The photo in figure 23 comes from a long article in the *New York Times* about key players in the food movement and their influence. It featured Alice Waters praising the organic garden Michelle Obama created at the White House.[10] In a paragraph that also cites the work of Michael Pollan and Eric Schlosser, the article mentions me as "a ubiquitous and widely quoted critic of commercial food manufacturers." I particularly like

FIGURE 23. In my NYU office showing off my collection of kids' cereal boxes. The photo appeared in an article in the *New York Times* on March 29, 2009, about the newly emerging food movement.

the photo because it displays some of the kids' cereal boxes I've collected over the years. I'm holding up the package of the whole-grain version of Alpha-Bits that had just been released, which proclaims the contents as having "0 grams of sugar." Cereal companies frequently change the designs of their boxes to reflect current marketing trends, as well as in response to changing FDA rules about nutrition labeling and health claims. Knowing that an unsweetened kids' cereal was unlikely to sell well enough to remain on the market, I bought a box of Alpha-Bits the minute I could find one.[11] Sure enough, it soon vanished from supermarket shelves.

I started collecting cereal boxes when I realized how closely they reflect changes in nutrition labeling policy. In 1990, Congress passed a law to put "Nutrition Facts" labels on food packages and also to allow them to display certain health claims. Years later, I could not remember what labels looked like before 1990 and was unable to find examples. When I agreed to give some informal (unpaid) advice to nutritionists from Kellogg's about a product they were considering, I realized their cereal-box files would show how nutrition labeling had changed over the years. I asked if I could go through Kellogg files to see the packaging changes for Froot Loops, All-Bran, and Rice Krispies from the time those cereals were first introduced. The nutrition staff agreed, and some weeks later I flew to Battle Creek, Michigan, for several days of research at Kellogg headquarters. On arrival, I learned that company lawyers had nixed that idea. Instead, the nutrition staff handed me a gift: complete sets of color images of boxes of those three cereals, which I got to take home with me. These and the others I've collected are a goldmine of information, but I am still mulling over how best to use them. Perhaps they could illustrate a history of US nutrition labeling policy, if I can ever get around to it.

Just as I don't keep track of print interviews, I don't track TV interviews. In the prepandemic days, most TV interviewers filmed me in my office. Studio interviews take longer and are a nuisance to get to, and I've only rarely done major interviews, like the one with Peter Jennings. Because my TV interviews end up as such brief clips, I think of them as long-shot opportunities to structure stories the way I'd like to see them done. Occasionally, one surprises me—my appearance on *The Daily Show*, for example. The segment involved an interview with a man who sold unfiltered, unchlorinated "raw" water at an exorbitant price. In my most professorial tone, I said drinking untreated water is risky, and "water is water." This clip still makes me laugh every time I watch it.[12]

Public Lectures

I have had my share of disastrous speaking experiences, mainly having to do with my foot-dragging transition from the old 35-millimeter slides to PowerPoint in 2003. Slides were hazardous. I still shudder to recall the sixty-slide talk I was giving in an enormous hotel ballroom to an audience of more than a thousand, when slide #6 got stuck. The projector was so far away that I could not see what was happening, but in trying to unjam the slide, the projectionist dropped the carousel, and the rest of the slides fell out. While he was trying to retrieve them, I was left to ad lib the whole presentation. Not my best talk ever. The next two talks I gave were in places where they had stopped using slide projectors altogether but hadn't warned me. I had no choice; it was time to switch to PowerPoint.

I also have had miserable speaking experiences when I was scheduled as the last speaker on a panel. The first was when I was on an otherwise all-male panel run by a male moderator who did not hold earlier speakers to time limits, leaving me with ten minutes in which to give my forty-minute slide talk. After a few more such occasions, I finally realized that I had to discuss timing with moderators in advance and to remind them to leave me enough time if previous panelists were going on too long.

I can never predict how my talks will be received. I was hugely flattered when the US State Department invited me to Rome in 2009 to give the annual George McGovern Lecture in celebration of World Food Day. This took place in an elegant auditorium at the headquarters of FAO, the United Nations Food and Agriculture Organization (figure 24). The lecture honored McGovern, the former Democratic senator from South Dakota, for his work as the first director of the Food for Peace program, an initiator of the World Food Program, and the US ambassador to FAO. I particularly admired him for chairing the Senate Select Committee on Nutrition and Human Needs, which produced the first set of dietary goals for prevention of chronic disease in 1977.[13]

My talk was introduced by Ertharin Cousin, then the US ambassador to FAO. I discussed the food industry's role in obesity, its

FIGURE 24. Giving the George McGovern annual World Food Day lecture at the Food and Agriculture Organization in Rome, October 16, 2009, in front of the flags of UN member countries. This lecture invitation felt like an honor because it came from the US State Department.

opposition to public health obesity prevention measures, and the need for social, economic, and political—rather than technical— solutions to hunger and malnutrition. I used genetically modified foods as an example of technical solutions. When I finished, Ambassador Cousin thanked me but assured the audience that my remarks did not represent the views of the American government. I thought this was funny—I was there at the behest of the State Department, after all—but the FAO nutritionists were mortified. When I asked my State Department host why I had been invited, she explained that one purpose of such invitations is to demonstrate to the world that the United States welcomes differing viewpoints.

Each new book generates further speaking invitations, and I've never had an easy time turning them down. Every group that invites me is worth speaking to, but in self-defense I had to set some limits. I decided that I would accept invitations to give plenary talks at conferences, but not breakout sessions, and that I would have to decline invitations for guest lecturing to classes. And I would expect hosts to pay all my travel expenses.

Once again, I recognize my extraordinary privilege. My NYU salary, and now retirement funds, take care of my financial needs. But even when I don't really need the money, I want hosts to pay me for speaking to their groups. Counterintuitive as it may seem, I learned the hard way that the better I am paid, the better I am treated. Some of my most uncomfortable speaking experiences—curtailed speaking time, absent hosts, no introductions, being abandoned in strange cities—have been no-fee talks that made me understand the meaning of "No good deed goes unpunished." If hosts are paying an honorarium, even a small one, they treat me more respectfully. By another stroke of good fortune, I am now represented by the Steven Barclay Agency, which takes care of all the financial and logistical negotiations for my public speaking and makes my life much easier.

Since some of my hosts might be food companies, I also had to create a conflict-of-interest policy. I finally settled on one that lets me accept reimbursements for travel, hotels, meals, and meeting registrations, because these quickly add up. But I do not accept honoraria, consulting fees, or any other personal payments from food, beverage, or supplement companies. In lieu of such payments, I ask the companies to make an equivalent donation to the NYU Library's food studies collection or to my NYU department's fund for student travel. This policy may not be perfect—I benefit indirectly from donations made in my name—but it makes me think carefully about the conflicts inherent in arrangements with for-profit companies. As I demonstrate in *Unsavory Truth*, recipients of funding from food companies (or any other for-profit company) are largely unaware of how the funding influences opinions, research questions, or interpretation of research results.

I began this chapter with how lucky I feel to be doing this work. I am a living example of the adage "Do what you love and you will never have to work a day in your life."[14] I still reserve mornings for writing and afternoons for catching up with email, reading, meetings, or interviews. Only the email feels like work: there is just so much of it, with so many requests requiring a thoughtful response. Everything else is what I most want to do, and I can't wait to get to it every morning.

12 *The Books* ✓

I enjoy writing books. I like collecting everything I can find on a topic, sorting out what the research means, and trying to explain it clearly. When I'm working on a book, I am completely engrossed. Everything else just disappears. Book projects get me through hard times. Just as *Nutrition in Clinical Practice* gave me something to focus on during the breakup of my second marriage, this book was my lifeline during the coronavirus pandemic.

For me, a book is a three-year project: one year for the research, one for the writing, and one for production. I begin by collecting what's been published on whatever I'm writing about and organizing everything into files. When I'm ready to start writing, I open the file folder, read what's in it, and get to work. I try to write so anyone can understand what I'm saying, just the same way I speak. I prepare the references as I go along, which makes the first draft a slow process. If I seem especially productive, it is not because I write quickly. I don't. Instead I write consistently—one to three hours a day, almost every day, including weekends. Three hours is my upper limit: after an hour or so of intense concentration, I start making mistakes. I forget to save my work, enter changes in the wrong file, or delete something I shouldn't. Writing every day, even for just an hour, maintains momentum. In some way that I truly do not understand, it lets me pick up the next day right where I left off. If I miss a day, it's like starting over from scratch.

Once I have an early draft that covers the points I want to make, I give it to Mal to read. He spent decades as a nutrition scientist and is especially skilled at picking up on issues that need clarification or finding places where I need to tone down my tendency to overstate. With later drafts, I organize a personal peer review: I ask friends and colleagues to read what I've written and tell me what they don't understand or find jarring. I revise accordingly. I find the entire process thoroughly engaging.

Getting Published

The publishing process is more complicated, as it involves many other people. I like to have a publishing commitment before I start writing. This requires writing a book proposal—a twenty-page (double-spaced) description of what the book is about, what's new or special about it, and who it is for. These are hard to write because I don't really know what a book will cover until I'm done with it. The proposal goes to my agent, who uses it to negotiate with publishers. The first decision is whether to try for an academic or a trade press. Academic publishers give authors more control and keep books in print longer but pay minimal or no advances (the immediate payments that are deducted from future royalties, if there are any). Trade publishers often have more effective marketing departments, aim for a wider audience, and pay larger advances. But if a book doesn't sell, they quickly drop it and cut their losses.

Thanks to my NYU salary, I never needed the money from advances, but agents get a percentage of them, which is how they get paid. Most of my advances have been in the low- to mid-five figures. *What to Eat* and, surprisingly, *Feed Your Pet Right* were the only ones that went into six. Nearly all of the money I've earned from books has come from the advances. None has ever sold enough copies to earn out its advance and pay royalties. I still get a couple of thousand a year in royalties from UC Press for *Food Politics* and *Safe Food,* but I do not remember getting an advance for those books. Instead, the press paid for the developmental editor who helped me shape them.

Once I turn in a manuscript, it is at the mercy of peer reviewers (for academic books), and of the publisher's editors, copyeditors, designers, production managers, and marketers, all of whom have their own ideas about what a book should say and look like. My book is always my first priority, but all the rest of the people involved in it are working on other books at the same time. It isn't always easy to get their attention. Book production, at least for me, is rarely a smooth process.

Writing the book is the smoothest part. Perhaps if I were truly a best-selling author, the publication process would prove less onerous. Each of my books has gone through its own set of difficulties with production. In several cases, the editor who enthusiastically acquired my book left to take another job, abandoning me to someone far less interested. But getting books out into the world is worth the trouble. I want my ideas to be up for debate, and I am endlessly pleased to hear from readers who tell me that my work has meant something to them. And each of my books has paved the way to the next.

Once *Food Politics* went into production, I began dealing with the chapters that were set aside for a second book. These covered food safety and the then-emerging field of food biotechnology. Outbreaks of foodborne illness were affecting hundreds of thousands of people a year, yet hardly anyone seemed upset about that. In contrast, nobody was getting sick from eating genetically modified foods, but they were perceived as "Frankenfoods." Fortunately, I stumbled across the literature on risk communication. This research explains why public reactions to familiar safety hazards like food poisoning differ from reactions to things like GMOs, which are technological, foreign, imposed, under corporate control and, therefore, anxiety producing.[1]

These contrasting attitudes gave me a structure for exploring the history and politics of food safety. With the help of developmental editor, John Bergez, my task was to weave these two sets of chapters into a coherent story.[2] John's questions and prompts were similar to the ones he had for *Food Politics:* Why do readers need to know about this? What does what you are writing about mean for readers? *Safe Food* came out in 2003. When I was telling Bambi Shieffelin, my NYU anthropologist neighbor, what it was about, she said, "Oh, it's the evil twin of *Food Politics.*" A few years later, my UC Press editor, Stan Holwitz, suggested I update *Safe Food*, and the press published an expanded edition in 2010.

After *Food Politics* and *Safe Food* came out, my agent at the time, Lydia Wills, thought I should write a trade book for a wider audience. I suggested something along the lines of "Marion Nestle's Nutrition Book" (although I would not have called it that), and wrote a proposal. Lydia arranged interviews with ten publishers, but by the time I got to the last one she had an offer I couldn't refuse from Rebecca Saletan, an editor at North Point Press, an imprint of Farrar, Straus, and Giroux (FSG). I felt honored to be doing a book with such a distinguished literary publisher.

But before I could even start on it, Becky left to take a job with another publisher. There went my champion at the press. The assigned editor had no interest in working with me, but Lydia had another client, Paul Elie, who was an editor at FSG and agreed to take me on. I plunged ahead and began drafting chapters about what is in food, why we need it, and what happens to it in the body. I got as far as digestion but then reached an impasse. I could easily explain how food carbohydrates, fats, and proteins are broken down into sugars, fatty acids, and amino acids, the common molecular subunits that get reassembled into our own body parts. But when I had to talk about how those subunits are further broken down—metabolized—to produce energy and waste products, I could not figure out how to do it without getting into more biochemistry than most readers would care about. I was stuck.

go around grocery store

Still struggling with this impasse in the summer of 2004, I discussed it with my new partner, Mal Nesheim. He had an idea: Could I consider doing something more accessible, like going around a supermarket and discussing the food and nutrition issues that come up in each section? Indeed I could. And this would be fun to do. I filed away what I'd already written and started exploring supermarkets.

That was the genesis of *What to Eat.* I spent much of the next year on supermarket field trips, often with Mal's assistance. I wrote chapters to answer the questions I thought anyone might have about why supermarkets are arranged the way they are, and what goes on in the produce, meat, dairy, fish, and packaged foods sections. My explorations made it clear that nothing about supermarkets is accidental. They are set up to maximize sales by keeping customers in the store as long as possible. Stores place the most profitable items where they are most visible: the front of the store, the ends of aisles, and the checkout counters. Food companies pay to have their products shelved at eye level in those impossible-to-miss locations. When it came to surveying individual sections of the market, the fish counter seemed especially complicated; sorting out one fish from another and balancing health benefits against toxins (methylmercury, PCBs) and environmental concerns (excessive bycatch, overfishing), is more than anyone—eater or fish seller—can be expected to manage.

"What to Eat"

What to Eat has been my best-selling book (more than one hundred thousand copies if you count all editions), not least because of FSG's effective marketing. Like *Food Politics,* this book was reviewed widely and won a James Beard book award (this time in the reference

FIGURE 25. Waiting to sign copies of *What to Eat* at NYU's Fales Library after my first talk about the book on May 3, 2006.

category), and was translated into Hebrew.[3] While working on this memoir, I signed a contract with FSG to update and extensively revise *What to Eat* for a second edition.

Writing Collaboratively

I did much of the research for *What to Eat* at the Wegmans grocery store in Ithaca, New York, because that's where Mal has lived since he was a graduate student at Cornell. At the time, that particular Wegmans had eight center aisles devoted to packaged foods. One of them, 110 feet long, displayed pet foods—cat food on one side and dog food on the other. I thought any food that occupied so much supermarket real estate deserved its own chapter in *What to Eat*, but the manuscript was already way too long.

FIGURE 26. This not particularly flattering portrait of me doing battle with Kellogg's cereal characters illustrated my interview with the Israeli newspaper *Haaretz* (September 21, 2007), following the publication of the Hebrew translation of *What to Eat*. The cartoonist is Itamar Daube.

I also could see that a chapter on pet foods would take serious work. I had a beloved dog, Pokey, as a child and several cats when my kids were young, but I have not had pets for years, and I found pet foods puzzling. They do not come with the Nutrition Facts labels required on foods for humans. Instead, they are labeled as animal feed, and I did not understand what the labels meant. But Mal did. He had a doctorate in animal nutrition and knew all about feed labeling rules. He is a careful researcher, and, as I knew from some previous projects we had done together, he does not mind if our joint efforts end up in my writing voice. If I did not understand pet food labels, other people also might not understand them. I thought a *What to Eat* for dogs and cats would be a good joint project for us.

When word got out that we were doing this, *The Bark* magazine (its motto is "Dog is my copilot") invited us to become its food editors, something I consider as one of my proudest professional accomplishments. With our *Bark* press credentials, we could go to pet food trade shows and conferences and meet product makers and marketers, as well as the terrific community of people who care deeply about what dogs and cats are fed. We wrote articles about pet food for *The Bark* as well as for professional journals.[4]

Our human-nutritionist colleagues could not understand why we were interested in pet food. But we saw it as anything but trivial, not least because these products are made from by-products of human food production that would otherwise be wasted. This makes pet food an integral part of our food system. Our decision to write this book was soon vindicated. Within a month of our having signed a contract for a book on pet food with the Free Press (an imprint of Simon & Schuster), a Canadian pet food manufacturer announced what was then the largest recall of food products ever recorded— more than one hundred brands of pet foods. These recalls were a major food safety story in 2007.

The products sickened cats and dogs because they contained melamine, a cheap nitrogen-rich compound typically used to make plastic dishes. When introduced into food, melamine impairs kidney function. Chinese suppliers of wheat gluten, an expensive ingredient used as a source of protein, had substituted melamine for it. They could do this because tests for protein content cannot tell the difference between the nitrogen in protein and that in melamine. This food safety disaster got front-page attention.

I was following the melamine scandal with great interest and planned to do a chapter on it for our forthcoming pet food book. But the chapter expanded into a lengthy investigative report as I learned more about the profound grief of pet owners who lost pets to contaminated food, and about the greed, dishonesty, and lack of concern about safety throughout the pet-food supply chain. The chapter outgrew any reasonable length. Now what? I told Stan Holwitz about it, and he said UC Press would publish it as a separate book. That was the origin of *Pet Food Politics: The Chihuahua in the Coal Mine,* which came out in 2008. Its point: because pet foods are essential food system components, if they are unsafe, foods for humans are also unsafe. Sure enough, soon after the book's publication in 2008, another melamine scandal erupted in China, this one involving infant formula. Melamine-infused formula sickened more than three hundred thousand babies, killed several, and resulted in severe punishment for the Chinese perpetrators.[5]

In the meantime, Mal and I were working on the more general book, the equivalent of *What to Eat* for pets. We divided up the chapters, wrote drafts, and passed them back and forth. Our book ended up as an analysis of the pet food industry—its structure, major players, function in the food system, and influence. We wanted the book's title to convey that this was far more than a book on how to feed pets (although it covered that too), but we were overruled by the publisher's marketing team. The misleadingly titled *Feed Your Pet Right* was published in 2010.[6]

We thought (and still think) we did a great job on the book, but just about everyone else was unhappy with it. Veterinarians thought we were too critical of their cozy relationships with pet food companies. Because we do not view commercial pet foods as poison, and see them as an excellent use of the by-products of human food production, the alternative pet-food community wrote us off too. We disappeared from *The Bark*'s masthead and were never invited to

FIGURE 27. Mal Nesheim and I were interviewed by the *San Francisco Chronicle* for an article that appeared on June 23, 2010, about our book *Feed Your Pet Right*. We enjoyed the photo shoot at the kitchens run by the *Chronicle*'s food section. The Australian Shepherds, pets of a food-section staff member, had just been fed meals prepared from recipes in our book.

write for it again. The book did not sell well, and Simon & Schuster relegated it to their print-on-demand list. We still hope to get a chance to do a revised, updated, and better-titled edition someday.

Next came the calorie book. When Stan Holwitz suggested I write an updated edition of *Safe Food,* he also had another idea: a book about calories. This was brilliant. Nobody understands calories. They are too abstract—they can't be seen, smelled, tasted, or estimated precisely—and they are largely ignored in the fat-versus-carbohydrate debates about weight gain. I would be able to use the discarded chapters on nutrition from *What to Eat.* Even better, a book about calories would be something Mal and I could work on together. He knew the science of energetics better than I did, and our ways of understanding calories would complement each other. The timing was perfect. Everyone seemed to be arguing about whether all calories were the same ("A calorie is a calorie") or whether calories from sugars affect metabolism differently. Mal and I could contribute some nuance to that debate.

Our view is that when it comes to weight gain or maintenance, a calorie is indeed a calorie, but the foods the calories come from matter greatly to overall health. Because it is impossible to count calories accurately without using fancy equipment, the best way to monitor calorie intake is to use a bathroom scale. If your weight is going up and you don't want that to continue, you need to eat less. That, of course, is never easy in a world in which food companies push products at us constantly, everywhere, at all times of day, and in large (and, therefore, highly caloric) amounts.

Our book *Why Calories Count: From Science to Politics* came out in 2012 and won an award from the International Association of Culinary Professionals in the food matters category. By the time it appeared, Stan had retired from UC Press. Mal and I ended up working with Kate Marshall, who edits UC Press's food and culture series and has been my esteemed editor and friend ever since.

Using Cartoons

For decades I have clipped and filed cartoons by topic for use in teaching and lectures, and include them in my books whenever I can. Reprinting them requires formal permission from the cartoonist or copyright holder, and often a hefty fee. While working on *Why Calories Count,* I needed permission to reproduce a couple of cartoons by artists represented by the Cartoonist Group. That is how I met Sara Thaves, its owner. During my negotiations with Sara about fees, she asked: "Are you the Marion Nestle who wrote *Food Politics?*" And then she said, "I've always wanted to do a cartoon book about food politics." What a coincidence: me too. I wrote a proposal, and Lydia sold the book to Rodale Press.

The process could not have been more of a pleasure. Sara pulled 1,200 cartoons about food politics from her files and sent them to me. I spread them out on the floor, organized them into piles by topic, picked my favorite two hundred out of the lot, and wrote text to go with them. This book took just a few weeks to write, less than any other book I'd ever done. The cartoons did all the work. The Rodale book designers, Amy King and Mike Smith, did a spectacular job of fitting the cartoons into the text, and the resulting full-color book is gorgeous.

On the Friday before the book was to go to press, my editor at Rodale, Alex Postman, called to say that the book had one blank page at the end, and would I like to add a cartoon of myself if they could get someone to do it over the weekend? Would I ever. I love Clay Bennett's work and was delighted that he agreed to do this. I use this cartoon as the last slide in almost every talk I give (figure 28). *Eat, Drink, Vote: An Illustrated Guide to Food Politics* ("with Selections from the Vaults of the Cartoonist Group") was published in 2013. It too won an award from the International Association of Culinary Professionals in the food matters category.

Vote with your fork.
Even better, vote with your vote!

Bennett

FIGURE 28. This portrait of me appeared as the last-minute last page of *Eat, Drink, Vote*. Clay Bennett, the editorial cartoonist for the *Chattanooga Times Free Press*, produced it over the weekend before the book went to press. He signed a copy to me: "To my fellow rabble-rouser Marion—Your comrade, Clay Bennett."

Losing and Finding an Agent

My longtime agent, Lydia Wills, had a suggestion for my next project. Would I consider doing a book about sodas, as part of an elaborate project involving one of her other clients? I thought this was an exciting idea. Sodas, when consumed in large amounts, are strongly associated with poor diets, weight gain, and chronic disease. In some cities and countries, antisoda advocacy had succeeded in removing sodas from schools and getting them taxed as a means of reducing consumption. Lydia worked out an agreement for authorship and royalties. Having worked with Lydia on *Food Politics* and all subsequent books, I signed it without giving it a second thought. Lydia sold the book to Oxford University Press, which made the best offer. My Oxford editor would be Max Sinsheimer, who usually worked on encyclopedias. I had written a couple of entries for him for his *Oxford Companion to Sugar and Sweets,* and I greatly enjoyed working with him.[7] This would be Max's first nonencyclopedia book with Oxford, and I knew it would be in good hands.

But after I wrote the book, I was suddenly confronted with legal challenges based on the contract I'd signed (the details are too much of a digression to bother with here, and best recounted over a glass of wine). I am not a litigious person—I did not even have a personal lawyer—and I spent many sleepless nights fretting over the threatened lawsuits. Eventually Max came up with a workable compromise and helped me negotiate my way out of this. I had loved working with Lydia, but she had gotten me into this situation; she knew it and apologized, but the damage was done. From this, I learned two hard lessons. First, I needed to read contracts carefully. Second, I would have to find another agent who would look after my interests more effectively.

While I was mulling over how to do that, *Soda Politics* won the James Beard Book Award in the writing and literature category, and Max and I went out to celebrate. Max was leaving Oxford University Press, moving away from New York, and thinking of setting up a literary agency. Would I like to be his first client? I would indeed. We celebrated further when *Soda Politics* won the Jane Grigson Award for Distinguished Scholarship from the International Association of

Culinary Professionals. This memoir is our third book together since *Soda Politics*.

Taking on Conflicted Interests

In researching *Soda Politics*, I came across studies funded by Coca-Cola and the American Beverage Association. These almost invariably produced results that soda companies could use for marketing purposes or to counter the idea that sugary drinks are not good for health. I included examples of such studies in a chapter in that book. While I was working on that chapter, I kept coming across studies funded by other food, beverage, and supplement companies with results that favored the sponsor's commercial interests. Companies announced the results in press releases extolling the superior health benefits of their products. I was so annoyed by this seemingly get-what-you-pay-for research that in March 2015 I began posting examples of such studies at FoodPolitics.com, five at a time. Despite pleading with readers to send me examples of industry-funded studies with results that did *not* favor the sponsor's interests, I found few. I did this for an entire year. By March 2016, I had posted 168 industry-funded studies. Of these, 156 had favorable results; only 12 did not.

During the year I was posting those studies, *Soda Politics* went into production. It was still in production in August 2015 when the *New York Times* published a front-page article about Coca-Cola's funding of research. The company was sponsoring the work of the Global Energy Balance Network, a group of researchers who argued that physical activity was more important than diet (soda intake, for example) in maintaining a healthy body weight, despite much evidence to the contrary. The reporter interviewed me for the story, and the *Times* displayed my quote as a banner headline across the top of an inside page where it could not be missed.[8]

In the following week, at least thirty reporters called to ask for further comment. They were shocked. They could not believe Coca-Cola would pay for that kind of research, researchers would accept Coca-Cola's funding, or universities would allow their faculty to accept such funding. Their reactions shocked *me*. If reporters found these arrangements unbelievable, other people would too. Clearly, I had another book to write.

For this, I was well prepared. I had been writing about industry influence on nutrition research, practice, and public policy since 2001.[9] Max got to work and sold the proposal to Basic Books, a trade publisher well respected for its ability to promote academic-type books to a wide audience. The manuscript I turned in exceeded the length allowed in my contract by twenty thousand words. Cutting it down meant deleting two chapters and eliminating words wherever I could. This hurt, but surely made *Unsavory Truth: How the Food Industry Skews the Science of What We Eat* easier to read when it came out in 2018.

The book did not get much publicity, generated few reviews, and sold poorly. It also won no prizes, although the *Hagstrom Report* ranked it among the best agriculture books of the year. I was disappointed that it got so little attention from mainstream media. Conflicts of interest in food research are apparently of less public interest than those in drug or climate-change research.

The book was also largely ignored by the nutrition research community and got the full silent treatment from my American nutrition colleagues. This was disappointing, if understandable. Money for research is hard to come by. As is well established, researchers do not believe that industry funding influences their work and do not recognize its effects. I felt better about the book's reception when an advocacy group in Brazil arranged for a Portuguese translation and the most exhilarating book tour I have ever had.[10] I gave talks in Brasilia, Saõ Paulo, and Rio de Janeiro to large and enthusiastic audiences of book buyers. This was my first and only experience of feeling like a rock star.

Summarizing My Work

During the years I was working on *Soda Politics* and *Unsavory Truth,* Kate Marshall at UC Press was urging me to do a short book that would pull together my ideas about food politics. For several years, we discussed and rejected a variety of approaches but finally agreed that a Q&A format might work. My friend Kerry Trueman agreed to write the questions, and the result was our coauthored book *Let's Ask Marion: What You Need to Know About the Politics of Food, Nutrition, and Health.* In a four-by-six-inch format and with a clever cover—red cloth with the title and our names in white conversation bubbles—it is our version of Mao's Little Red Book.[11] But its publication could not have come at a worse time: September 2020, the height of the coronavirus pandemic. The entire book-tour plan for bookstore readings and conference lectures scheduled in multiple cities had to be scrapped.

And with that, we come to the book you are reading. It is my sixth book with UC Press, which seems just the right place for a personal account of my academic life. It also feels special. It is UC Press's first memoir in its California Series in Food and Culture, putting it firmly in the genre of "foodoir."

Conclusion

Some Final Thoughts

In a sense, this book is a case study of the particular barriers faced and dealt with by one woman growing up in post–World War II America. Mine were low expectations—familial and societal, adopted as my own—along with institutional biases, lack of mentorship, and the demands of family and child care, which are always greater for women. I had a hard time imagining what I might want to do within the constraints of what I would be *allowed* to do. I tried to conform to societal expectations and make the best of whatever situation I was in, but it took me decades to realize that I was better at things I liked doing and that I really did have choices and could act on them.

In another sense, my life illustrates the profound advantages that became available to women, at least those who were white, at that precise—and now understood to be unique—moment in history. Only then was it possible for someone from a poor family like mine to get a first-rate, debt-free education; to achieve a solidly middle-class life (with safe and comfortable housing, excellent public schools, and comprehensive health care) on a modest academic salary; and to have lifetime job security. These are benefits beyond comprehension for most young people in the United States today. It was my great fortune to enter the workforce just as doors for women's education and advancement were beginning to open. And despite my inability to balance a scientific career with family life, I had the opportunity to invent the field that made possible the productive career I have so greatly enjoyed.

None of this makes it any easier to say what the story of my life could possibly mean to anyone else. Interviewers often ask me (trust me, these are genuine examples): "Why does your work matter in the world?" "What are some of the significant social, ethical, or political implications of the work you do?" "How would you assess your legacy?" Such questions stop me cold. I cannot possibly assess the impact of my own work. Surely, that impact must be for others to determine.

Students often say, "I want to do what you do. Tell me how." Sometimes people write, "I read your book; it changed my life." Or, they say, "I read your book; it changed my diet" (after reading *What to Eat*), or "I lost weight" (*Soda Politics*), or "I went into food studies" (*Food Politics*). This must be evidence of impact, but I have not kept track of such comments and cannot quantify them. They are anecdotes, not science.

Given my innately skeptical way of looking at the world, I find it easier to recognize where I have *not* had influence. Despite my best efforts, nutrition professionals continue to have financial ties to food companies without recognizing or acknowledging the influence of such ties, even though conflicted interests contribute to public distrust of nutrition research and advice. I hoped that *Unsavory Truth* would encourage nutrition researchers and practitioners to push back against food industry influence. But I don't see that happening. I've done what I can: it's up to younger colleagues to take up this cause.

I do have a tangible legacy. It includes the books I've written, the now-burgeoning field of food studies, and the NYU library's vast collection of materials about food and cooking. For these, I have received plenty of recognition in the form of awards, invitations, and celebrations. I love getting awards, despite my embarrassment and lingering doubts about whether I really deserve them. Because I did not come through a traditional doctoral program in nutrition, attract traditional mentors, or work in traditional academic departments, I have never had colleagues who could or would nominate me for awards. Asking to be nominated was not something I would ever be comfortable doing. Consequently, I never expected any of the awards I've received.

I have a window case in my office (blocking my view of a brick wall) filled with glass objects and medals for lifetime achievement from, among others, the James Beard Foundation (Leadership, Who's Who), the International Association of Culinary Professionals (Trailblazer), Heritage Radio (Hall of Fame), Les Dames d'Escoffier (Grand Dame), and my alma mater, Berkeley's School of Public Health (Public Health Hero). The honorary doctorates from Kentucky's Transylvania University and the City University of New York came as total surprises. I considered it an enormous honor when Michael Pollan named me as the #2 foodie in America (second only to Michelle Obama), and Mark Bittman listed me as the #1 foodie to be thankful for. Bittman, who generously wrote the foreword to *Soda Politics*, more recently called *Food Politics* "the most important work on contemporary nutrition."[1]

I try not to let this recognition go to my head or to take it too seriously, especially because some awards seem ironic. In 2015, for example, *Women's Health* listed me first among four women honored as "Game Changers in Science and Medicine." I could not believe it was including me in the same category as Mary-Claire King, who discovered the gene for breast cancer, and Elizabeth Blackburn, the codiscoverer of telomeres, the caps at the end of chromosomes that prevent the aging of DNA. But the one other woman in this group was Elizabeth Holmes, described as the "youngest female self-made billionaire, at 31" for having founded Theranos, a company that claimed—fraudulently, as it turned out—to be able to analyze blood chemistry from just a drop of blood.[2] This reminded me of the Health Quality Award I shared with Newt Gingrich in 2005.

Elizabeth Blackburn, whom I had known at UCSF, has a Nobel Prize, and I saw her in Stockholm in 2016 when we both were invited to participate in the Nobel week dialogue "The Future of Food: Your Plate, Our Planet." My talk—about food politics, of course—was titled "Who Makes Our Food Choices?"[3] This was as close to the Nobel Prizes as I was ever going to get, and it was a glorious event. When else would someone like me ever get a chance to meet the songwriter, author, and poet Patti Smith, who was in Stockholm to celebrate the literature prize awarded to Bob Dylan? There she was, sitting two seats away at the concert the night before the award ceremonies.[4] She graciously agreed to a photo, which I knew would impress my family, friends, and colleagues more than anything else I could ever possibly do (figure 29).

In 2018, I was again invited by the Nobel Prize committee to speak at a food symposium, this time in Yokohama, Japan. During that year and the next, I taught at the University of Gastronomy in Italy, went on book tour in Brazil, and spoke at meetings in Switzerland, the Netherlands, France, Portugal, China, Italy, Great Britain, and Chile. All of that was possible because I had the time; I retired from NYU in September 2017.

My retirement was the result of a tenure-contract buyout. While I was teaching at Berkeley in 2015, I received an email from my school's dean, Dominic Brewer. The school, by then called the Steinhardt School of Culture, Education, and Human Development, was having financial problems, needed to downsize, and was offering an exceptionally generous package to buy out the tenure contracts of long-standing senior faculty. I qualified for the buyout on the grounds of both age and length of service, but was not sure I was ready to retire. My identity is closely linked to what I do, and I did not want to stop teaching. At the same time, I thought it would be unseemly *not*

FIGURE 29. With Patti Smith at the concert the night before the 2016 Nobel Prize ceremonies in Stockholm. I gave a talk at its food conference. She sang "A Hard Rain's a-Gonna Fall" in honor of Bob Dylan, who had won the Nobel Prize in Literature but did not attend the celebration.

to accept the offer. I would soon be turning eighty, long beyond the age anyone should be hanging on to a tenured position at a university. That impending birthday was no secret: the Fales Library, the Steinhardt School, my department, and Clark Wolf were jointly organizing public celebrations (see figure 30).

While trying to decide what to do, I went to discuss my options with Dean Brewer. "Oh no!" he said, "We didn't mean this for you." With that reassurance, I could negotiate the softest retirement ever. I would be able to keep my office and continue teaching, and retirement would make little difference in my day-to-day professional life. The university no longer pays me, but its retirement plan—another great advantage of tenured university positions—takes care of my

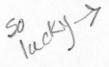

so lucky →

FIGURE 30. NYU held a weeklong series of events to celebrate my retirement, this one a reception at the Fales Library on April 26, 2018. Its walls were lined with blown-up copies of articles about the department and covers of my books. I am flanked by the food writers and teachers Meryl Rosofsky (*left*) and Betty Fussell (*right*).

financial needs. The main difference: I now teach only short courses on food systems politics, policy, and advocacy on a pass/fail basis (which allows students to listen, learn, and interact without worrying about grades, and also eliminates that chore). The other difference, of course, is that I had more time to travel—until COVID-19 put a stop to all that.

I began this memoir by explaining that my rationale for writing it was to address questions I'm constantly asked, and that the COVID-19 pandemic gave me the time to reflect on them. To conclude this account, I have three more frequently asked questions to address: "What keeps you going?," "What's driving you forward at the moment?," and "What makes you hopeful?"

On this last, plenty. For one thing, I still love the field I work in. I still believe that studying food is an exceptionally effective and accessible way to get at the most vexing societal problems that affect all of us. Food is about taste and pleasure, but it is also about nutrition, health, community, and culture. I am hard pressed to think of a problem in society that cannot be understood more deeply by examining the role of food. Just consider how food relates to hunger and chronic disease, environmental pollution, or climate change; to systems of agricultural production and distribution; to the ways foods are sold, prepared, and consumed; or to how societies deal with such matters as immigration, racial and gender discrimination, and incarceration. These food problems result directly from capitalist—or, if you prefer, neoliberal—economic and political systems. Talking about capitalism scares people, but everyone eats. Everyone can grasp food issues and say something about them. And talking about food helps everyone understand how capitalist economies lead to institutional discrimination, inequities, and environmental damage.

Despite the flaws in its methods and my field's too-cozy relationship with food companies, I still love studying and teaching about the nutritional aspects of food. I love how everyone can relate to what gets eaten and the passion so many people bring to that relationship. I love how nutrition demands critical thinking. I love the scientific challenges of nutrition research and still believe that the question of how to measure the effects of what people eat is a thrilling intellectual pursuit.

Given the complexity of daily diets, it is easy to understand why studies so often yield ambiguous results or apparently negligible differences and require complicated statistical tests to decide whether the differences are real or could have occurred by chance. Nutrition scientists do the best they can with them. Some statisticians now argue that the flaws in nutrition research are so serious that the field needs a complete overhaul.[5] I disagree, especially because these critics propose no better alternatives for such research. This leaves us with the need for careful interpretation, which is what I find most fascinating about this field.

As a public health nutritionist, I want everyone to have access to diets that are healthy and sustainable. I want my nutrition colleagues to care and be willing to do something about the social and economic inequities that act as barriers to such diets. Here is another situation in which I wish I had more influence. The field of nutrition seems to be moving precisely in the opposite direction. Instead of promoting healthy diets for all, researchers are focusing on "precision" nutrition, an approach based on the idea that one diet is *not* for all; instead, diets should be tailored to individual expressions of genetics and metabolism.[6] This approach will undoubtedly yield fascinating scientific insights, but is unlikely to help solve world hunger, reduce chronic disease, or mitigate the environmental damage induced by food production and consumption. We need and should be advocating for a compelling global campaign to address all three simultaneously—triple-duty diets—as was argued by two *Lancet* commissions in 2019.[7]

This campaign necessarily must involve much stronger regulation of food industry marketing and lobbying practices and should argue forcefully for reduced consumption of what are now called ultraprocessed foods. These constitute the specific category of junk foods defined as industrially produced, unable to be made in home kitchens, containing artificial ingredients (for color, texture, and flavor), and including much added sugar and salt. Ultraprocessed foods have been strongly demonstrated by research to lead to excessive calorie intake, weight gain, and chronic disease.[8] We would all do better if we ate more real food and less of highly processed food products. In 2022, I outlined my specific aspirations for the elements of food advocacy campaigns in an article for the *American Journal of Public Health*.[9]

As for what keeps me going, I have two quick answers. One is a feeling of responsibility. Carolyn Heilbrun, the first woman to get tenure in Columbia University's English department, once wrote of women who had succeeded in academia: "We should make use of our security, our seniority, to take risks, to make noise, to be courageous, to become unpopular."[10] I've tried my best to do just that.

The second is this: I teach students. I have the great good fortune to be able to teach young people who are passionately interested in food issues, and for all the right reasons. They want to use food to change the world. They want food to be produced in ways that are healthier for people and the planet, and to make such food available and accessible to everyone—the poor and disenfranchised as well as the rich and privileged. They are not afraid to confront the damaging consequences of capitalism. They understand how profits drive corporate practices and what's wrong with corporate control of food systems. They want systems to change.

I consider it a privilege to teach these students and anyone else interested in advocating for healthier and more sustainable food systems. I cannot think of a better way to learn about effective advocacy than through food. I encourage students to get involved in food issues as a means of exercising their rights as citizens in a democratic society. They can choose the specific issues they want to work on. But I want students as well as readers of my books to understand that advocacy really can produce results. If students—and you—don't advocate for better food systems, who will? The future is yours. If what I write and teach encourages advocacy for a better future, I still have plenty more work to do.

Acknowledgments

Memoirs depend on memory, unreliable as it is, and mine is no better than anyone else's. I am a nonfiction writer and felt uneasy writing about events that might not have happened the way I remember them. I would not have been able to write this book without the early encouragement to take on this project from friends and colleagues, especially Stefani Bardin, Robby Cohen, Kathleen Finlay, Betty Fussell, Ray Goldberg, Vivian Gornick, Jan Poppendieck, Ricardo Salvador, Alix Kates Shulman, and Kerry Trueman.

I am grateful to those who helped me check facts about our shared experiences: long-standing friends from UCSF days, Bobby Baron, Jim Cone, and Melinda Lee Jackson; Vince Casalaina, Narsai David, and Iliana Matisse from *Over Easy;* Hanmin Liu about his 1986 workshop in Shanghai; Linda Fried, Rozanne Gold, Gary Taubes, Bret Thorn, Clark Wolf, and Margo Wootan for details I struggled to remember; and my NYU colleagues Jennifer Berg, Melissa Metrick, Krishnendu Ray, and Lisa Sasson, who also helped with details from our shared past. UCSF librarians Rachel Taketa and Erin Hurley helped with documents and dates.

This pandemic made it especially hard to obtain copies of photographs, but NYU librarians Janet Bunde, Charlotte Priddle, and Elizabeth Benchley Verrelli, along with Shane Miller of NYU's photo bureau, helped dig them out. The pandemic also complicated the always difficult process of obtaining permission to use the photos and cartoons. I was able to get most permissions on my own, but Eitan Sasson and Idan Sasson merit my enormous appreciation for their three-country effort to track down the cartoonist for the Israeli newspaper *Haaretz.* Special thanks to Jessie YuChen for taking the photos used in three of the illustrations, and to Michael Brennan, Mitchell Davis, and Fernanda Nunes for social media support.

My personal hero medals go to friends, colleagues, and family who read and commented on various stages of the entire manuscript: Mal Nesheim, of course; my own peer reviewers Loma Flowers, Jocelyn Harris, and Laura Shapiro; my children, Charles and Rebecca Nestle; and UC Press's official peer reviewers, one anonymous and the three who confessed—Lia Fernald, Barry Popkin, and Andy Smith. I took your suggestions to heart and did the best I could to follow most of them. Reading page proofs is particularly heroic. For keeping so many errors out of this book, I thank Mal and Rebecca, but also Stefani Bardin and Joanne Csete. Joanne has done this for several of my books and I am ever in awe of her skills and generosity.

At UC Press, my deepest thanks go to Kate Marshall for taking on this project and recruiting Jenny Wapner for developmental editing. Her suggestions were always constructive and helped streamline the book. I thank Lia Tjandra for the splendid cover design; Enrique Ochoa-Kaup for helping me stay on track with UC Press procedures; Erika Būky for meticulous copyediting, eliminating errors, and keeping me out of trouble; Judy Loeven for keen-eyed proofreading; Thérèse Shere for her deft indexing; and production manager Julie Van Pelt—I so enjoyed our Zoom consultations.

I am eternally grateful to my agent, Max Sinsheimer, for his extraordinary generosity in working with me on the proposal, reading multiple versions of the manuscript (way beyond any call of duty), and his ongoing counsel in response to countless sticking points. It is a joy to work with you Max, and I am proud to have been your first client.

That leaves family. My Moss and Zittell cousins always bring joy. Everlasting thanks to my children, Charles and Rebecca Nestle, not only for reading and critiquing this manuscript but also for our weekly half-hour Zoom meetings throughout the pandemic. They helped me get through it. Last, but certainly not least, I thank my partner, Mal Nesheim, for his patience, wisdom, and steady support for this project and so much else in my life.

Notes

Note: All URLs were active as of March 2022.

Introduction

1. Marion Nestle, key player. Activist Facts. https://www.activistfacts.com/person/3381-marion-nestle-dr/.

2. The first three quotations come from "Praise for Marion Nestle" (the "praise pages") at the beginning of my book with Kerry Trueman, *Let's Ask Marion: What You Need to Know About the Politics of Food, Nutrition, and Health*. University of California Press; 2020. The "badass" designation is from *Whole Living*'s food issue, November 2012:97–107. I was in good company; the others named were chef Dan Barber ("The Flavor Seeker"), agrarian philosopher Wendell Berry ("The Patriarch"), the Land Institute's Wes Jackson ("The Grain Guru"), and FoodCorps ("The Organizers").

3. My official title is Paulette Goddard Professor of Nutrition, Food Studies, and Public Health, Emerita. I love holding it. Goddard was married to Charlie Chaplin and starred in his *Modern Times*. She later married Erich Maria Remarque, the author of *All Quiet on the Western Front*. She left her estate to NYU, which uses it to endow professorships, among other purposes. See Lorch D. Paulette Goddard left N.Y.U. $20 million. *New York Times*, May 18, 1990.

4. Pierce JP, Gilpin E, Burns DM, et al. Does tobacco advertising target young people to start smoking? Evidence from California. *JAMA*. 1991;266:3154–3158.

5. On precisely this point, see Colwell R, McGrayne SB. *A Lab of One's Own: One Woman's Personal Journey through Sexism in Science*. Simon & Schuster; 2020.

Chapter 1. A Long, Slow Start

1. *Jews without Money* (International Publishers, 1942, but newer editions are still in print) is a harrowing novel about living in poverty by Michael Gold (1894–1967). Gold is a pseudonym for Granich. Mike Gold was a brother of Manny Granich, who ran the summer camp at Higley Hill discussed in this chapter.

2. See Restaurant guild at issue in strike. *New York Times,* January 20, 1939; This is no April Fool's Day joke; The Brass Rail strike is settled. *New York Times,* April 2, 1942. My father's name is not mentioned in either article but does appear in clippings in the scrapbook, now in NYU's Tamiment Library.

3. In 1998, 2009, and 2018, I went to Higley Hill reunions, but had been at the camp too early to know most of the participants. With the director of NYU's Tamiment collection, I helped organize the 2009 celebration of its acquisition of Higley Hill camp materials and photographs; the collection includes a video of the event. For a contemporary description, see Heller P. Local camp nurtured young progressives. *Barre Montpelier Times Argus,* December 2, 2016. Updated October 27, 2018.

4. Berkeley tuition costs for state residents were nearly $15,000 per semester in 2022. Estimated total costs were $40,000, but by living in a co-op students could save approximately $10,000.

5. Our assigned books included the anthropologist Ruth Benedict's *Patterns of Culture* (1934), which described ways of living that differed greatly from those in the United States. I am still in touch with the teaching assistant in that class, Renata Polt.

6. I was repeatedly told a clearly apocryphal story about my husband's name. When his father's family arrived at Ellis Island in the early 1900s, they saw a sign for Nestlé's milk and said, "Okay, we'll take that one."

7. See Oldham K. U.S. Supreme Court strikes down loyalty oaths for Washington State employees on June 1, 1964. HistoryLinkOrg. February 14, 2003. The military oath is still required today, but in a slightly different form.

8. Haderlie went on to a distinguished career in marine biology. Among his publications is this monumental book: Morris RH, Abbott DP, Haderlie EC. *Intertidal Invertebrates of California.* Stanford University Press; 1980. Also see Denny M. *Conversations with Marco Polo: The Remarkable Life of Eugene C. Haderlie.* XLibris; 2006.

9. Sanders R. Biochemist Howard Schachman, an advocate for research ethics, dies at 97. *Berkeley News,* August 10, 2016.

10. Nestle M. *Purification and Properties of a Nuclease from* Serratia marcescens. Dissertation. University of California, Berkeley; 1968.

11. My thesis papers, all by Nestle M and Roberts WK: (1) Separation of ribonucleosides and ribonucleotides by a one-dimensional paper chromatographic system. *Anal Biochem.* 1968;22:349–351; (2) An extracellular nuclease from *Serratia marcescens.* I. Purification and some properties of the enzyme. *J Biol Chem.* 1969;244:5213–5218; (3) An extracellular nuclease from *Serratia marcescens.* II. Specificity of the enzyme. *J Biol Chem.* 1969;244:5219–5225.

12. See Cohen R, Zelnik RE, eds. *The Free Speech Movement: Reflections on Berkeley in the 1960s.* University of California Press; 2002. The first editor, Robby Cohen, is a colleague at NYU. I am ever amazed that he studies as history the events I lived through.

13. Barr A, Levy P. *The Official Foodie Handbook.* Arbor House; 1984.

14. Felsenstein J. Obituary: Allan Charles Wilson (1934–1991). *Nature.* 1991;343:19.

Chapter 2. My First Academic Job

1. Nestle M, Sussman M. The effect of cyclic-AMP on morphogenesis and enzyme accumulation in *Dictyostelium discoideum. Devel Biol.* 1972;28: 545–554.

2. Rosenthal NB. Consciousness raising: from revolution to re-evaluation. *Psychol Women Quart.* 1984;8(4):309–326.

3. Jon and Myla did marry and have children. Using their merged last names, Kabat-Zinn, Jon went on to become a celebrated professor of medicine and a well-known author and advocate of mindful meditation.

4. See Baker RB, Washington HA, Olakanmi O, et al. African American physicians and organized medicine, 1846–1968: origins of a racial divide. *JAMA.* 2008;300(3):306–314. The 1968 quote comes from an online timeline of medical history referred to in the article.

5. National Research Council, Food and Nutrition Board. *Recommended Dietary Allowances.* 8th rev. ed. National Academy of Sciences; 1974.

6. Williams RD, Mason HL, Wilder RM, Smith BF. Observations of induced thiamine (vitamin B1) deficiency in man. *Arch Intern Med.* 1940;66(4): 785–799.

7. Hodges RE, Baker EM, Hood J, Sauberlich HE, March SC, Canham JE. Experimental scurvy in man. *Am J Clin Nutr.* 1969;22(5):535–548.

8. Barraclough G. The great world crisis I. *New York Rev Books,* January 23, 1975, and Wealth and power: the politics of food and oil. *New York Rev Books,* August 7, 1975.

Chapter 3. Second Job

1. A look at UCSF in the 1970s. *UCSF News.* 1970;3(March–April). Also see UCSF Philip R. Lee Institute for Health Policy Studies. Philip R. Lee (1924–2020). https://healthpolicy.ucsf.edu/philip-r-lee-md. Lee was assistant secretary for health under Presidents Lyndon B. Johnson and Bill Clinton, chancellor of UCSF from 1969 to 1972, and a major proponent of justice in health care.

2. Bill Reinhardt had been on the medical school faculty since 1939; he was dean from 1963 to 1966 and given much credit for having led UCSF's transformation into a leading research university.

3. Bobby Baron has had a long career on the UCSF medical faculty. He was a coauthor on my first paper on nutrition policy in 1983 (cited below in n. 7). In 2014 we wrote an article on nutrition in medical education for *JAMA Internal Medicine* on progress made in this area (not much). See Nestle M, Baron RB. Nutrition in medical education: from counting hours to measuring competence. *JAMA Intern Med.* 2014;174(6):843–844. Bobby's daughter Haley came to NYU for a master's degree in food studies in 2015. Jim Cone is the medical director of the World Trade Center Health Registry in the New York City Health Department. Erica Goode had an undergraduate degree in nutrition; she became a private practitioner in integrative medicine and taught medical students until her death in 2019.

4. The great irony of my difficulties with Doris Calloway is that we ended up with a family connection. She later married Bob Nesheim, my partner's older brother. Well before Mal and I got together, she chaired the federal 1995 Dietary Guidelines Advisory Committee, on which I served, and we worked closely together. When I had dinner with her and Bob after one of the committee meetings, she apologized for her lack of support for my early efforts at UCSF. She had not meant the rebuff personally; rather she was dismayed that the medical school did not value nutrition enough to have recruited one of her better-trained graduates or colleagues.

5. Nestle M, Evans C, eds. *Nutrition UCSF: A Resource Guide to Courses, Services, and Research.* UCSF; 1980. On the creation of NutritionUCSF, see Nestle M. Nutrition instruction for health professions students and practitioners: strategies for the 1980s. *J Parenter Enteral Nutr.* 1982;6(3):191–193.

6. Nestle M. Our changing (not always wise) diet habits [review of *Jane Brody's Nutrition Book*]. *San Francisco Chronicle/Examiner Review,* April 19, 1981.

7. Nestle M, Lee PR, Baron RB. Nutrition policy update. In: Weininger J, Briggs GM, eds. *Nutrition Update,* Vol. 1. John Wiley and Sons; 1983:285–313.

8. The Asian edition was published by Maruzen, Singapore, 1986, and the Greek edition by GK Parisianes, Athens, 1987.

9. Anne Engammare McBride. Tweet. January 5, 2019. https://twitter.com /annemcbride/status/1081680687789494272?s=03. At the time of writing, Anne was director of programs at the James Beard Foundation. Her tweet referred to University of Arizona Commission on the Status of Women. Avoiding gender bias in reference writing. This document is undated but refers to research published as late as 2009.

10. See the website of the John Tung Foundation at https://www.jtf.org.tw /JTF01/01-04.asp (it can be translated into English via Google Translate). Also see Lo Y. John Tung (1914–1986) of I-Feng Enamelling. Industrial History of Hong Kong Group; December 16, 2014.

Chapter 4. Back to School

1. In 1987, the groups involved in San Francisco's Coalition of Homeless Shelter Providers established a more formal organization, the Coalition on Homelessness, still in existence in 2022.

2. The quote is from the description of Marty Forman's work as USAID's first director of nutrition and as a "nutrition visionary and pioneer" in chapter 1 of USAID. *Nourishing Lives and Building the Future: The History of Nutrition at USAID.* June 25, 2019. https://www.usaid.gov/documents/1864/history-nutrition-usaid-chapter-1.

3. As of 2022, Hanmin Liu is president of the Wildflowers Institute in San Francisco, which works to strengthen communities.

Chapter 5. Working for the Feds

1. This chapter draws on the log I kept of events related to the *Surgeon General's Report* from June 30, 1987, to July 27, 1988; the press conference briefing book; the slides I used in talks about the report; the report itself; my 2009 oral history interviews with Judith Weinraub; and the letter from Mike McGinnis to the head of NYU's faculty search committee, April 12, 1988.

2. Among my ODPHP colleagues, Linda Meyers went on to become executive director of the Food and Nutrition Board at the National Academy of Sciences; Peggy Hamburg went from heading the New York City Department of Health to appointments as assistant secretary for health and FDA commissioner; and Cathie Woteki served as undersecretary at USDA, dean of the College of

Agriculture at the University of Iowa, and science adviser to President Joe Biden.

3. Nestle M, Woteki CE. Trends in American dietary patterns: research issues and policy implications. In: Bronner F, ed. *Nutrition and Health: Topics and Controversies*. CRC Press; 1995:1–44.

4. Office of the Surgeon General. *Smoking and Health: Report of the Advisory Committee to the Surgeon General of the Public Health Service*. US Department of Health, Education, and Welfare; 1964.

5. Rosellini L. Rebel with a cause: Koop. *US News & World Report*. 1988;104(May 30):55–64.

6. MADD succeeded in at least one way: Koop's office sponsored a workshop on drunk driving later that year. See *Surgeon General's Workshop on Drunk Driving: Proceedings*. HHS; December 14–18, 1988. https://www.ncjrs.gov/pdffiles1 /Digitization/118732NCJRS.pdf.

7. Department of Health and Human Services, Public Health Service. *The Surgeon General's Report on Nutrition and Health*. Publ. No. (PHS) 88-50210. US Government Printing Office; 1988. The acknowledgments begin: "The *Surgeon General's Report on Nutrition and Health* was prepared under the general editorship of the Department of Health and Human Services' Nutrition Policy Board. . . . Managing Editor was Marion Nestle, Ph.D., M.P.H., Office of Disease Prevention and Health Promotion."

8. Leary WE. Major U.S. report on the diet urges reduction in fat intake. *New York Times*, July 28, 1988.

9. Collins G. The cookies that ate a new market. *New York Times*, August 24, 1994.

10. Glinsmann WH, Irausquin H, Park YK. Evaluation of health aspects of sugars contained in carbohydrate sweeteners: report from FDA's Sugars Task Force, 1986. *J Nutr*. 1986;116(11S):s1–s216.

11. Taubes's book, *The Case against Sugar* (Knopf; 2016), documents the sugar industry's influence on a previous government report on sugars, a matter I discuss in my book *Unsavory Truth*. The quotation comes from an email that Taubes sent to Hailey Eber, a reporter for the *Washington Post* on October 24, 2018, and shared with me.

12. McGinnis M, Nestle M. The Surgeon General's Report on Nutrition and Health: policy implications and implementation strategies. *Am J Clin Nutr*. 1989;49:23–28.

13. Pollan M. *Food Rules: An Eater's Manual*. Penguin; 2009.

14. Wilson DB. Koop the intruder. *Boston Globe,* August 9, 1988; McCarthy C. Koop's diet advice is stale stuff. *Washington Post,* August 6, 1988; Dr. Koop's timid war on fat. *New York Times,* July 31, 1988.

15. Specter M. Reduce fat in diets, Koop urges: broad report links nutrition to cause of most deaths in '87. *Washington Post,* July 28, 1988.

16. Gordon A. *What We Don't Talk About When We Talk About Fat.* Beacon Press; 2020:34–35.

17. On Blackburn, see Roberts S. Dr. George Blackburn, who worked to help you eat better, dies at 81. *New York Times,* March 7, 2017.

18. Examples: The Surgeon General's Report on Nutrition and Health: new federal dietary guidance policy. *J Nutr Educ.* 1988;20(5):252–254; Promoting health and preventing disease: national nutrition objectives for 1990 and 2000. *Food Technol.* 1988;42(2):103–107; Nutrition in medical education: new policies needed for the 1990s. *J Nutr Educ.* 1988;20(1 Suppl):S1-S6; with Porter DV. Federal nutrition policies: impact on dietetic practice. *J Am Diet Assoc.* 1989; 89:944–947.

19. Theories X and Y are based on the work of Douglas McGregor, *The Human Side of Enterprise.* McGraw-Hill; 1960. This in turn was based on Abraham Maslow's theories of human motivation: see, for example, A theory of human motivation. *Psychol Rev.* 1943;50(4):370–396.

Chapter 6. Finally, NYU

1. During my years at NYU, the name of the school was changed to the School of Education and later to the Steinhardt School of Culture, Education, and Human Development.

2. The unpublished report: Nestle M. Nutrition improvement: an evaluation of the nutritional quality of meals served in HRA food assistance and distribution programs. Human Resources Administration; November 15, 1990.

3. The photograph of Mayor Koch appeared in Harris EA. Ran city, but didn't own a piece of it. *New York Times,* February 1, 2013. I wrote "How I ended up living in Ed Koch's famous Greenwich Village apartment" for *The Atlantic,* February 12, 2013. On James Beard's living arrangements in the late 1930s, see Birdsall B. *The Man Who Ate Too Much: The Life of James Beard.* W.W. Norton & Company; 2020:104–106.

4. Human Nutrition Information Service. *USDA's Eating Right Pyramid* (Home and Garden Bull. No. 249). USDA; March 1991. Although this version was

never released, the USDA sent prepublication copies to selected reporters. I wrote about this history in Dietary advice for the 1990s: the political history of the food guide pyramid. *Caduceus* 1993;9:136–153; In defense of the USDA Food Guide Pyramid. *Nutr Today.* 1998;33(5):189–197; and chapter 2 in *Food Politics.* University of California Press; 2002:51–66.

5. Gladwell M. US rethinks, redraws the food groups. *Washington Post,* April 13, 1991.

6. Sugarman C, Gladwell M. U.S. drops new food chart. *Washington Post,* April 27, 1991. Also see Pyramid decision due: two options remaining. *CNI Nutr Week,* January 3, 1992. Malcolm Gladwell explained the origin of his story to me in a 1993 telephone conversation.

7. Burros M. Are cattlemen now guarding the henhouse? *New York Times,* May 8, 1991; and Testing of food pyramid comes full circle. *New York Times,* March 25, 1992.

8. Human Nutrition Information Service. *USDA's Food Guide Pyramid* (Home and Garden Bull. No. 249). Washington, DC: USDA, April 1992. See Sugarman C. The $855,000 pyramid: revised U.S. food-group chart is released. *Washington Post,* April 28, 1992.

9. Pyramid survives delay; new graphic to become symbol of a healthy diet. *CNI Nutr Week,* May 1, 1992.

Chapter 7. Joining the Food World

1. Gifford D, Baer-Sinnott S. *The Oldways Table: Essays and Recipes from the Culinary Think Tank.* Ten Speed Press; 2007.

2. I discuss some of these events in my foreword to Nancy Jenkins's *The New Mediterranean Diet Cookbook.* Bantam Books; 2009:xi–xiii.

3. Lewis B. Oat bran: no magic bullet against cholesterol. *Los Angeles Times,* February 21, 1991.

4. I describe my relationship with Oldways in my book *Unsavory Truth: How the Food Industry Skews the Science of What We Eat,* in the chapter on disclosure, pp. 173–175. Oldways lists its Mediterranean Diet and Traditions Conferences from 1991 to 2011 at https://oldwayspt.org/system/files/atoms/files/OldwaysConferenceEventList.pdf.

5. Nestle M. Traditional models of healthy eating: alternatives to technofood. *J Nutr Educ.* 1994;26:241–245.

6. *Quality* refers to the purity, antioxidant content, and degree of rancidity of oils. *Integrity* refers to the accuracy and honesty of the labeling (whether Italian

oils really come from Italian olives, for example). Both are ongoing issues for what is now called the International Olive Council.

7. Nestle M, ed. Mediterranean diets: science and policy implications. *Am J Clin Nutr*. 1995;61(suppl):1313s–1427s. I also wrote the introductory essay: Mediterranean diets: historical and research overview: pp. 1313s–1320s.

8. Oldways. This month in Oldways' history. I am listed as cochair of the Mediterranean diet conference in January 1993, but nothing is said about the 1995 Mediterranean diet supplement. https://oldwayspt.org/about-us/founder-history/oldways-timeline/month-oldways-history.

9. Nestle M. Mediterranean Diet Month Memory—Day 26. Oldways, May 26, 2013. https://oldwayspt.org/blog/mediterranean-diet-month-memory-day-26.

10. Lawson C. Julia Child boiling, answers her critics. *New York Times,* June 20, 1990.

11. This episode from *The French Chef,* Julia Child's gateau in a cage, is available at https://www.dailymotion.com/video/x2gtnft.

12. Letter from Julia Child to author, October 2, 1995.

13. Burros M. A new view on training food experts. *New York Times,* June 19, 1996.

14. Letter from Julia Child to author, November 23, 1998.

Chapter 8. Inventing Food Studies

1. This chapter draws on my earlier accounts: Nestle M. Writing the food studies revolution. *Food, Culture & Society.* 2010;13(2):159–168; Berg J, Nestle M, Bentley A. Food studies. In: Katz SH, Weaver WW, eds. *The Scribner Encyclopedia of Food and Culture,* Vol. 2. Charles Scribner's Sons; 2003:16–18; and Nestle M. Foreword: Cookbooks and food studies canons. In: Taylor MJ, Wolf C, eds. *100 Classic Cookbooks, 501 Classic Recipes.* Rizzoli; 2012:8–9. Also see Byrne T. Feature: the origin of food studies movement in the USA 1943–1996. *The Feed: Food, Culture,* March 8, 2019.

2. Mitchell Davis knew that Barkan, a distinguished professor, was writing a food column for the Italian magazine *Gambero Rosso.* We went to Barkan's lecture at NYU's Casa Italiana and immediately recruited him to the committee to give it some academic gravitas.

3. Burros M. A new view on training food experts. *New York Times,* June 19, 1996.

4. Association for the Study of Food and Society. Food Studies Programs. http://www.food-culture.org/food-studies-programs/.

5. Grabar M. Food fetish on campus. James Martin Center for Academic Renewal, March 12, 2014. https://www.jamesgmartin.center/2014/03/food-fetish-on-campus/.

6. Michael Schrader retired from *Nation's Restaurant News* in 2005. The NYU library displays a plaque acknowledging his gift of the Anne Kane Schrader Cookbook and Nutrition Collection. He died in 2007 at age sixty-eight under shocking circumstances. See Frumkin P. NRN copy editor leaves legacy of excellence, education. *Nation's Restaurant News,* January 15, 2007; and Haas B. Juan Ortega. Man, 21, charged in fatal stabbing. *South Florida Sun Sentinel,* January 4, 2007.

7. Marion Nestle Food Studies Collection & Finding Aids. This site lists all donated or acquired collections of books, papers, menus, pamphlets, and oral histories related to food studies. https://guides.nyu.edu/speccol/food-studies#:~:text=The%20Marion%20Nestle%20Food%20Studies,activity%20of%20New%20York%20City.

Chapter 9. Writing *Food Politics*

1. Most of my writings are listed (and available) at FoodPolitics.com under the "Publications" tab. Early examples of papers with *policy* in the titles include the following: with Porter DV. National nutrition monitoring policy: the continuing need for legislative intervention. *J Nutr Educ.* 1990;22(3):141-144; with Guttmacher S. Evolution of federal dietary guidance policy: from food adequacy to chronic disease prevention. *Caduceus.* 1990;6(2):43-67; Hunger in the United States: rationale, methods, and policy implications of state hunger surveys. *J Nutr Educ.* 1992;24:18s-22s; Dietary recommendations for cancer prevention: public policy implementation. *J Natl Cancer Inst Monographs.* 1992;12:153-157; Societal barriers to improved school lunch programs: rationale for recent policy recommendations. *School Food Serv Res Rev.* 1992;16(1):5-10; Nutrition policy: children in poverty. In: Karp RJ, ed. *Malnourished Children in the United States: Caught in the Cycle of Poverty.* Springer Publishing Co.; 1993:235-249.

2. Dietary advice for the 1990s: the political history of the food guide pyramid. *Caduceus.* 1993;9:136-153; Food lobbies, the food pyramid, and U.S. nutrition policy. *Int J Health Serv.* 1993;23:483-496; Dietary supplement advertising: a matter of politics, not science. *J Nutr Educ.* 1999;31:278-282; with Caldwell D and Rogers W. School nutrition services. In: Marx E, Wooley SF, Northrop D, eds. *Health Is Academic: A Guide to Coordinated School Health Programs.* Teachers College Press; 1998:195-223.

3. The FDA disbanded this committee in 2017. I first wrote about biotechnology in an editorial (Food biotechnology: truth in advertising. *Bio/Technol.* 1992;10:1056) and then in book chapters: Agricultural biotechnology, policy, and nutrition. In: Murray TJ, Mehlman MJ, eds. *Encyclopedia of Ethical, Legal, and Policy Issues in Biotechnology.* John Wiley & Sons, Inc; 2000:66–76; and Food biotechnology: politics and policy implications. In: Kiple KF, Ornelas-Kiple CK, eds. *The Cambridge World History of Food and Nutrition,* Vol. 2:7.7. Cambridge University Press; 2000:1643–1662. The selling of Olestra. *Public Health Rep.* 1998;113:508–520.

4. Nestle M, Wing R, Birch L, et al. Behavioral and social influences on food choice. *Nutr Rev.* 1998;56:s50–s64; Nestle M, Jacobson MF. Halting the obesity epidemic: a public health policy approach. *Public Health Rep.* 2000;115:12–24.

5. Nestle M. Soft drink "pouring rights": marketing empty calories. *Public Health Rep.* 2000;115:308–319.

6. Nestle M. Food company sponsorship of nutrition research and professional activities: A conflict of interest? *Public Health Nutr.* 2001;4:1015–1022. I returned to this topic in depth in *Unsavory Truth* (2018).

7. Stan Holwitz retired from UC Press in 2009 and died in 2018 at age eighty-eight.

8. Spicoli J. Here is Michael Lomonaco's story of 9/11. Cougar Board. September 11, 2019. https://www.cougarboard.com/board/message.html?id=22264258.

9. Mandelbaum-Schmid J. A healthy dose of Marion Nestle. *Walking Magazine,* September–October 2000:52–54; Jaret P. Changing the way America eats. *Health,* July–August 2001:136–146. Among other women described in this article were Sara Baer-Sinnott of Oldways and Bonnie Liebman of the Center for Science in the Public Interest.

Chapter 10. The Fun Begins

1. Rampton S. *Toxic Sludge Is Good for You: Lies, Damned Lies, and the Public Relations Industry.* Common Courage Press; 1995.

2. Milloy S. New nutrition book choking on bad science. Fox News. February 22, 2002. https://www.foxnews.com/story/new-nutrition-book-choking-on-bad-science.

3. The Sugar Association's letter and my rebuttal are posted at FoodPolitics.com, under "Controversies" at the bottom of the Media page.

4. The Crankster website no longer exists, but this group's review of *Food Politics* is available on the website of the American Council on Science and Health:

Food industry to blame for fat? https://www.acsh.org/news/2002/03/12/food-industry-to-blame-for-fat. The Activist Facts profile: see Marion Nestle: Key Player at https://www.activistfacts.com/person/3381-marion-nestle-dr/. Also see Amer S. Dishonor roll: here comes trouble. *Restaurant Business,* June 2, 2002:16–32. I appear on page 28. Other honorees were a class-action lawyer, animal rights activists, greedy landlords, anti-immigration congressional representatives, and the State of New Jersey (high overhead costs for restaurants).

5. Efforts by UN agencies produced two reports: *Diet, Nutrition and the Prevention of Chronic Diseases: Report of the Joint WHO/FAO Expert Consultation.* WHO Tech Rep Series, No. 916, 2003; and WHO. *Global Strategy on Diet, Physical Activity, and Health.* May 26, 2004. I wrote about Derek Yach's subsequent career with PepsiCo in my book *Soda Politics: Taking on Big Soda (and Winning).* Later, he became president of the Foundation for a Smoke-Free World, established by Philip Morris International.

6. Julie Creswell. Chewing out the food industry. *Fortune,* February 18, 2002:36.

7. The ABC News special *How to Get Fat without Even Trying* aired on December 8, 2003, and is available on YouTube: https://www.youtube.com/watch?v=ZH-9acC7Msw.

8. The TIME/ABC News Summit on Obesity was held June 2–4, 2004, in Williamsburg, Virginia.

9. Steinberg J, Seelye KQ. Controversy claims senior CNN executive. *New York Times,* February 14, 2005; O'Brien T. Can Angelina Jolie really save the world? *New York Times,* January 30, 2005; Parker C. China's Xi Jinping defends globalization from the Davos stage. World Economic Forum, January 17, 2017. https://www.weforum.org/agenda/2017/01/chinas-xi-jinping-defends-globalization-from-the-davos-stage/.

10. Kamp D, Rosenfeld M. The Food Snob's Dictionary, Volume I. *Vanity Fair,* December 2003:284–286. The authors added new items and more living people to create a book with the same title (Broadway Books; 2007). My entry is on page 72, this time between "Mouthfeel" and "New American."

11. *Food Politics* translations: The Chinese edition, in simplified characters, was published by the Social Sciences Academic Press, Beijing, 2004. The Japanese edition was published by the Tuttle-Mori Agency, Inc., Tokyo, 2005.

12. See NCQA. Clinton, Gingrich among those to be honored for improving health care quality. *Quality Digest,* February 28, 2005. https://www.qualitydigest.com/inside/quality-insider-news/clinton-gingrich-among-those-be-honored-improving-health-care-quality.

13. Hicks J. Newt Gingrich's changing stance on health-care mandates (Fact Checker biography). *Washington Post*, December 12, 2011.

14. Cognard-Black J. The feminist food revolution. *Ms.* 2010;20(3):36–39.

15. The slow road to paradise. *San Francisco 7 × 7*, August 2008:108.

16. For links to my speech and other sources, see Bard College's Prison Initiative: organic food politics! FoodPolitics.com, June 16, 2010. Also see Hirsch J. Convict cultivation: growing organic behind bars. *Modern Farmer*, August 29, 2013.

Chapter 11. How I Do It

1. Mintz died in 2015 at age ninety-three. The book that made him a hero in Puerto Rico is *Worker in the Cane: A Puerto Rican Life History*. W. W. Norton & Company; 1974.

2. Bergman B. Troy Duster's garden of plugged-in scholarship, and how it grew. UCNet, August 26, 2014. Also see Asimov A. UC Berkeley shutting down rare pipeline for doctorates of color: its supporters are fighting back. *San Francisco Chronicle*, December 26, 2020.

3. Congress could not reach agreement on the provisions of the Farm Bill in 2012 and did not pass it until 2014. See National Sustainable Agriculture Coalition. The 2012 farm bill (that never was): year in review. January 11, 2013. https://sustainableagriculture.net/blog/2012-farm-bill-in-review/. My articles on the farm bill are Utopian dream: a new farm bill. *Dissent.* 2012;Spring:15–19; and The farm bill drove me insane. *Politico,* March 17, 2016. https://www.politico.com/agenda/story/2016/03/farm-bill-congress-usda-food-policy-000070/.

4. I never saw Tony Hendra again. See Genzlinger N. Tony Hendra, a multiplatform humorist, is dead at 79. *New York Times.* March 5, 2021. On the creation of the Food Network, see Salkin A. *From Scratch: The Uncensored History of the Food Network.* G. P. Putnam's Sons; 2013.

5. For a splendid account of the making of the 1997 edition of *The Joy of Cooking,* see Parsons R. A heaping cupful of conflict. *Los Angeles Times,* November 5, 1997. He writes: "It seemed that every cookbook writer in America was either working on the revision or wondering why she or he had not been asked. . . . So frantic was the action at the end that entire chapters were rewritten and whole groups of chapters were eliminated after the book was in bound galley—normally a stage at which only minimal copy editing changes are made."

6. O'Neill M. It's a new 'Joy,' but is it the old love? The cookbook now speaks in a corporate tone. *New York Times,* November 5, 1997. Maria Guarnaschelli died in 2021. See Moskin J. Maria Guarnaschelli, book editor who changed what we

cook, dies at 79. *New York Times,* February 11, 2021. On the history of the *Joy of Cooking* prior to the 1996 edition, see Mendelsohn A. *Stand Facing the Stove: The Story of the Women Who Gave America the Joy of Cooking.* Henry Holt; 1996.

7. I explained the blog's origins in a post in 2017: This blog's 10th anniversary week: how it started. FoodPolitics.com. May 17, 2017.

8. *Time.* The 140 best Twitter feeds of 2011: "When journalists need to understand how an agricultural policy or nutrition guideline will affect public health, they call Marion Nestle. So you may as well go straight to the source on her Twitter feed. . . . Nestle has an unparalleled ability to parse USDA reports and cut through the hype to deliver sane, informed nutritional information you can use." http://content.time.com/time/specials/packages/article/0,28804,2058946_2059043_2059034,00.html. Travis J. Twitter's science stars, the sequel. *Science,* October 6, 2014. https://www.sciencemag.org/news/2014/10/twitters-science-stars-sequel; Srinivas S. Ten super smart health twitter feeds to follow now. *Guardian,* February 19, 2015. https://www.theguardian.com/lifeandstyle/2015/feb/19/top-10-tweeters-health-twitter-food-healthcare-research-policy.

9. Kaufman L, Severson K. Stand-alone food section faces demise in Bay Area. *New York Times,* November 13, 2013. My columns for the *Chronicle* are posted on FoodPolitics.com under "Publications," just above the chronological list of articles.

10. Martin A. Is a food revolution now in season? *New York Times,* March 22, 2009.

11. Post introduced the "healthier" version of Alpha-Bits in 2005, dropped it, and then tried it again for a few months in 2008. On its introduction, see Warner M. Altering Alpha-Bits: not as simple as A B C. *New York Times,* August 11, 2005.

12. *The Daily Show.* A deep dive into the "raw water" craze. Comedy Central, April 18, 2018. https://www.youtube.com/watch?v=WjJJeFDk8Ok. I was interviewed by the deadpan Desi Lydic, whose main interview was with the remarkable founder of Live Water, Mukhande Singh.

13. Select Committee on Nutrition and Human Needs, US Senate. *Dietary Goals for the United States,* February 1977. These were the first US government dietary recommendations for chronic disease prevention. Political pushback forced the committee to issue revised goals later that year, as I describe in *Food Politics.*

14. I can't resist getting scholarly. The adage is usually ascribed to Confucius, but incorrectly. See Quote Investigator, September 2, 2014. https://quoteinvestigator.com/2014/09/02/job-love/.

Chapter 12. The Books

1. Few genetically modified foods are found in the produce sections of US supermarkets (the most likely are papayas from Hawai'i and a pink pineapple), but most US field corn, soybeans, and sugar beets are genetically modified. No known harm has come from eating GM foods or products, but the herbicide glyphosate, used with crops genetically modified to resist it, is a suspected carcinogen. See Gillam C. *Whitewash: The Story of a Weed Killer, Cancer, and the Corruption of Science*. Island Press; 2017; and *The Monsanto Papers: Deadly Secrets, Corporate Corruption, and One Man's Search for Justice*. Island Press; 2021.

2. I hoped to work with John Bergez again on this book, but he died in 2015.

3. The cartoon illustrated an article by Shahar Smooha: Marion, Marion please report to the deli counter. *Haaretz*, September 21, 2007:88–92.

4. See, for example, Nesheim MC, Nestle M. Pet Food. In: Allen G, Albala K, eds. *The Business of Food: Encyclopedia of the Food and Drink Industries*. Greenwood Press; 2007:297–301; Additional information on melamine in pet food [letter]. *J Am Vet Med Assoc*. 2007;231:1647; Recall follow up. Who knew? Melamine, the not-so-secret ingredient. *The Bark*, April 2008:34–36.

5. See Huang E. Ten years after China's infant milk tragedy, parents still won't trust their babies to local formula. *Quartz*, July 16, 2018.

6. Figure 27 illustrated May M. Challenging the pet-food dogma. *San Francisco Chronicle*, June 23, 2010.

7. My entries are "Soda" and, with Daniel Bowman Simon, "Sugar lobbies." *Oxford Companion to Sugar and Sweets*. Oxford University Press; 2015:623–624 and 681–682.

8. O'Connor A. Coca-Cola funds scientists who shift blame for obesity away from bad diets. *New York Times*, August 9, 2015. I am quoted as saying: "The Global Energy Balance Network is nothing but a front group for Coca-Cola. Coca-Cola's agenda here is very clear: Get these researchers to confuse the science and deflect attention from dietary intake."

9. Nestle M. Food company sponsorship of nutrition research and professional activities: A conflict of interest? *Public Health Nutr*. 2001;4:1015–1022. More recent articles: Conflict of interest in the regulation of food safety: a threat to scientific integrity. *JAMA Intern Med*. 2013;173(22):2036–2038; Corporate funding of food and nutrition research: science or marketing? *JAMA Intern Med*. 2016;176(1):13–14; Food industry funding of nutrition research: the relevance of history for current debates. *JAMA Intern Med*. 2016;176(11):1685–1686.

10. The Portuguese edition is *Uma Verdade Indigesta: Como A Indústria Alimentícia Manipula A Ciência Do Que Comemos*. Elefante Editora; 2019. It contains a foreword by Paula Johns, director-president of ACT Promoção da Saúde, the advocacy group sponsoring the book and my visit.

11. *Quotations from Chairman Mao Tse-tung*, published by the People's Liberation Army General Political Department in 1964, had a red cover and was pocket-sized. Hence Mao's Little Red Book.

Conclusion

1. Perlroth N. Michael Pollan: The world's 7 most powerful foodies. *Forbes,* November 2, 2011; Bittman M. Opinionator: No turkeys here. *New York Times,* November 19, 2011; Bittman M. *Animal, Vegetable. Junk: A History of Food, from Sustainable to Suicidal.* Houghton Mifflin Harcourt; 2021:179.

2. Game Changers: Women in science and medicine. *Women's Health,* October 2015:146. For a quick overview of Elizabeth Holmes's story, see Hartmans A., Leskin P. The rise and fall of Elizabeth Holmes, the Theranos founder whose federal fraud trial is delayed until 2021. *Business Insider,* August 11, 2020; U.S. Attorney's Office, Northern District of California. Theranos founder Elizabeth Holmes found guilty of investor fraud. January 4, 2022. https://www.justice.gov/usao-ndca/pr/theranos-founder-elizabeth-holmes-found-guilty-investor-fraud.

3. Food politics: Who makes our food choices? Marion Nestle at the Nobel Week Dialogue. December 9, 2016. https://www.youtube.com/watch?v=r4VDp8Yw4tI.

4. See Petrusich A. A transcendent Patti Smith accepts Bob Dylan's Nobel Prize. *New Yorker,* December 10, 2016. Also see Smith P. Cultural comment: How does it feel. *New Yorker,* December 14, 2016.

5. See, for example: Ioannidis JPA. Implausible results in human nutrition research. *BMJ.* 2013;347:f6698; Ioannidis JPA. The challenge of reforming nutritional epidemiologic research. *JAMA.* 2018;320(10):969–970.

6. Stover PJ, King JC. More nutrition precision, better decisions for the health of our nation. *J Nutr.* 2020;150:3058–3060; Kaiser J. NIH's "precision nutrition" bet aims for individualized diets. *Science.* 2021;371:552.

7. I view these articles as game-changing: Willett W, Rockström J, Loken B, Springmann M, Lang T, Vermeulen S, et al. Food in the Anthropocene: the EAT-Lancet Commission on healthy diets from sustainable food systems. *Lancet.* 2019;393(10170):447–492; Swinburn BA, Kraak VI, Allender S, et al. The global syndemic of obesity, undernutrition, and climate change: The Lancet Commission report. *Lancet.* 2019;393(10173):791–846.

8. Also game-changing: Monteiro CA, Cannon G, Levy RB, et al. Ultra-processed foods: what they are and how to identify them. *Public Health Nutr.* 2019;22(5):936–941; Hall KD, Ayuketah A, Bernstein S, et al. Ultra-processed diets cause excess calorie intake and weight gain: a one-month inpatient randomized controlled trial of ad libitum food intake. *Cell Metab.* 2019(July 2;30(1):67–77.e3; Pagliai G, Dinu M, Madarena MP, Bonaccio M, Iacoviello L. Consumption of ultra-processed foods and health status: a systematic review and meta-analysis. *Br J Nutr.* 2021;125(3):308–318.

9. Nestle M. Regulating the food industry: an aspirational agenda. *Am J Public Health.* 2022: in press.

10. Heilbrun CG. *Writing a Woman's Life.* Ballantine Books; 1988:131.

Illustration Credits

Index

to publish, 162, 167, 193; social
norms and expectations, 2, 24,
31, 33, 230. *See also* women in
academia
Carmona, Richard, 184
cartoons, 10*fig.*, 219*fig.*, 224, 225*fig.*
Case against Sugar, The (Taubes),
246n11
Center for Consumer Freedom, 180
Center for Science in the Public
Interest (CSPI), 48, 62, 163–64,
166, 179
cereals and cereal boxes, 207–8,
207*fig.*, 254n11
Child, Julia, 35, 136–40, 147
Child, Paul, 137
childhood experiences, 2, 6, 9–24;
Eva's arrival and presence, 15–16,
17, 18, 19; family finances, 9, 11–12,
18, 19, 25, 56–57; family moves, 15,
16, 17–18, 19; food experiences,
20–21, 21–22; going to camp at
Higley Hill, 21–22, 23*fig.*; jobs in my
teen years, 22, 24; my childhood
doubts and anxieties, 13, 15, 16–17,
18, 19; my father's death, 9, 18; my
parents and me, 12–13, 15–16, 18, 19;
my parents' backgrounds and
relationship, 9–12, 17, 18; my
parents' political beliefs, 9, 12,
14*fig.*; my sense of myself and my
future options, 16–17, 19, 24–25
children: child care as a career
challenge, 31, 33, 38–40; childhood
obesity, 164, 174; as targets of
food-industry marketing, 164, 174.
See also school foods
children's cereals, 207–8, 207*fig.*,
254n11
China travel, 81–83, 84*fig.*
cholesterol, 95, 103, 129

chronic disease: diet and, 100, 101–2;
as focus of the *Surgeon General's
Report*, 99; socioeconomic status
and, 99
CIA (Culinary Institute of America),
135, 150
civil rights and antiwar movements,
34–35
Claiborne, Craig, 64–65, 65*fig.*
Clinton, Hillary, 186
Coalition of Homeless Shelter
Providers (San Francisco), my
fieldwork with, 76–79
Coca-Cola, 166, 227–28
Cognard-Black, Jennifer, 186–87
Collins, Francis, 184–85
Committee for Health Rights in
Central America, 73
Communist Party, communist
sympathies: Higley Hill camp and,
22; my parents' Party membership,
9, 12. *See also* anticommunism
Cone, Jim, 59, 244n3
conflicts of interest, between the food
industry and food and nutrition
professionals, 131–33, 134, 166,
211–12, 227–28, 231
Conley, Dalton, 197
cookbooks: establishing library
collections for the NYU food
studies program, 156–58; my early
experiences with, 27, 30. *See also
specific titles and authors*
cooking experiences. *See* food and
cooking experiences
coronary artery disease, 102. *See also*
chronic disease
Cousin, Ertharin, 209, 210
COVID-19 pandemic, 199
Craig Claiborne's Gourmet Diet
(Claiborne and Franey), 64–65

federal nutrition policy. *See* dietary guidance; food and nutrition policy; ODPHP

Feed Your Pet Right (Nestle and Nesheim), 214, 218–23, 222*fig.*

Feldman, Charles, 154

Feminine Mystique, The (Friedan), 31

feminism, second-wave, 31, 42–43

"Feminist Food Revolution, The" (Cognard-Black), 186–87

Ferro-Luzzi, Anna, 133

Finkelstein, Jim, 108

Fishman, Bob, 67–68

Flowers, Loma, 57

food advocacy/food movement: gender issues in, 186–87; my hopes for, 237–38; as a social movement, 197

Food and Agriculture Organization (FAO) World Food Day lecture (Rome, 2009), 209–10, 210*fig.*

food and cooking experiences: childhood food experiences, 20–21, 21–22; cooking at home as a young woman, 30, 35, 137; in Hong Kong and Shanghai, 81, 83; laboratory squid, 40; at Oldways Preservation and Exchange Trust conferences, 130; *Over Easy* cooking demonstrations, 64–65

Food and Drug Administration. *See* FDA

food and nutrition policy: the Farm Bill of 2012, 198, 253n3; food industry influence and, 89, 125–26; my interest and training in, 69, 75, 76, 79, 87, 162; nutrition labeling requirements, 207–8; policy-related critiques of the 1988 *Surgeon General's Report*, 103–4; the Senate Select Committee on Nutrition and Human Needs dietary goals (1977), 209; views on industry regulation, 103–4, 237. See also *Surgeon General's Report on Nutrition and Health*

food assistance programs: federal programs, 76, 79; my New York assessment fieldwork, 119–20; my San Francisco assessment fieldwork, 76–79

Food for People, Not for Profit (Center for Science in the Public Interest), 48, 51–52

food industry: and the COVID-19 pandemic, 199; developing my interest in industry influence and practices, 163–65; and federal nutrition policy and guidance, 89, 125–26, 165; industry-funded research and other potential conflicts for food and nutrition professionals, 131–33, 134, 166, 211–12, 227–28, 231; marketing practices, 4, 164, 174, 217; pet foods, 218–21; responses to the *Surgeon General's Report*, 100, 102; as topic of World Food Day lecture (Rome, 2009), 209–10; values of, 1; views on industry regulation, 103, 237

food insecurity and food access, 52, 99. *See also* food assistance programs

food labeling, 207–8; pet foods, 219–20

Food Matters (newspaper column), 205–6

food movement. *See* food advocacy/ food movement

Food Politics (Nestle), 2, 162–75; background and inspiration for, 4,

Global Energy Balance Network, 227
GMO foods, 165, 215–16, 251n3 (ch. 9),
    255n1
Goddard, Paulette, 241n3
Gold, Mike (Granich), 242n1
Gold, Rozanne, 114
Goldstein, Darra, 168
Goode, Erica, 59, 244n3
Gordon, Aubrey, 103–4
Gourmet magazine, 156
government agricultural policy, 104,
    125–26, 198, 253n3
government food assistance
    programs, 76, 79
government nutrition policy. *See*
    dietary guidance; food and
    nutrition policy; ODPHP
government work and advisory
    positions: after *Food Politics*, 192;
    FDA advisory committee service,
    165. See also *Surgeon General's Report
    on Nutrition and Health*; Washing-
    ton, DC, 1980s: AT ODPHP
Granich, George, 21
Granich, Grace, 21–22
Granich, Max (Manny), 21–22, 242n1
Granich, Mike (Mike Gold), 242n1
Grossman, Larry, 37
Guarnaschelli, Maria, 201–2, 203,
    253–54n6
Gussow, Joan, 133, 148

Haber, Barbara, 137
Haderlie, Eugene, 30, 242n8
Hall, Zach: career, 36, 52, 53, 56, 66;
    and my Brandeis salary negotia-
    tions, 43; my relationship with, 36,
    38, 52, 66, 68, 70, 72; and my UCSF
    hiring, 53
Hamburg, Peggy, 91, 245n2 (ch. 5)
Hamilton, Dorothy Cann, 146

Hanover, Donna, 201
Harris, Suzanne, 90, 94
Harry Chapin Media Award, 185
Harvard School of Public Health,
    48–49, 133
Hawkes, Corinna, 196
health and nutrition. *See* chronic
    disease; nutrition science and
    research; obesity and weight gain
Heilbrun, Carolyn, 238
Helsing, Elisabet, 133
Hendra, Tony, 201
Hersh, Stephanie, 138
HFCS (high-fructose corn syrup), 179
HHS (Department of Health and
    Human Services), 88. *See also*
    dietary guidance; ODPHP; *Surgeon
    General's Report on Nutrition and
    Health*
high-fructose corn syrup (HFCS), 179
Higley Hill camp, 21–22, 23*fig.*,
    242nn1,3
Hoff, Syd (a.k.a. Redfield), 9, 10*fig.*
Holmes, Elizabeth, 232
Holwitz, Stan, 168–69, 169–70, 171,
    176, 216, 221, 223
home economics, as a discipline, 108
Home Economics and Nutrition
    Department (NYU SEHNAP). *See*
    New York City, 1988–2003: AT NYU
homeless community services: my
    field work assessing food programs,
    76–79, 119–20
Hong Kong visit (1986), 81, 81*fig.*
honors, awards, and recognition, 158,
    185–89, 231–33; Food Revolution
    pantheon article (2009), 206–7,
    207*fig.*; IACP awards, 223, 224,
    226–27, 232; James Beard founda-
    tion, 185–86, 217–18, 232
Huffman, Sue, 201

IACP (International Association of Culinary Professionals) awards, 223, 224, 226–27, 232
Indian Health Service (IHS) speaking invitation, 91–92
Indonesia trip, 85–86
Instagram, 205
International Association of Culinary Professionals (IACP) awards, 223, 224, 226–27, 232
International Olive Oil Council (IOOC), 131–32, 133, 134–35

Jacobson, Michael, 48, 62, 86, 91, 166, 179
Jakarta visit (1986), 85–86
James, Brent, 186
James Beard Foundation and awards, 128–29, 146, 153, 185, 217–18, 232
Jaret, Peter, 174
Jenkins, Nancy Harmon, 129, 135, 137
Jennings, Peter, 183–84
Jews without Money (Gold), 242n1
John Tung Foundation, 73
Jolie, Angelina, 185
Jones, Richard, 66
Joy of Cooking, The (Rombauer and Becker) (1997 edition), 201–3, 253n5
junk foods, 164, 237. *See also* food industry; ultraprocessed foods

Kabat-Zinn, John, 43, 243n3
Kabat-Zinn, Myla, 43, 243n3
Kaltreider, Nancy, 72–73. *See also* therapists and their advice
Katz, Jonathan Ned, 157
Kellogg's, 208, 219
Kenner, Max, 187
King, Mary-Claire, 232
Kirshenblatt-Gimblett, Barbara, 154, 168

Koch, Ed, 122, 123*fig.*, 124
Koop, C. Everett, 98–99, 100, 103. See also *Surgeon General's Report on Nutrition and Health*
Kornhauser, William, 197
Kovner, Amy, 42, 43
KQED television: *Over Easy* program appearances, 63–65, 65*fig.*
Krevans, Julius, 53, 56, 59, 67

labeling, 207–8; pet foods, 219–20
Lappé, Frances Moore, 48
Lashof, Joyce, 73
lectures. *See* speaking engagements; teaching
Lee, Philip, 55, 65–66, 69–70, 73, 79, 244n1
Lefer, Gary, 115–16
Let's Ask Marion (Nestle and Trueman), 229
Lewis, Richard, 152
Liebman, Bonnie, 62
litigation: beef industry suit against Oprah Winfrey, 179; Sugar Association litigation threat, 178–80
Liu, Hanmin, 82, 245n3
Lomonaco, Michael, 146, 173
Los Angeles, high school years in, 16, 17–19, 23–24. *See also* childhood experiences

MADD (Mothers Against Drunk Driving), 98, 246n6
Madigan, Edward, 125
management theory and styles, 106, 107, 247n19; resistance to my NYU management style, 116–17
maple syrup, at Higley Hill, 22, 23*fig.*
Marcus, Ann, 117, 121, 143–44, 148, 149, 190, 191
Margen, Sheldon, 60, 73, 80, 93, 94

New York City, 1930s–1950s. *See* childhood experiences

New York City, 1988–2003: AT NYU (SEHNAP HOME ECONOMICS AND NUTRITION DEPARTMENT CHAIR), 3–4, 108–92; building relationships with the press and commenting on the USDA food pyramid, 124–27; cleaning and equipping the teaching kitchen, 112–14; the department's status when I was hired, 108–10, 112–14; establishing the food studies program, 141–61; expanding my academic interests, 127, 135–36; faculty and staff relations, 116–17, 142, 145, 190–91; feeling secure and settled, 111–12, 127; financial challenges, 114, 115, 117; getting involved with the food world, 128–40; getting the job, 105, 108–12; improving the department and its programs, 115–18, 141; my concerns about the pressure to publish, 162, 167; my 9/11 experience, 172–73; my resignation from the department chair position, 189–92; my subsidized Greenwich Village apartment, 3, 121–24, 123*fig.*; my summer assessing City-run homeless food programs, 119–20; my teaching experiences, 194, 195–96; producing *Food Politics*, 162–75; responses to *Food Politics*, 176–92; travel opportunities, 128. See also *Food Politics*; food world involvement; NYU food studies program; personal life

New York City, 2003–: TEACHING, WRITING, AND PUBLIC ENGAGEMENT, 193–229; engaging with the public, 199–212; keeping up with food and nutrition news and research, 193–95, 206; my enthusiasm for my work, 2, 193, 212, 213, 236–38; my teaching methods and experiences, 195–99; NYU teaching and official retirement, 196, 199, 233–35, 235*fig.*, 241n3. *See also* public engagement; writing and publishing; *specific book titles*

New York Times: on Coca-Cola's nutrition research funding, 227–28; Food Guide Pyramid story, 125; Jane Brody's column, 48, 64–65; on the 1997 edition of *The Joy of Cooking*, 203; relationships with *Times* reporters, 4, 124; on the *Surgeon General's Report* release, 100; 2009 Food Revolution article, 206–7, 207*fig.*

9/11 attacks, 172–73

Nobel Prize week talks (2016, 2018), 233

North Point Press, 216

nutrition, "precision," 237

Nutrition Facts labeling, 207–8

Nutrition in Clinical Practice (Nestle), 2, 66, 73, 96, 167, 213

nutrition policy. *See* food and nutrition policy

nutrition science and research: the challenges of nutrition research, 50–51, 236–37; Julia Child's views on nutritionists, 136, 138, 139, 140, 147; credentialing in the field, 74–75, 76; developing the UCSF nutrition curriculum, 59–61; evaluating and keeping up with, 193–95, 206; food-industry influence and research funding, 166, 227–28; food world attention to/views of, 129; my graduate studies in nutrition and public health, 69–70, 73, 74–79; my growth as a nutrition scientist, 61–62; my hopes for the future of the field, 237; my research at Brandeis, 37, 38; nutrition scientists at the first Oldways Mediterranean Diet conference, 133; nutrition viewed as a low-status field, 54; poorly designed/controlled studies, 49–50, 51; popular interest in the 1970s, 48, 61; sociopolitical questions and, 51–52, 237

NutritionUCSF program, 61, 62

NYU: adjunct faculty at, 109; Fales Library food studies collection, 156–58, 231; my current title, 241n3; soft drinks at, 166. *See also* New York City, 1988–2003: AT NYU; New York City, 2003–: TEACH-ING, WRITING, AND PUBLIC ENGAGEMENT; NYU food studies program

NYU food studies program, 136, 139, 140, 141–61, 231; background and approval of, 141–47; building academic community and respect, 153–56; constructing the teaching kitchen, 151–52; establishing the library collections, 156–58; faculty recruitment, 148–51, 161; incorporating agriculture, 148, 158–61; interdisciplinary nature of, 148, 151; Kirshenblatt-Gimblett, Barbara, 144; making food central to the curriculum, 144–48; reactions to/opinions about the new program, 147–48, 158–59; working with Clark Wolf, 145–46, 147, 151–52

NYU Press, 167

Oakville Grocery, 145

oat bran, 129

Obama, Michelle, 186, 206, 232

obesity and weight gain: ABC News special and summit on, 183–84; childhood obesity, 164, 174; diet and, 100, 102, 237; diet vs. exercise and, 227; as focus of the *Surgeon General's Report*, 99, 103; food industry influence on, as topic of World Food Day lecture (Rome, 2009), 209–10; my father's obesity, 17; sociological and food-systems views of, 99, 103–4, 164–65, 174; *Why Calories Count*, 223, 224

Occupy Big Food speech, 200*fig*.

ODPHP (Office of Disease Prevention and Health Promotion), 79, 88, 107. *See also* dietary guidance; *Surgeon General's Report on Nutrition and Health*; Washington, DC, 1980s: AT ODPHP

Oldways Preservation and Exchange Trust, 128–35; connecting with, 128–29; editing the Mediterranean Diet conference papers, 133–35; my conflict-of-interest concerns, 131–33, 134; participating in Oldways conferences, 129–31, 133; reflecting on my connection with, 135–36

Olestra, 165

olive oil, 131–33, 248–49n6 (ch. 7)

Oliver, Jamie, 186

Over Easy (television program), 63–65, 65*fig*.

Oxford Companion to Sugar and Sweets, 226, 255n7

Oxford University Press, 167, 226

Packard, Phil, 74, 80

Parasecoli, Fabio, 150

Prize week talks (2016, 2018), 233; Occupy Big Food demonstration, 200*fig.*; in Southeast Asia (1986), 80–86; speaking fees and conflict-of-interest concerns, 211–12; World Food Day lecture (Rome, 2009), 209–10, 209*fig.*

Specter, Michael, 103

Spurlock, Morgan, 186–87

Stanford University, my application to, 25

Steingarten, Jeffrey, 146

Stent, Gunther, 31

Steven Barclay Agency, 211

sugar and sugars, 95, 100, 101–2; Puerto Rico field course on (2004), 196–97; sugar vs. sugars, 179

Sugar Association litigation threat, 178–80

Sugarman, Carol, 124, 125–26

sugary drinks, 166, 179, 225–26

supermarkets, 217, 218

Super Size Me (film), 187

Surgeon General's Report on Nutrition and Health (1988), 88; my publications based on, 97, 105, 246n3; my reassessment of, 104; public release press conference, 97–99, 101*fig.*; report development and publication restrictions and challenges, 89, 94–99; responses and critiques, 101–2, 103–4

Sussman, Maurice, 37, 39

Sussman, Raquel, 37, 39

Suttie, John, 148

Sweetness and Power: The Place of Sugar in Modern History (Mintz), 133

Taubes, Gary, 101–2, 246n11

Taylor, Marvin, 138, 156–58

teaching, 193, 195–99, 238; at Brandeis, 40–42, 46*fig.*, 52; collaborative teaching experiences, 196–97; gender-based pay inequities, 42–44; my lecture methods, 62, 198–99, 208–9; my official NYU retirement, 233–35, 235*fig.*; at/for NYU, 195–98, 199, 235; the rewards and satisfactions of, 33, 42, 46*fig.*, 52, 238; at UC Berkeley and abroad, 198; at UCSF, 53, 54–55, 59–62, 194

television: *The French Chef,* 136, 137; my television appearances, 63–65, 65*fig.*, 181, 183–84, 201, 208

Thailand visit, 83, 85

Thaler, Pat Koch, 122

Thaves, Sara, 224

Theranos, 232–33

therapists and their advice, 72–73, 106, 110, 115–16, 122, 127, 191

thiamine deficiency study, 50

tobacco industry, 4, 163, 178. *See also* smoking and antismoking advocacy

Toxic Sludge Is Good for You (Rampton), 177

traditional foods and diets, 130–31; Mediterranean diets, 132–33. *See also* Oldways Preservation and Exchange Trust

travel, overseas, 73, 80–86, 122, 130, 228–29, 233

Trichopoulos, Dimitrios, 133

Trichopoulou, Antonia, 133, 134–35

triple-duty diets, 237

Truman, Harry, 28

Tung, John, 81, 81*fig.*

Tung Foundation, 73, 81*fig.*

Twitter, 204–5

California Studies in Food and Culture

DARRA GOLDSTEIN, EDITOR

Founded in 1893,
UNIVERSITY OF CALIFORNIA PRESS
publishes bold, progressive books and journals
on topics in the arts, humanities, social sciences,
and natural sciences—with a focus on social
justice issues—that inspire thought and action
among readers worldwide.

The UC PRESS FOUNDATION
raises funds to uphold the press's vital role
as an independent, nonprofit publisher, and
receives philanthropic support from a wide
range of individuals and institutions—and from
committed readers like you. To learn more, visit
ucpress.edu/supportus.